M000026815

THIS IS YOUR **PASSBOOK**® FOR ...

ADMINISTRATIVE AIDE

NLC®

NATIONAL LEARNING CORPORATION®
passbooks.com

PASSBOOK® SERIES

THE *PASSBOOK® SERIES* has been created to prepare applicants and candidates for the ultimate academic battlefield – the examination room.

At some time in our lives, each and every one of us may be required to take an examination – for validation, matriculation, admission, qualification, registration, certification, or licensure.

Based on the assumption that every applicant or candidate has met the basic formal educational standards, has taken the required number of courses, and read the necessary texts, the *PASSBOOK® SERIES* furnishes the one special preparation which may assure passing with confidence, instead of failing with insecurity. Examination questions – together with answers – are furnished as the basic vehicle for study so that the mysteries of the examination and its compounding difficulties may be eliminated or diminished by a sure method.

This book is meant to help you pass your examination provided that you qualify and are serious in your objective.

The entire field is reviewed through the huge store of content information which is succinctly presented through a provocative and challenging approach – the question-and-answer method.

A climate of success is established by furnishing the correct answers at the end of each test.

You soon learn to recognize types of questions, forms of questions, and patterns of questioning. You may even begin to anticipate expected outcomes.

You perceive that many questions are repeated or adapted so that you can gain acute insights, which may enable you to score many sure points.

You learn how to confront new questions, or types of questions, and to attack them confidently and work out the correct answers.

You note objectives and emphases, and recognize pitfalls and dangers, so that you may make positive educational adjustments.

Moreover, you are kept fully informed in relation to new concepts, methods, practices, and directions in the field.

You discover that you arre actually taking the examination all the time: you are preparing for the examination by "taking" an examination, not by reading extraneous and/or supererogatory textbooks.

In short, this PASSBOOK®, used directedly, should be an important factor in helping you to pass your test.

ADMINISTRATIVE AIDE

DUTIES

An employee in this class assists an administrative supervisor or department head in providing administrative services to a county or local department or unit. The incumbent receives assignments in such areas as payroll, budget preparation, personnel administration and other office management. Supervision may be exercised over a support staff. The incumbent receives close supervision and guidance from an administrative supervisor while learning departmental operations and procedures. Once experienced in the position, the employee would be expected to exercise independent judgment and initiative in carrying out assignments. Does related work as required.

SCOPE OF THE EXAMINATION

The written test will cover knowledge, skills and/or abilities in such areas as:

1. Evaluating conclusions in light of known facts;
2. Understanding and interpreting written material;
3. Understanding and interpreting tabular material; and
4. Report writing and record keeping.

HOW TO TAKE A TEST

I. YOU MUST PASS AN EXAMINATION

A. *WHAT EVERY CANDIDATE SHOULD KNOW*

Examination applicants often ask us for help in preparing for the written test. What can I study in advance? What kinds of questions will be asked? How will the test be given? How will the papers be graded?

As an applicant for a civil service examination, you may be wondering about some of these things. Our purpose here is to suggest effective methods of advance study and to describe civil service examinations.

Your chances for success on this examination can be increased if you know how to prepare. Those "pre-examination jitters" can be reduced if you know what to expect. You can even experience an adventure in good citizenship if you know why civil service exams are given.

B. *WHY ARE CIVIL SERVICE EXAMINATIONS GIVEN?*

Civil service examinations are important to you in two ways. As a citizen, you want public jobs filled by employees who know how to do their work. As a job seeker, you want a fair chance to compete for that job on an equal footing with other candidates. The best-known means of accomplishing this two-fold goal is the competitive examination.

Exams are widely publicized throughout the nation. They may be administered for jobs in federal, state, city, municipal, town or village governments or agencies.

Any citizen may apply, with some limitations, such as the age or residence of applicants. Your experience and education may be reviewed to see whether you meet the requirements for the particular examination. When these requirements exist, they are reasonable and applied consistently to all applicants. Thus, a competitive examination may cause you some uneasiness now, but it is your privilege and safeguard.

C. *HOW ARE CIVIL SERVICE EXAMS DEVELOPED?*

Examinations are carefully written by trained technicians who are specialists in the field known as "psychological measurement," in consultation with recognized authorities in the field of work that the test will cover. These experts recommend the subject matter areas or skills to be tested; only those knowledges or skills important to your success on the job are included. The most reliable books and source materials available are used as references. Together, the experts and technicians judge the difficulty level of the questions.

Test technicians know how to phrase questions so that the problem is clearly stated. Their ethics do not permit "trick" or "catch" questions. Questions may have been tried out on sample groups, or subjected to statistical analysis, to determine their usefulness.

Written tests are often used in combination with performance tests, ratings of training and experience, and oral interviews. All of these measures combine to form the best-known means of finding the right person for the right job.

II. HOW TO PASS THE WRITTEN TEST

A. NATURE OF THE EXAMINATION

To prepare intelligently for civil service examinations, you should know how they differ from school examinations you have taken. In school you were assigned certain definite pages to read or subjects to cover. The examination questions were quite detailed and usually emphasized memory. Civil service exams, on the other hand, try to discover your present ability to perform the duties of a position, plus your potentiality to learn these duties. In other words, a civil service exam attempts to predict how successful you will be. Questions cover such a broad area that they cannot be as minute and detailed as school exam questions.

In the public service similar kinds of work, or positions, are grouped together in one "class." This process is known as *position-classification*. All the positions in a class are paid according to the salary range for that class. One class title covers all of these positions, and they are all tested by the same examination.

B. FOUR BASIC STEPS

1) Study the announcement

How, then, can you know what subjects to study? Our best answer is: "Learn as much as possible about the class of positions for which you've applied." The exam will test the knowledge, skills and abilities needed to do the work.

Your most valuable source of information about the position you want is the official exam announcement. This announcement lists the training and experience qualifications. Check these standards and apply only if you come reasonably close to meeting them.

The brief description of the position in the examination announcement offers some clues to the subjects which will be tested. Think about the job itself. Review the duties in your mind. Can you perform them, or are there some in which you are rusty? Fill in the blank spots in your preparation.

Many jurisdictions preview the written test in the exam announcement by including a section called "Knowledge and Abilities Required," "Scope of the Examination," or some similar heading. Here you will find out specifically what fields will be tested.

2) Review your own background

Once you learn in general what the position is all about, and what you need to know to do the work, ask yourself which subjects you already know fairly well and which need improvement. You may wonder whether to concentrate on improving your strong areas or on building some background in your fields of weakness. When the announcement has specified "some knowledge" or "considerable knowledge," or has used adjectives like "beginning principles of…" or "advanced … methods," you can get a clue as to the number and difficulty of questions to be asked in any given field. More questions, and hence broader coverage, would be included for those subjects which are more important in the work. Now weigh your strengths and weaknesses against the job requirements and prepare accordingly.

3) Determine the level of the position

Another way to tell how intensively you should prepare is to understand the level of the job for which you are applying. Is it the entering level? In other words, is this the position in which beginners in a field of work are hired? Or is it an intermediate or advanced level? Sometimes this is indicated by such words as "Junior" or "Senior" in the class title. Other jurisdictions use Roman numerals to designate the level – Clerk I, Clerk II, for example. The word "Supervisor" sometimes appears in the title. If the level is not indicated by the title, check the description of duties. Will you be working under very close supervision, or will you have responsibility for independent decisions in this work?

4) Choose appropriate study materials

Now that you know the subjects to be examined and the relative amount of each subject to be covered, you can choose suitable study materials. For beginning level jobs, or even advanced ones, if you have a pronounced weakness in some aspect of your training, read a modern, standard textbook in that field. Be sure it is up to date and has general coverage. Such books are normally available at your library, and the librarian will be glad to help you locate one. For entry-level positions, questions of appropriate difficulty are chosen – neither highly advanced questions, nor those too simple. Such questions require careful thought but not advanced training.

If the position for which you are applying is technical or advanced, you will read more advanced, specialized material. If you are already familiar with the basic principles of your field, elementary textbooks would waste your time. Concentrate on advanced textbooks and technical periodicals. Think through the concepts and review difficult problems in your field.

These are all general sources. You can get more ideas on your own initiative, following these leads. For example, training manuals and publications of the government agency which employs workers in your field can be useful, particularly for technical and professional positions. A letter or visit to the government department involved may result in more specific study suggestions, and certainly will provide you with a more definite idea of the exact nature of the position you are seeking.

III. KINDS OF TESTS

Tests are used for purposes other than measuring knowledge and ability to perform specified duties. For some positions, it is equally important to test ability to make adjustments to new situations or to profit from training. In others, basic mental abilities not dependent on information are essential. Questions which test these things may not appear as pertinent to the duties of the position as those which test for knowledge and information. Yet they are often highly important parts of a fair examination. For very general questions, it is almost impossible to help you direct your study efforts. What we can do is to point out some of the more common of these general abilities needed in public service positions and describe some typical questions.

1) General information

Broad, general information has been found useful for predicting job success in some kinds of work. This is tested in a variety of ways, from vocabulary lists to questions about current events. Basic background in some field of work, such as sociology or economics, may be sampled in a group of questions. Often these are principles which have become familiar to most persons through exposure rather than through formal training. It is difficult to advise you how to study for these questions; being alert to the world around you is our best suggestion.

2) Verbal ability

An example of an ability needed in many positions is verbal or language ability. Verbal ability is, in brief, the ability to use and understand words. Vocabulary and grammar tests are typical measures of this ability. Reading comprehension or paragraph interpretation questions are common in many kinds of civil service tests. You are given a paragraph of written material and asked to find its central meaning.

3) Numerical ability

Number skills can be tested by the familiar arithmetic problem, by checking paired lists of numbers to see which are alike and which are different, or by interpreting charts and graphs. In the latter test, a graph may be printed in the test booklet which you are asked to use as the basis for answering questions.

4) Observation

A popular test for law-enforcement positions is the observation test. A picture is shown to you for several minutes, then taken away. Questions about the picture test your ability to observe both details and larger elements.

5) Following directions

In many positions in the public service, the employee must be able to carry out written instructions dependably and accurately. You may be given a chart with several columns, each column listing a variety of information. The questions require you to carry out directions involving the information given in the chart.

6) Skills and aptitudes

Performance tests effectively measure some manual skills and aptitudes. When the skill is one in which you are trained, such as typing or shorthand, you can practice. These tests are often very much like those given in business school or high school courses. For many of the other skills and aptitudes, however, no short-time preparation can be made. Skills and abilities natural to you or that you have developed throughout your lifetime are being tested.

Many of the general questions just described provide all the data needed to answer the questions and ask you to use your reasoning ability to find the answers. Your best preparation for these tests, as well as for tests of facts and ideas, is to be at your physical and mental best. You, no doubt, have your own methods of getting into an exam-taking mood and keeping "in shape." The next section lists some ideas on this subject.

IV. KINDS OF QUESTIONS

Only rarely is the "essay" question, which you answer in narrative form, used in civil service tests. Civil service tests are usually of the short-answer type. Full instructions for answering these questions will be given to you at the examination. But in case this is your first experience with short-answer questions and separate answer sheets, here is what you need to know:

1) Multiple-choice Questions

Most popular of the short-answer questions is the "multiple choice" or "best answer" question. It can be used, for example, to test for factual knowledge, ability to solve problems or judgment in meeting situations found at work.

A multiple-choice question is normally one of three types—

- It can begin with an incomplete statement followed by several possible endings. You are to find the one ending which *best* completes the statement, although some of the others may not be entirely wrong.
- It can also be a complete statement in the form of a question which is answered by choosing one of the statements listed.
- It can be in the form of a problem – again you select the best answer.

Here is an example of a multiple-choice question with a discussion which should give you some clues as to the method for choosing the right answer:

When an employee has a complaint about his assignment, the action which will *best* help him overcome his difficulty is to
- A. discuss his difficulty with his coworkers
- B. take the problem to the head of the organization
- C. take the problem to the person who gave him the assignment
- D. say nothing to anyone about his complaint

In answering this question, you should study each of the choices to find which is best. Consider choice "A" – Certainly an employee may discuss his complaint with fellow employees, but no change or improvement can result, and the complaint remains unresolved. Choice "B" is a poor choice since the head of the organization probably does not know what assignment you have been given, and taking your problem to him is known as "going over the head" of the supervisor. The supervisor, or person who made the assignment, is the person who can clarify it or correct any injustice. Choice "C" is, therefore, correct. To say nothing, as in choice "D," is unwise. Supervisors have and interest in knowing the problems employees are facing, and the employee is seeking a solution to his problem.

2) True/False Questions

The "true/false" or "right/wrong" form of question is sometimes used. Here a complete statement is given. Your job is to decide whether the statement is right or wrong.

SAMPLE: A roaming cell-phone call to a nearby city costs less than a non-roaming call to a distant city.

This statement is wrong, or false, since roaming calls are more expensive.

This is not a complete list of all possible question forms, although most of the others are variations of these common types. You will always get complete directions for answering questions. Be sure you understand *how* to mark your answers – ask questions until you do.

V. RECORDING YOUR ANSWERS

Computer terminals are used more and more today for many different kinds of exams.

For an examination with very few applicants, you may be told to record your answers in the test booklet itself. Separate answer sheets are much more common. If this separate answer sheet is to be scored by machine – and this is often the case – it is highly important that you mark your answers correctly in order to get credit.

An electronic scoring machine is often used in civil service offices because of the speed with which papers can be scored. Machine-scored answer sheets must be marked with a pencil, which will be given to you. This pencil has a high graphite content which responds to the electronic scoring machine. As a matter of fact, stray dots may register as answers, so do not let your pencil rest on the answer sheet while you are pondering the correct answer. Also, if your pencil lead breaks or is otherwise defective, ask for another.

Since the answer sheet will be dropped in a slot in the scoring machine, be careful not to bend the corners or get the paper crumpled.

The answer sheet normally has five vertical columns of numbers, with 30 numbers to a column. These numbers correspond to the question numbers in your test booklet. After each number, going across the page are four or five pairs of dotted lines. These short dotted lines have small letters or numbers above them. The first two pairs may also have a "T" or "F" above the letters. This indicates that the first two pairs only are to be used if the questions are of the true-false type. If the questions are multiple choice, disregard the "T" and "F" and pay attention only to the small letters or numbers.

Answer your questions in the manner of the sample that follows:

32. The largest city in the United States is
   A. Washington, D.C.
   B. New York City
   C. Chicago
   D. Detroit
   E. San Francisco

1) Choose the answer you think is best. (New York City is the largest, so "B" is correct.)
2) Find the row of dotted lines numbered the same as the question you are answering. (Find row number 32)
3) Find the pair of dotted lines corresponding to the answer. (Find the pair of lines under the mark "B.")
4) Make a solid black mark between the dotted lines.

VI. BEFORE THE TEST

Common sense will help you find procedures to follow to get ready for an examination. Too many of us, however, overlook these sensible measures. Indeed, nervousness and fatigue have been found to be the most serious reasons why applicants fail to do their best on civil service tests. Here is a list of reminders:

- Begin your preparation early – Don't wait until the last minute to go scurrying around for books and materials or to find out what the position is all about.
- Prepare continuously – An hour a night for a week is better than an all-night cram session. This has been definitely established. What is more, a night a week for a month will return better dividends than crowding your study into a shorter period of time.
- Locate the place of the exam – You have been sent a notice telling you when and where to report for the examination. If the location is in a different town or otherwise unfamiliar to you, it would be well to inquire the best route and learn something about the building.
- Relax the night before the test – Allow your mind to rest. Do not study at all that night. Plan some mild recreation or diversion; then go to bed early and get a good night's sleep.
- Get up early enough to make a leisurely trip to the place for the test – This way unforeseen events, traffic snarls, unfamiliar buildings, etc. will not upset you.
- Dress comfortably – A written test is not a fashion show. You will be known by number and not by name, so wear something comfortable.
- Leave excess paraphernalia at home – Shopping bags and odd bundles will get in your way. You need bring only the items mentioned in the official notice you received; usually everything you need is provided. Do not bring reference books to the exam. They will only confuse those last minutes and be taken away from you when in the test room.
- Arrive somewhat ahead of time – If because of transportation schedules you must get there very early, bring a newspaper or magazine to take your mind off yourself while waiting.
- Locate the examination room – When you have found the proper room, you will be directed to the seat or part of the room where you will sit. Sometimes you are given a sheet of instructions to read while you are waiting. Do not fill out any forms until you are told to do so; just read them and be prepared.
- Relax and prepare to listen to the instructions
- If you have any physical problem that may keep you from doing your best, be sure to tell the test administrator. If you are sick or in poor health, you really cannot do your best on the exam. You can come back and take the test some other time.

VII. AT THE TEST

The day of the test is here and you have the test booklet in your hand. The temptation to get going is very strong. Caution! There is more to success than knowing the right answers. You must know how to identify your papers and understand variations in the type of short-answer question used in this particular examination. Follow these suggestions for maximum results from your efforts:

1) Cooperate with the monitor

The test administrator has a duty to create a situation in which you can be as much at ease as possible. He will give instructions, tell you when to begin, check to see that you are marking your answer sheet correctly, and so on. He is not there to guard you, although he will see that your competitors do not take unfair advantage. He wants to help you do your best.

2) Listen to all instructions

Don't jump the gun! Wait until you understand all directions. In most civil service tests you get more time than you need to answer the questions. So don't be in a hurry. Read each word of instructions until you clearly understand the meaning. Study the examples, listen to all announcements and follow directions. Ask questions if you do not understand what to do.

3) Identify your papers

Civil service exams are usually identified by number only. You will be assigned a number; you must not put your name on your test papers. Be sure to copy your number correctly. Since more than one exam may be given, copy your exact examination title.

4) Plan your time

Unless you are told that a test is a "speed" or "rate of work" test, speed itself is usually not important. Time enough to answer all the questions will be provided, but this does not mean that you have all day. An overall time limit has been set. Divide the total time (in minutes) by the number of questions to determine the approximate time you have for each question.

5) Do not linger over difficult questions

If you come across a difficult question, mark it with a paper clip (useful to have along) and come back to it when you have been through the booklet. One caution if you do this – be sure to skip a number on your answer sheet as well. Check often to be sure that you have not lost your place and that you are marking in the row numbered the same as the question you are answering.

6) Read the questions

Be sure you know what the question asks! Many capable people are unsuccessful because they failed to *read* the questions correctly.

7) Answer all questions

Unless you have been instructed that a penalty will be deducted for incorrect answers, it is better to guess than to omit a question.

8) Speed tests

It is often better NOT to guess on speed tests. It has been found that on timed tests people are tempted to spend the last few seconds before time is called in marking answers at random – without even reading them – in the hope of picking up a few extra points. To discourage this practice, the instructions may warn you that your score will be "corrected" for guessing. That is, a penalty will be applied. The incorrect answers will be deducted from the correct ones, or some other penalty formula will be used.

9) Review your answers

If you finish before time is called, go back to the questions you guessed or omitted to give them further thought. Review other answers if you have time.

10) Return your test materials

If you are ready to leave before others have finished or time is called, take ALL your materials to the monitor and leave quietly. Never take any test material with you. The monitor can discover whose papers are not complete, and taking a test booklet may be grounds for disqualification.

VIII. EXAMINATION TECHNIQUES

1) Read the general instructions carefully. These are usually printed on the first page of the exam booklet. As a rule, these instructions refer to the timing of the examination; the fact that you should not start work until the signal and must stop work at a signal, etc. If there are any *special* instructions, such as a choice of questions to be answered, make sure that you note this instruction carefully.

2) When you are ready to start work on the examination, that is as soon as the signal has been given, read the instructions to each question booklet, underline any key words or phrases, such as *least, best, outline, describe* and the like. In this way you will tend to answer as requested rather than discover on reviewing your paper that you *listed without describing*, that you selected the *worst* choice rather than the *best* choice, etc.

3) If the examination is of the objective or multiple-choice type – that is, each question will also give a series of possible answers: A, B, C or D, and you are called upon to select the best answer and write the letter next to that answer on your answer paper – it is advisable to start answering each question in turn. There may be anywhere from 50 to 100 such questions in the three or four hours allotted and you can see how much time would be taken if you read through all the questions before beginning to answer any. Furthermore, if you come across a question or group of questions which you know would be difficult to answer, it would undoubtedly affect your handling of all the other questions.

4) If the examination is of the essay type and contains but a few questions, it is a moot point as to whether you should read all the questions before starting to answer any one. Of course, if you are given a choice – say five out of seven and the like – then it is essential to read all the questions so you can eliminate the two that are most difficult. If, however, you are asked to answer all the questions, there may be danger in trying to answer the easiest one first because you may find that you will spend too much time on it. The best technique is to answer the first question, then proceed to the second, etc.

5) Time your answers. Before the exam begins, write down the time it started, then add the time allowed for the examination and write down the time it must be completed, then divide the time available somewhat as follows:

- If 3-1/2 hours are allowed, that would be 210 minutes. If you have 80 objective-type questions, that would be an average of 2-1/2 minutes per question. Allow yourself no more than 2 minutes per question, or a total of 160 minutes, which will permit about 50 minutes to review.
- If for the time allotment of 210 minutes there are 7 essay questions to answer, that would average about 30 minutes a question. Give yourself only 25 minutes per question so that you have about 35 minutes to review.

6) The most important instruction is to *read each question* and make sure you know what is wanted. The second most important instruction is to *time yourself properly* so that you answer every question. The third most important instruction is to *answer every question*. Guess if you have to but include something for each question. Remember that you will receive no credit for a blank and will probably receive some credit if you write something in answer to an essay question. If you guess a letter – say "B" for a multiple-choice question – you may have guessed right. If you leave a blank as an answer to a multiple-choice question, the examiners may respect your feelings but it will not add a point to your score. Some exams may penalize you for wrong answers, so in such cases *only*, you may not want to guess unless you have some basis for your answer.

7) Suggestions
   a. Objective-type questions
      1. Examine the question booklet for proper sequence of pages and questions
      2. Read all instructions carefully
      3. Skip any question which seems too difficult; return to it after all other questions have been answered
      4. Apportion your time properly; do not spend too much time on any single question or group of questions
      5. Note and underline key words – *all, most, fewest, least, best, worst, same, opposite,* etc.
      6. Pay particular attention to negatives
      7. Note unusual option, e.g., unduly long, short, complex, different or similar in content to the body of the question
      8. Observe the use of "hedging" words – *probably, may, most likely,* etc.
      9. Make sure that your answer is put next to the same number as the question
      10. Do not second-guess unless you have good reason to believe the second answer is definitely more correct
      11. Cross out original answer if you decide another answer is more accurate; do not erase until you are ready to hand your paper in
      12. Answer all questions; guess unless instructed otherwise
      13. Leave time for review

   b. Essay questions
      1. Read each question carefully
      2. Determine exactly what is wanted. Underline key words or phrases.
      3. Decide on outline or paragraph answer

4. Include many different points and elements unless asked to develop any one or two points or elements
5. Show impartiality by giving pros and cons unless directed to select one side only
6. Make and write down any assumptions you find necessary to answer the questions
7. Watch your English, grammar, punctuation and choice of words
8. Time your answers; don't crowd material

8) Answering the essay question

Most essay questions can be answered by framing the specific response around several key words or ideas. Here are a few such key words or ideas:

M's: manpower, materials, methods, money, management
P's: purpose, program, policy, plan, procedure, practice, problems, pitfalls, personnel, public relations
   a. Six basic steps in handling problems:
      1. Preliminary plan and background development
      2. Collect information, data and facts
      3. Analyze and interpret information, data and facts
      4. Analyze and develop solutions as well as make recommendations
      5. Prepare report and sell recommendations
      6. Install recommendations and follow up effectiveness

   b. Pitfalls to avoid
      1. *Taking things for granted* – A statement of the situation does not necessarily imply that each of the elements is necessarily true; for example, a complaint may be invalid and biased so that all that can be taken for granted is that a complaint has been registered
      2. *Considering only one side of a situation* – Wherever possible, indicate several alternatives and then point out the reasons you selected the best one
      3. *Failing to indicate follow up* – Whenever your answer indicates action on your part, make certain that you will take proper follow-up action to see how successful your recommendations, procedures or actions turn out to be
      4. *Taking too long in answering any single question* – Remember to time your answers properly

IX. AFTER THE TEST

Scoring procedures differ in detail among civil service jurisdictions although the general principles are the same. Whether the papers are hand-scored or graded by machine we have described, they are nearly always graded by number. That is, the person who marks the paper knows only the number – never the name – of the applicant. Not until all the papers have been graded will they be matched with names. If other tests, such as training and experience or oral interview ratings have been given, scores will be combined. Different parts of the examination usually have different weights. For example, the written test might count 60 percent of the final grade, and a rating of training and experience 40 percent. In many jurisdictions, veterans will have a certain number of points added to their grades.

After the final grade has been determined, the names are placed in grade order and an eligible list is established. There are various methods for resolving ties between those who get the same final grade – probably the most common is to place first the name of the person whose application was received first. Job offers are made from the eligible list in the order the names appear on it. You will be notified of your grade and your rank as soon as all these computations have been made. This will be done as rapidly as possible.

People who are found to meet the requirements in the announcement are called "eligibles." Their names are put on a list of eligible candidates. An eligible's chances of getting a job depend on how high he stands on this list and how fast agencies are filling jobs from the list.

When a job is to be filled from a list of eligibles, the agency asks for the names of people on the list of eligibles for that job. When the civil service commission receives this request, it sends to the agency the names of the three people highest on this list. Or, if the job to be filled has specialized requirements, the office sends the agency the names of the top three persons who meet these requirements from the general list.

The appointing officer makes a choice from among the three people whose names were sent to him. If the selected person accepts the appointment, the names of the others are put back on the list to be considered for future openings.

That is the rule in hiring from all kinds of eligible lists, whether they are for typist, carpenter, chemist, or something else. For every vacancy, the appointing officer has his choice of any one of the top three eligibles on the list. This explains why the person whose name is on top of the list sometimes does not get an appointment when some of the persons lower on the list do. If the appointing officer chooses the second or third eligible, the No. 1 eligible does not get a job at once, but stays on the list until he is appointed or the list is terminated.

X. HOW TO PASS THE INTERVIEW TEST

The examination for which you applied requires an oral interview test. You have already taken the written test and you are now being called for the interview test – the final part of the formal examination.

You may think that it is not possible to prepare for an interview test and that there are no procedures to follow during an interview. Our purpose is to point out some things you can do in advance that will help you and some good rules to follow and pitfalls to avoid while you are being interviewed.

What is an interview supposed to test?
The written examination is designed to test the technical knowledge and competence of the candidate; the oral is designed to evaluate intangible qualities, not readily measured otherwise, and to establish a list showing the relative fitness of each candidate – as measured against his competitors – for the position sought. Scoring is not on the basis of "right" and "wrong," but on a sliding scale of values ranging from "not passable" to "outstanding." As a matter of fact, it is possible to achieve a relatively low score without a single "incorrect" answer because of evident weakness in the qualities being measured.

Occasionally, an examination may consist entirely of an oral test – either an individual or a group oral. In such cases, information is sought concerning the technical knowledges and abilities of the candidate, since there has been no written examination for this purpose. More commonly, however, an oral test is used to supplement a written examination.

Who conducts interviews?

The composition of oral boards varies among different jurisdictions. In nearly all, a representative of the personnel department serves as chairman. One of the members of the board may be a representative of the department in which the candidate would work. In some cases, "outside experts" are used, and, frequently, a businessman or some other representative of the general public is asked to serve. Labor and management or other special groups may be represented. The aim is to secure the services of experts in the appropriate field.

However the board is composed, it is a good idea (and not at all improper or unethical) to ascertain in advance of the interview who the members are and what groups they represent. When you are introduced to them, you will have some idea of their backgrounds and interests, and at least you will not stutter and stammer over their names.

What should be done before the interview?

While knowledge about the board members is useful and takes some of the surprise element out of the interview, there is other preparation which is more substantive. It *is* possible to prepare for an oral interview – in several ways:

1) Keep a copy of your application and review it carefully before the interview

This may be the only document before the oral board, and the starting point of the interview. Know what education and experience you have listed there, and the sequence and dates of all of it. Sometimes the board will ask you to review the highlights of your experience for them; you should not have to hem and haw doing it.

2) Study the class specification and the examination announcement

Usually, the oral board has one or both of these to guide them. The qualities, characteristics or knowledges required by the position sought are stated in these documents. They offer valuable clues as to the nature of the oral interview. For example, if the job involves supervisory responsibilities, the announcement will usually indicate that knowledge of modern supervisory methods and the qualifications of the candidate as a supervisor will be tested. If so, you can expect such questions, frequently in the form of a hypothetical situation which you are expected to solve. NEVER go into an oral without knowledge of the duties and responsibilities of the job you seek.

3) Think through each qualification required

Try to visualize the kind of questions you would ask if you were a board member. How well could you answer them? Try especially to appraise your own knowledge and background in each area, *measured against the job sought*, and identify any areas in which you are weak. Be critical and realistic – do not flatter yourself.

4) Do some general reading in areas in which you feel you may be weak

For example, if the job involves supervision and your past experience has NOT, some general reading in supervisory methods and practices, particularly in the field of human relations, might be useful. Do NOT study agency procedures or detailed manuals. The oral board will be testing your understanding and capacity, not your memory.

5) Get a good night's sleep and watch your general health and mental attitude

You will want a clear head at the interview. Take care of a cold or any other minor ailment, and of course, no hangovers.

What should be done on the day of the interview?

Now comes the day of the interview itself. Give yourself plenty of time to get there. Plan to arrive somewhat ahead of the scheduled time, particularly if your appointment is in the fore part of the day. If a previous candidate fails to appear, the board might be ready for you a bit early. By early afternoon an oral board is almost invariably behind schedule if there are many candidates, and you may have to wait. Take along a book or magazine to read, or your application to review, but leave any extraneous material in the waiting room when you go in for your interview. In any event, relax and compose yourself.

The matter of dress is important. The board is forming impressions about you – from your experience, your manners, your attitude, and your appearance. Give your personal appearance careful attention. Dress your best, but not your flashiest. Choose conservative, appropriate clothing, and be sure it is immaculate. This is a business interview, and your appearance should indicate that you regard it as such. Besides, being well groomed and properly dressed will help boost your confidence.

Sooner or later, someone will call your name and escort you into the interview room. *This is it.* From here on you are on your own. It is too late for any more preparation. But remember, you asked for this opportunity to prove your fitness, and you are here because your request was granted.

What happens when you go in?

The usual sequence of events will be as follows: The clerk (who is often the board stenographer) will introduce you to the chairman of the oral board, who will introduce you to the other members of the board. Acknowledge the introductions before you sit down. Do not be surprised if you find a microphone facing you or a stenotypist sitting by. Oral interviews are usually recorded in the event of an appeal or other review.

Usually the chairman of the board will open the interview by reviewing the highlights of your education and work experience from your application – primarily for the benefit of the other members of the board, as well as to get the material into the record. Do not interrupt or comment unless there is an error or significant misinterpretation; if that is the case, do not hesitate. But do not quibble about insignificant matters. Also, he will usually ask you some question about your education, experience or your present job – partly to get you to start talking and to establish the interviewing "rapport." He may start the actual questioning, or turn it over to one of the other members. Frequently, each member undertakes the questioning on a particular area, one in which he is perhaps most competent, so you can expect each member to participate in the examination. Because time is limited, you may also expect some rather abrupt switches in the direction the questioning takes, so do not be upset by it. Normally, a board member will not pursue a single line of questioning unless he discovers a particular strength or weakness.

After each member has participated, the chairman will usually ask whether any member has any further questions, then will ask you if you have anything you wish to add. Unless you are expecting this question, it may floor you. Worse, it may start you off on an extended, extemporaneous speech. The board is not usually seeking more information. The question is principally to offer you a last opportunity to present further qualifications or to indicate that you have nothing to add. So, if you feel that a significant qualification or characteristic has been overlooked, it is proper to point it out in a sentence or so. Do not compliment the board on the thoroughness of their examination – they have been sketchy, and you know it. If you wish, merely say, "No thank you, I have nothing further to add." This is a point where you can "talk yourself out" of a good impression or fail to present an important bit of information. Remember, *you close the interview yourself.*

The chairman will then say, "That is all, Mr. _____, thank you." Do not be startled; the interview is over, and quicker than you think. Thank him, gather your belongings and take your leave. Save your sigh of relief for the other side of the door.

How to put your best foot forward

Throughout this entire process, you may feel that the board individually and collectively is trying to pierce your defenses, seek out your hidden weaknesses and embarrass and confuse you. Actually, this is not true. They are obliged to make an appraisal of your qualifications for the job you are seeking, and they want to see you in your best light. Remember, they must interview all candidates and a non-cooperative candidate may become a failure in spite of their best efforts to bring out his qualifications. Here are 15 suggestions that will help you:

1) Be natural – Keep your attitude confident, not cocky

If you are not confident that you can do the job, do not expect the board to be. Do not apologize for your weaknesses, try to bring out your strong points. The board is interested in a positive, not negative, presentation. Cockiness will antagonize any board member and make him wonder if you are covering up a weakness by a false show of strength.

2) Get comfortable, but don't lounge or sprawl

Sit erectly but not stiffly. A careless posture may lead the board to conclude that you are careless in other things, or at least that you are not impressed by the importance of the occasion. Either conclusion is natural, even if incorrect. Do not fuss with your clothing, a pencil or an ashtray. Your hands may occasionally be useful to emphasize a point; do not let them become a point of distraction.

3) Do not wisecrack or make small talk

This is a serious situation, and your attitude should show that you consider it as such. Further, the time of the board is limited – they do not want to waste it, and neither should you.

4) Do not exaggerate your experience or abilities

In the first place, from information in the application or other interviews and sources, the board may know more about you than you think. Secondly, you probably will not get away with it. An experienced board is rather adept at spotting such a situation, so do not take the chance.

5) If you know a board member, do not make a point of it, yet do not hide it

Certainly you are not fooling him, and probably not the other members of the board. Do not try to take advantage of your acquaintanceship – it will probably do you little good.

6) Do not dominate the interview

Let the board do that. They will give you the clues – do not assume that you have to do all the talking. Realize that the board has a number of questions to ask you, and do not try to take up all the interview time by showing off your extensive knowledge of the answer to the first one.

7) Be attentive

You only have 20 minutes or so, and you should keep your attention at its sharpest throughout. When a member is addressing a problem or question to you, give him your undivided attention. Address your reply principally to him, but do not exclude the other board members.

8) Do not interrupt

A board member may be stating a problem for you to analyze. He will ask you a question when the time comes. Let him state the problem, and wait for the question.

9) Make sure you understand the question

Do not try to answer until you are sure what the question is. If it is not clear, restate it in your own words or ask the board member to clarify it for you. However, do not haggle about minor elements.

10) Reply promptly but not hastily

A common entry on oral board rating sheets is "candidate responded readily," or "candidate hesitated in replies." Respond as promptly and quickly as you can, but do not jump to a hasty, ill-considered answer.

11) Do not be peremptory in your answers

A brief answer is proper – but do not fire your answer back. That is a losing game from your point of view. The board member can probably ask questions much faster than you can answer them.

12) Do not try to create the answer you think the board member wants

He is interested in what kind of mind you have and how it works – not in playing games. Furthermore, he can usually spot this practice and will actually grade you down on it.

13) Do not switch sides in your reply merely to agree with a board member

Frequently, a member will take a contrary position merely to draw you out and to see if you are willing and able to defend your point of view. Do not start a debate, yet do not surrender a good position. If a position is worth taking, it is worth defending.

14) Do not be afraid to admit an error in judgment if you are shown to be wrong

The board knows that you are forced to reply without any opportunity for careful consideration. Your answer may be demonstrably wrong. If so, admit it and get on with the interview.

15) Do not dwell at length on your present job

The opening question may relate to your present assignment. Answer the question but do not go into an extended discussion. You are being examined for a *new* job, not your present one. As a matter of fact, try to phrase ALL your answers in terms of the job for which you are being examined.

Basis of Rating

Probably you will forget most of these "do's" and "don'ts" when you walk into the oral interview room. Even remembering them all will not ensure you a passing grade. Perhaps you did not have the qualifications in the first place. But remembering them will help you to put your best foot forward, without treading on the toes of the board members.

Rumor and popular opinion to the contrary notwithstanding, an oral board wants you to make the best appearance possible. They know you are under pressure – but they also want to see how you respond to it as a guide to what your reaction would be under the pressures of the job you seek. They will be influenced by the degree of poise you display, the personal traits you show and the manner in which you respond.

ABOUT THIS BOOK

This book contains tests divided into Examination Sections. Go through each test, answering every question in the margin. At the end of each test look at the answer key and check your answers. On the ones you got wrong, look at the right answer choice and learn. Do not fill in the answers first. Do not memorize the questions and answers, but understand the answer and principles involved. On your test, the questions will likely be different from the samples. Questions are changed and new ones added. If you understand these past questions you should have success with any changes that arise. Tests may consist of several types of questions. We have additional books on each subject should more study be advisable or necessary for you. Finally, the more you study, the better prepared you will be. This book is intended to be the last thing you study before you walk into the examination room. Prior study of relevant texts is also recommended. NLC publishes some of these in our Fundamental Series. Knowledge and good sense are important factors in passing your exam. Good luck also helps. So now study this Passbook, absorb the material contained within and take that knowledge into the examination. Then do your best to pass that exam.

EXAMINATION SECTION

EXAMINATION SECTION
TEST 1

DIRECTIONS: Each question or incomplete statement is followed by several suggested answers or completions. Select the one that BEST answers the question or completes the statement. *PRINT THE LETTER OF THE CORRECT ANSWER IN THE SPACE AT THE RIGHT.*

1. In almost every organization, there is a nucleus of highly important functions commonly designated as *management.* Which of the following statements BEST characterizes *management?*   1.____

    A.   Getting things done through others
    B.   The highest level of intelligence in any organization
    C.   The process whereby democratic and participative activities are maximized
    D.   The *first among equals*

2. Strategies in problem-solving are important to anyone aspiring to advancement in the field of administration. Which of the following is BEST classified as the first step in the process of problem-solving?   2.____

    A.   Collection and organization of data
    B.   The formulation of a plan
    C.   The definition of the problem
    D.   The development of a method and methodology

3. One of the objectives of preparing a budget is to   3.____

    A.   create optimistic goals which each department can attempt to meet
    B.   create an overall company goal by combining the budgets of the various departments
    C.   be able to compare planned expenditures against actual expenditures
    D.   be able to identify accounting errors

4. The rise in demand for *systems* personnel in industrial and governmental organizations over the past five years has been extraordinary.
In which of the following areas would a *systems* specialist assigned to an agency be LEAST likely to be of assistance?   4.____

    A.   Developing, recommending, and establishing an effective cost and inventory system
    B.   Development and maintenance of training manuals
    C.   Reviewing existing work procedures and recommending improvements
    D.   Development of aptitude tests for new employees

5. Management experts have come to the conclusion that the traditional forms of motivation used in industry and government, which emphasize authority over and economic rewards for the employee, are no longer appropriate.
To which of the following factors do such experts attribute the GREATEST importance in producing this change?   5.____

    A.   The desire of employees to satisfy material needs has become greater and more complex.

B. The desire for social satisfaction has become the most important aspect of the job for the average worker.
C. With greater standardization of work processes, there has been an increase in the willingness of workers to accept discipline.
D. In general, employee organizations have made it more difficult for management to fire an employee.

6. In preparing a budget, it is usually considered advisable to start the initial phases of preparation at the operational level of management.
Of the following, the justification that management experts usually advance as MOST reasonable for this practice is that operating managers, as a consequence of their involvement, will

    6._____

A. develop a background in finance or accounting
B. have an understanding of the organizational structure
C. tend to feel responsible for carrying out budget objectives
D. have the ability to see the overall financial picture

7. An administrative officer has been asked by his superior to write a concise, factual report with objective conclusions and recommendations based on facts assembled by other researchers.
Of the following factors, the administrative officer should give LEAST consideration to

    7._____

A. the educational level of the person or persons for whom the report is being prepared
B. the use to be made of the report
C. the complexity of the problem
D. his own feelings about the importance of the problem

8. In an agency, upon which of the following is a supervisor's effectiveness MOST likely to depend?
The

    8._____

A. degree to which a supervisor allows subordinates to participate in the decision-making process and the setting of objectives
B. degree to which a supervisor's style meets management's objectives and subordinates' needs
C. strength and forcefulness of the supervisor in pursuing his objectives
D. expertise and knowledge the supervisor has about the specific work to be done

9. For authority to be effective, which of the following is the MOST basic requirement?
Authority must be

    9._____

A. absolute   B. formalized   C. accepted   D. delegated

10. Management no longer abhors the idea of employees taking daily work breaks, but prefers to schedule such breaks rather than to allot to each employee a standard amount of free time to be taken off during the day as he wishes. Which of the following BEST expresses the reason management theorists give for the practice of scheduling such breaks?

    10._____

A. Many jobs fall into natural work units which are scheduled, and the natural time to take a break is at the end of the unit.

B. Taking a scheduled break permits socialization and a feeling of accomplishment.
C. Managers have concluded that scheduling rest periods seems to reduce the incidence of unscheduled ones.
D. Many office workers who really need such breaks are hesitant about taking them unless they are scheduled.

11. The computer represents one of the major developments of modern technology. It is widely used in both scientific and managerial activities because of its many advantages. Which of the following is NOT an advantage gained by management in the use of the computer?
A computer

11.____

A. provides the manager with a greatly enlarged memory so that he can easily be provided with data for decision making
B. relieves the manager of basic decision-making responsibility, thereby giving him more time for directing and controlling
C. performs routine, repetitive calculations with greater precision and reliability than employees
D. provides a capacity for rapid simulations of alternative solutions to problem solving

12. A supervisor of a unit in a division is usually responsible for all of the following EXCEPT

12.____

A. the conduct of subordinates in the achievement of division objectives
B. maintaining quality standards in the unit
C. the protection and care of materials and equipment in the unit
D. performing the most detailed tasks in the unit himself

13. You have been assigned to teach a new employee the functions and procedures of your office.
In your introductory talk, which of the following approaches is PREFERABLE?

13.____

A. Advise the new employee of the employee benefits and services available to him, over and above his salary.
B. Discuss honestly the negative aspects of departmental procedures and indicate methods available to overcome them.
C. Give the new employee an understanding of the general purpose of office procedures and functions and of their relevance to departmental objectives.
D. Give a basic and detailed explanation of the operations of your office, covering all functions and procedures.

14. It is your responsibility to assign work to several clerks under your supervision. One of the clerks indignantly refuses to accept an assignment and asks to be given something else. He has not yet indicated why he does not want the assignment, but is sitting there glaring at you, awaiting your reaction.
Of the following, which is the FIRST action you should take?

14.____

A. Ask the employee into your office in order to reprimand him and tell him emphatically that he must accept the assignment.
B. Talk to the employee privately in an effort to find the reason for his indignation and refusal, and then base your action upon your findings.

C. Let the matter drop for a day or two to allow the employee to cool off before you insist that he accept the assignment.
D. Inform the employee quietly and calmly that as his supervisor you have selected him for this assignment and that you fully expect him to accept it.

15. Administrative officers are expected to be able to handle duties delegated to them by their supervisors and to be able, as they advance in status, to delegate tasks to assistants.
When considering whether to delegate tasks to a subordinate, which of the following questions should be LEAST important to an administrative officer?
In the delegated tasks,

    15.____

A. how significant are the decisions to be made, and how much consultation will be involved?
B. to what extent is uniformity and close coordination of activity required?
C. to what extent must speedy-on-the-spot decisions be made?
D. to what extent will delegation relieve the administrative officer of his burden of responsibility?

16. A functional forms file is a collection of forms which are grouped by

    16.____

A. purpose   B. department   C. title   D. subject

17. All of the following are reasons to consult a records retention schedule except one.
Which one is that?
To determine

    17.____

A. whether something should be filed
B. how long something should stay in file
C. who should be assigned to filing
D. when something on file should be destroyed

18. Listed below are four of the steps in the process of preparing correspondence for filing. If they were to be put in logical sequence, the SECOND step would be

    18.____

A. preparing cross-reference sheets or cards
B. coding the correspondence using a classification system
C. sorting the correspondence in the order to be filed
D. checking for follow-up action required and preparing a follow-up slip

19. New material added to a file folder should USUALLY be inserted

    19.____

A. in the order of importance (the most important in front)
B. in the order of importance (the most important in back)
C. chronologically (most recent in front)
D. chronologically (most recent in back)

20. An individual is looking for a name in the white pages of a telephone directory. Which of the following BEST describes the system of filing found there?
A(n)_____ file

    20.____

A. alphabetic   B. sequential
C. locator   D. index

21. The MAIN purpose of a tickler file is to 21.____

    A. help prevent overlooking matters that require future attention
    B. check on adequacy of past performance
    C. pinpoint responsibility for recurring daily tasks
    D. reduce the volume of material kept in general files

22. Which of the following BEST describes the process of reconciling a bank statement? 22.____

    A. Analyzing the nature of the expenditures made by the office during the preceding month
    B. Comparing the statement of the bank with the banking records maintained in the office
    C. Determining the liquidity position by reading the bank statement carefully
    D. Checking the service charges noted on the bank statement

23. From the viewpoint of preserving agency or institutional funds, which of the following is the LEAST acceptable method for making a payment? 23.____
A check made out to

    A. cash   B. a company
    C. an individual   D. a partnership

24. In general, the CHIEF economy of using multicopy forms is in 24.____

    A. the paper on which the form is printed B. printing the form
    C. employee time   D. carbon paper

25. Suppose your supervisor has asked you to develop a form to record certain information needed. 25.____
The FIRST thing you should do is to

    A. determine the type of data that will be recorded repeatedly so that it can be pre-printed
    B. study the relationship of the form to the job to be accomplished so that the form can be planned
    C. determine the information that will be recorded in the same place on each copy of the form so that it can be used as a check
    D. find out who will be responsible for supplying the information so that space can be provided for their signatures

26. An administrative officer in charge of a small fund for buying office supplies has just written a check to Charles Laird, a supplier, and has sent the check by messenger to him. A half-hour later, the messenger telephones the administrative officer. He has lost the check. 26.____
Which of the following is the MOST important action for the administrative officer to take under these circumstances?

    A. Ask the messenger to return and write a report describing the loss of the check.
    B. Make a note on the performance record of the messenger who lost the check.
    C. Take the necessary steps to have payment stopped on the check.
    D. Refrain from doing anyting since the check may be found shortly.

27. A petty cash fund is set up PRIMARILY to   27.___

    A. take care of small investments that must be made from time to time
    B. take care of small expenses that arise from time to time
    C. provide a fund to be used as the office wants to use it with little need to maintain records
    D. take care of expenses that develop during emergencies, such as machine break-downs and fires

28. Of the following, which is usually the MOST important guideline in writing business letters?   28.___
A letter should be

    A. neat
    B. written in a formalized style
    C. written in clear language intelligible to the reader
    D. written in the past tense

29. Suppose you are asked to edit a policy statement. You note that personal pronouns like   29.___
you, we, and *I* are used freely.
Which of the following statements BEST applies to this use of personal pronouns?
It

    A. is proper usage because written business language should not be different from carefully spoken business language
    B. requires correction because it is ungrammatical
    C. is proper because it is clearer and has a warmer tone
    D. requires correction because policies should be expressed in an impersonal manner

30. Good business letters are coherent.   30.___
To be coherent means to

    A. keep only one unifying idea in the message
    B. present the total message
    C. use simple, direct words for the message
    D. tie together the various ideas in the message

31. Proper division of a letter into paragraphs requires that the writer of business letters   31.___
should, as much as possible, be sure that

    A. each paragraph is short
    B. each paragraph develops discussion of just one topic
    C. each paragraph repeats the theme of the total message
    D. there are at least two paragraphs for every message

32. An editor is given a letter with this initial paragraph: 32.___
 We have received your letter, which we read with interest, and we are happy to respond to your question. In fact, we talked with several people in our office to get ideas to send to you.
Which of the following is it MOST reasonable for the editor to conclude?
The paragraph is

A. concise
B. communicating something of value
C. unnecessary
D. coherent

33. As soon as you pick up the phone, a very angry caller begins immediately to complain   33.____
about city agencies and *red tape*. He says that he has been shifted to two or three different offices. It turns out that he is seeking information which is not immediately available
to you. You believe you know, however, where it can be found. Which of the following
actions is the BEST one for you to take?

    A. To eliminate all confusion, suggest that the caller write the mayor stating explicitly
what he wants.
    B. Apologize by telling the caller how busy city agencies now are, but also tell him
directly that you do not have the information he needs.
    C. Ask for the caller's telephone number and assure him you will call back after you
have checked further.
    D. Give the caller the name and telephone number of the person who might be able to
help, but explain that you are not positive he will get results.

34. Suppose that one of your duties is to dictate responses to routine requests from the pub-   34.____
lic for information. A letter writer asks for information which, as expressed in a one-sen-
tence, explicit agency rule, cannot be given out to the public.
Of the following ways of answering the letter, which is the MOST efficient?

    A. Quote verbatim that section of the agency rules which prohibits giving this informa-
tion to the public.
    B. Without quoting the rule, explain why you cannot accede to the request and sug-
gest alternative sources.
    C. Describe how carefully the request was considered before classifying it as subject
to the rule forbidding the issuance of such information.
    D. Acknowledge receipt of the letter and advise that the requested information is not
released to the public.

35. Suppose you assist in supervising a staff which has rather high morale, and your own   35.____
supervisor asks you to poll the staff to find out who will be able to work overtime this particular evening to help complete emergency work.
Which of the following approaches would be MOST likely to win their cooperation while
maintaining their morale?

    A. Tell them that the better assignments will be given only to those who work over-
time.
    B. Tell them that occasional overtime is a job requirement .
    C. Assure them they'll be doing you a personal favor.
    D. Let them know clearly why the overtime is needed.

36. Suppose that you have been asked to write and to prepare for reproduction new depart-   36.____
mental vacation leave regulations.
After you have written the new regulations, all of which fit on one page, which one of
the following would be the BEST method of reproducing 1000 copies?

    A. An outside private printer, because you can best maintain confidentiality using this
technique
    B. Xeroxing, because the copies will have the best possible appearance

C. Typing copies, because you will be certain that there are the fewest possible errors
D. Including it in the next company newsletter

37. Administration is the center, but not necessarily the source, of all ideas for procedural improvement.
The MOST significant implication that this principle bears for the administrative officer is that

    A. before procedural improvements are introduced, they should be approved by a majority of the staff
    B. it is the unique function of the administrative officer to derive and introduce procedural improvements
    C. the administrative officer should derive ideas and suggestions for procedural improvement from all possible sources, introducing any that promise to be effective
    D. the administrative officer should view employee grievances as the chief source of procedural improvements

37.____

38. Your bureau is assigned an important task.
Of the following, the function that you, as an administrative officer, can LEAST reasonably be expected to perform under these circumstances is

    A. division of the large job into individual tasks
    B. establishment of *production lines* within the bureau
    C. performance personally of a substantial share of all the work
    D. check-up to see that the work has been well done

38.____

39. Suppose that you have broken a complex job into its smaller components before making assignments to the employees under your jurisdiction.
Of the following, the LEAST advisable procedure to follow from that point is to

    A. give each employee a picture of the importance of his work for the success of the total job
    B. establish a definite line of work flow and responsibility
    C. post a written memorandum of the best method for performing each job
    D. teach a number of alternative methods for doing each job

39.____

40. As an administrative officer, you are requested to draw up an organization chart of the whole department.
Of the following, the MOST important characteristic of such a chart is that it will

    A. include all peculiarities and details of the organization which distinguish it from any other
    B. be a schematic representation of purely administrative functions within the department
    C. present a modification of the actual departmental organization in the light of principles of scientific management
    D. present an accurate picture of the lines of authority and responsibility

40.____

KEY (CORRECT ANSWERS)

1.	A	11.	B	21.	A	31.	B
2.	C	12.	D	22.	B	32.	C
3.	C	13.	C	23.	A	33.	C
4.	D	14.	B	24.	C	34.	A
5.	D	15.	D	25.	B	35.	D
6.	C	16.	A	26.	C	36.	B
7.	D	17.	C	27.	B	37.	C
8.	B	18.	A	28.	C	38.	C
9.	C	19.	C	29.	D	39.	D
10.	C	20.	A	30.	D	40.	D

———

TEST 2

DIRECTIONS: Each question or incomplete statement is followed by several suggested answers or completions. Select the one that BEST answers the question or completes the statement. *PRINT THE LETTER OF THE CORRECT ANSWER IN THE SPACE AT THE RIGHT.*

Questions 1-10.

DIRECTIONS: In each of Questions 1 through 10, a pair of related words written in capital letters is followed by four other pairs of words. For each question, select the pair of words which MOST closely expresses a relationship similar to that of the pair in capital letters.

SAMPLE QUESTION:

BOAT - DOCK
    A. airplane - hangar   B. rain - snow
    C. cloth - cotton   D. hunger - food

Choice A is the answer to this sample question since, of the choices given, the relationship between airplane and hangar is most similar to the relationship between boat and dock.

1. AUTOMOBILE - FACTORY   1.___

    A. tea - lemon   B. wheel - engine
    C. pot - flower   D. paper - mill

2. GIRDER - BRIDGE   2.___

    A. petal - flower   B. street - sidewalk
    C. meat - vegetable   D. sun - storm

3. RADIUS - CIRCLE   3.___

    A. brick - building   B. tie - tracks
    C. spoke - wheel   D. axle - tire

4. DISEASE - RESEARCH   4.___

    A. death - poverty   B. speech - audience
    C. problem - conference   D. invalid - justice

5. CONCLUSION - INTRODUCTION   5.___

    A. commencement - beginning   B. housing - motor
    C. caboose - engine   D. train - cabin

6. SOCIETY - LAW   6.___

    A. baseball - rules   B. jury - law
    C. cell - prisoner   D. sentence - jury

7. PLAN - ACCOMPLISHMENT   7.___

    A. deed - fact   B. method - success
    C. graph - chart   D. rules - manual

8. ORDER - GOVERNMENT   8._____

    A. chaos - administration   B. confusion - pandemonium
    C. rule - stability   D. despair - hope

9. TYRANNY - FREEDOM   9._____

    A. despot - mob   B. wealth - poverty
    C. nobility - commoners   D. dictatorship - democracy

10. FAX - LETTER   10._____

    A. hare - tortoise   B. lie - truth
    C. number - word   D. report - research

Questions 11-16.

DIRECTIONS: Answer Questions 11 through 16 SOLELY on the basis of the information
given in the passage below.

Inherent in all organized endeavors is the need to resolve the individual differences involved in conflict. Conflict may be either a positive or negative factor, since it may lead to creativity, innovation, and progress, on the one hand, or it may result, on the other hand, in a deterioration or even destruction of the organization. Thus, some forms of conflict are desirable, whereas others are undesirable and ethically wrong.

There are three management strategies which deal with interpersonal conflict. In the "divide-and-rule strategy", management attempts to maintain control by limiting the conflict to those directly involved and preventing their disagreement from spreading to the larger group. The "suppression-of-differences strategy" entails ignoring conflicts or pretending they are irrelevant. In the "working-through-differences strategy", management actively attempts to solve or resolve intergroup or interpersonal conflicts. Of the three strategies, only the last directly attacks and has the potential for eliminating the causes of conflict. An essential part of this strategy, however, is its employment by a committed and relatively mature management team.

11. According to the above passage, the *divide-and-rule strategy* for dealing with conflict is   11._____
the attempt to

    A. involve other people in the conflict
    B. restrict the conflict to those participating in it
    C. divide the conflict into positive and negative factors
    D. divide the conflict into a number of smaller ones

12. The word *conflict* is used in relation to both positive and negative factors in this passage.   12._____
Which one of the following words is MOST likely to describe the activity which the word
conflict, in the sense of the passage, implies?

    A. Competition   B. Cooperation
    C. Confusion   D. Aggression

13. According to the above passage, which one of the following characteristics is shared by   13._____
both the *suppression-of-differences strategy* and the *divide-and-rule strategy?*

    A. Pretending that conflicts are irrelevant
    B. Preventing conflicts from spreading to the group situation

11

C. Failure to directly attack the causes of conflict
D. Actively attempting to resolve interpersonal conflict

14. According to the above passage, the successful resolution of interpersonal conflict requires

    A. allowing the group to mediate conflicts between two individuals
    B. division of the conflict into positive and negative factors
    C. involvement of a committed, mature management team
    D. ignoring minor conflicts until they threaten the organization

14.___

15. Which can be MOST reasonably inferred from the above passage?
A conflict between two individuals is LEAST likely to continue when management uses

    A. the *working-through-differences strategy*
    B. the *suppression-of-differences strategy*
    C. the *divide-and-rule strategy*
    D. a combination of all three strategies

15.___

16. According to the above passage, a desirable result of conflict in an organization is when conflict

    A. exposes production problems in the organization
    B. can be easily ignored by management
    C. results in advancement of more efficient managers
    D. leads to development of new methods

16.___

Questions 17-23.

DIRECTIONS: Answer Questions 17 through 23 SOLELY on the basis of the information given in the passage below.

Modern management places great emphasis on the concept of communication. The communication process consists of the steps through which an idea or concept passes from its inception by one person, the sender, until it is acted upon by another person, the receiver. Through an understanding of these steps and some of the possible barriers that may occur, more effective communication may be achieved. The first step in the communication process is ideation by the sender. This is the formation of the intended content of the message he wants to transmit. In the next step, encoding, the sender organizes his ideas into a series of symbols designed to communicate his message to his intended receiver. He selects suitable words or phrases that can be understood by the receiver, and he also selects the appropriate media to be used-for example, memorandum, conference, etc. The third step is transmission of the encoded message through selected channels in the organizational structure. In the fourth step, the receiver enters the process by tuning in to receive the message. If the receiver does not function, however, the message is lost. For example, if the message is oral, the receiver must be a good listener. The fifth step is decoding of the message by the receiver, as for example, by changing words into ideas. At this step, the decoded message may not be the same idea that the sender originally encoded because the sender and receiver have different perceptions regarding the meaning of certain words.

Finally, the receiver acts or responds. He may file the information, ask for more information, or take other action. There can be no assurance, however, that communication has taken place unless there is some type of feedback to the sender in the form of an acknowledgement that the message was received.

17. According to the above passage, *ideation* is the process by which the   17.____

    A. sender develops the intended content of the message
    B. sender organizes his ideas into a series of symbols
    C. receiver tunes in to receive the message
    D. receiver decodes the message

18. In the last sentence of the passage, the word *feedback* refers to the process by which the   18.____
sender is assured that the

    A. receiver filed the information
    B. receiver's perception is the same as his own
    C. message was received
    D. message was properly interpreted

19. Which one of the following BEST shows the order of the steps in the communication pro-   19.____
cess as described in the passage?

    A. 1- ideation   2- encoding
        3- decoding   4- transmission
        5- receiving   6- action
        7- feedback to the sender

    B. 1- ideation   2- encoding
        3- transmission   4- decoding
        5- receiving   6- action
        7- feedback to the sender

    C. 1- ideation   2- decoding
        3- transmission   4- receiving
        5- encoding   6- action
        7- feedback to the sender

    D. 1- ideation   2- encoding
        3- transmission   4- receiving
        5- decoding   6- action
        7- feedback to the sender

20. Which one of the following BEST expresses the main theme of the passage?   20.____

    A. Different individuals have the same perceptions regarding the meaning of words.
    B. An understanding of the steps in the communication process may achieve better
       communication.
    C. Receivers play a passive role in the communication process.
    D. Senders should not communicate with receivers who transmit feedback.

21. The above passage implies that a receiver does NOT function properly when he   21.____

    A. transmits feedback   B. files the information
    C. is a poor listener   D. asks for more information

22. Which of the following, according to the above passage, is included in the SECOND step   22.___
of the communication process?

    A. Selecting the appropriate media to be used in transmission
    B. Formulation of the intended content of the message
    C. Using appropriate media to respond to the receiver's feedback
    D. Transmitting the message through selected channels in the organization

23. The above passage implies that the *decoding process* is MOST NEARLY the reverse of   23.___
the _____ process.

    A. transmission   B. receiving
    C. feedback   D. encoding

Questions 24-27.

DIRECTIONS: Answer Questions 24 through 27 SOLELY on the basis of the information
                  given in the paragraph below.

    *A personnel researcher has at his disposal various approaches for obtaining information,
analyzing it, and arriving at conclusions that have value in predicting and affecting the behavior of people at work. The type of method to be used depends on such factors as the nature
of the research problem, the available data, and the attitudes of those people being studied to
the various kinds of approaches. While the experimental approach, with its use of control
groups, is the most refined type of study, there are others that are often found useful in personnel research. Surveys, in which the researcher obtains facts on a problem from a variety
of sources, are employed in research on wages, fringe benefits, and labor relations. Historical
studies are used to trace the development of problems in order to understand them better
and to isolate possible causative factors. Case studies are generally developed to explore all
the details of a particular problem that is representative of other similar problems. A
researcher chooses the most appropriate form of study for the problem he is investigating.
He should recognize, however, that the experimental method, commonly referred to as the
scientific method, if used validly and reliably, gives the most conclusive results.*

24. The above statement discusses several approaches used to obtain information on partic-   24.___
ular problems.
Which of the following may be MOST reasonably concluded from the paragraph?
A(n)

    A. historical study cannot determine causative factors
    B. survey is often used in research on fringe benefits
    C. case study is usually used to explore a problem that is unique and unrelated to
       other problems
    D. experimental study is used when the scientific approach to a problem fails

25. According to the above paragraph, all of the following are factors that may determine the   25.___
type of approach a researcher uses EXCEPT

    A. the attitudes of people toward being used in control groups
    B. the number of available sources
    C. his desire to isolate possible causative factors
    D. the degree of accuracy he requires

26. The words *scientific method,* used in the last sentence of the paragraph, refer to a type of   26.____
study which, according to the paragraph,

    A. uses a variety of sources
    B. traces the development of problems
    C. uses control groups
    D. analyzes the details of a representative problem

27. Which of the following can be MOST reasonably concluded from the above paragraph?   27.____
In obtaining and analyzing information on a particular problem, a researcher employs
the method which is the

    A. most accurate   B. most suitable
    C. least expensive   D. least time-consuming

Questions 28-31.

DIRECTIONS: The graph below indicates at 5-year intervals the number of citations issued
for various offenses from the year 1990 to the year 2010. Answer Questions 28
through 31 according to the information given in this graph.

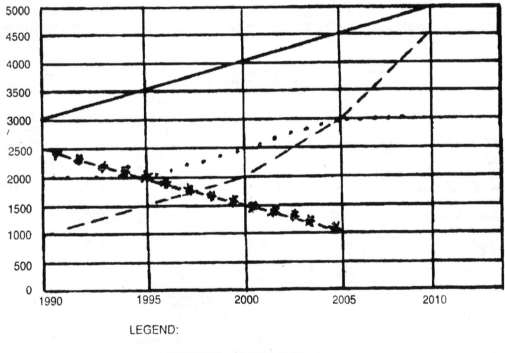

LEGEND:

——————— Parking Violatation

– – – Drug Use

• • • • Dangerous Weapons

✦✦✦ Improper Dress

28. Over the 20-year period, which offense shows an AVERAGE rate of increase of more   28.____
than 150 citations per year?

    A. Parking Violations   B. Dangerous Weapons
    C. Drug Use   D. None of the above

29. Over the 20-year period, which offense shows a CONSTANT rate of increase or decrease?   29.____

    A. Parking Violations   B. Drug Use
    C. Dangerous Weapons   D. Improper Dress

30. Which offense shows a TOTAL INCREASE OR DECREASE of 50% for the full 20-year period?   30.____

    A. Parking Violations   B. Drug Use
    C. Dangerous Weapons   D. Improper Dress

31. The percentage increase in total citations issued from 1995 to 2000 is MOST NEARLY   31.____

    A. 7%   B. 11%   C. 21%   D. 41%

Questions 32-35.

DIRECTIONS: The chart below shows the annual average number of administrative actions completed for the four divisions of a bureau. Assume that the figures remain stable from year to year.

                 Answer Questions 32 through 35 SOLELY on the basis of information given in the chart.

Administrative Actions	DIVISIONS				Totals
	W	X	Y	Z	
Telephone Inquiries Answered	8,000	6,800	7,500	4,800	27,100
Interviews Conducted	500	630	550	500	2,180
Applications Processed	15,000	18,000	14,500	9,500	57,000
Letters Typed	2,500	4,400	4,350	3,250	14,500
Reports Completed	200	250	100	50	600
Totals	26,200	30,080	27,000	18,100	101,380

32. In which division is the number of Applications Processed the GREATEST percentage of the total Administrative Actions for that division?   32.____

    A. W   B. X   C. Y   D. Z

33. The bureau chief is considering a plan that would consolidate the typing of letters in a separate unit. This unit would be responsible for the typing of letters for all divisions in which the number of letters typed exceeds 15% of the total number of Administrative Actions. Under this plan, which of the following divisions would CONTINUE to type its own letters?   33.____

    A. W and X   B. W, X, and Y
    C. X and Y   D. X and Z

34. The setting up of a central information service that would be capable of answering 25% of the whole bureau's telephone inquiries is under consideration. Under such a plan, the divisions would gain for other activities that time previously spent on telephone inquiries. Approximately how much total time would such a service gain for all four divisions if it requires 5 minutes to answer the average telephone inquiry? _____ hours.

    A. 500   B. 515   C. 565   D. 585

34.____

35. Assume that the rate of production shown in the table can be projected as accurate for the coming year and that monthly output is constant for each type of administrative action within a division. Division Y is scheduled to work exclusively on a 4-month long special project during that year. During the period of the project, Division Y's regular workload will be divided evenly among the remaining divisions.
Using the figures in the table, what would be MOST NEARLY the percentage increase in the total Administrative Actions completed by Division Z for the year?

    A. 8%   B. 16%   C. 25%   D. 50%

35.____

36. You have conducted a traffic survey at 10 two-lane bridges and find the traffic between 4:30 and 5:30 P.M. averages 665 cars per bridge that hour. You can't find the tabulation sheet for Bridge #7, but you know that 6066 cars were counted at the other 9 bridges. Determine from this how many must have been counted at Bridge #7.

    A. 584   B. 674   C. 665   D. 607

36.____

37. You pay temporary help $11.20 per hour and regular employees $12.00 per hour. Your workload is temporarily heavy, so you need 20 hours of extra regular employees' time to catch up. If you do this on overtime, you must pay time-and-a-half. If you use temporary help, it takes 25% more time to do the job.
What is the difference in cost between the two alternatives?

    A. $20 more for temporary   B. $40 more for temporary
    C. $80 more for regular   D. $136 more for regular

37.____

38. An experienced clerk can process the mailing of annual forms in 9 days. A new clerk takes 14 days to process them.
If they work together, how many days MOST NEARLY will it take to do the processing?

    A. $4\frac{1}{2}$ B. $5\frac{1}{2}$ C. $6\frac{1}{2}$ D. 7

38.____

39. A certain administrative aide is usually able to successfully handle 27% of all telephone inquiries without assistance. In a particular month, he receives 1200 inquiries and handles 340 of them successfully on his own. How many more inquiries has he handled successfully in that month than would have been expected of him based on his usual rate?

    A. 10   B. 16   C. 24   D. 44

39.____

40. Suppose that on a scaled drawing of an office building floor, 1/2 inch represents three feet of actual floor dimensions.
A floor which is, in fact, 75 feet wide and 132 feet long has which of the following dimensions on this scaled drawing? _____ inches wide and _____ inches long.

    A. 9.5; 20.5   B. 12.5; 22
    C. 17; 32   D. 25; 44

40.____

41. In a division of clerks and stenographers, 15 people are currently employed, 20% of whom are stenographers.
If management plans are to maintain the current number of stenographers, but to increase the clerical staff to the point where 12% of the total staff are stenographers, what is the MAXIMUM number of additional clerks that should be hired to meet these plans?

    A. 3   B. 8   C. 10   D. 12

42. Suppose that a certain agency had a 2005 budget of $1,100,500. The 2006 budget was 7% higher than that of 2005, and the 2007 budget was 8% higher than that of 2006. Of the following, which one is MOST NEARLY that agency's budget for 2007?

    A. $1,117,624   B. $1,261,737
    C. $1,265,575   D. $1,271,738

Question's 43-50.

DIRECTIONS: Your office keeps a file card record of the work assignments for all the employ-ees in a certain bureau. On each card is the employee's name, a work assign-ment code number, and the date of this assignment. In this filing system, the employee's name is filed alphabetically, the work assignment code is filed numerically, and the date of the assignment is filed chronologically (earliest date first).

Each of Questions 43 through 50 represents five cards to be filed, numbered (1) through (5) shown in Column I. Each card is made up of the employee's name, a work assignment code number shown in parentheses, and the date of this assignment. The cards are to be filed according to the following rules:

First: File in alphabetical order;
Second: When two or more cards have the same employee's name, file according to the work assignment number, beginning with the lowest number.
Third: When two or more cards have the same employee's name and same assign-ment number, file according to the assignment date beginning with earliest date.
Column II shows the cards arranged in four different orders. Pick the answer (A, B, C, or D) in Column II which shows the cards arranged correctly accord-ing to the above filing rules.

SAMPLE QUESTION:

Column I				Column II				
(1) Cluney	(486503)	6/17/07	A.	2,	3,	4,	1,	5
(2) Roster	(246611)	5/10/06	B.	2,	5,	1,	3,	4
(3) Altool	(711433)	10/15/07	C.	3,	2,	1,	4,	5
(4) Cluney	(527610)	12/18/06	D.	3,	5,	1,	4,	2
(5) Cluney	(486500)	4/8/07						

The correct way to file the cards is:

(3) Altool	(711433)	10/15/07
(5) Cluney	(486500)	4/8/07
(1) Cluney	(486503)	6/17/07
(4) Cluney	(527610)	12/18/06
(2) Roster	(246611)	5/10/06

The correct filing order is shown by the numbers in front of each name (3, 5, 1, 4, 2). The answer to the sample question is the letter in Column II in front of the numbers 3, 5, 1, 4, 2. This answer is D.

43.   43.____

		Column I			Column II				
(1)	Prichard	(013469)	4/6/06	A.	5,	4,	3,	2,	1
(2)	Parks	(678941)	2/7/06	B.	1,	2,	5,	3,	4
(3)	Williams	(551467)	3/6/05	C.	2,	1,	5,	3,	4
(4)	Wilson	(551466)	8/9/02	D.	1,	5,	4,	3,	2
(5)	Stanhope	(300014)	8/9/02						

44.   44.____

(1)	Ridgeway	(623809)	8/11/06	A.	5,	1,	3,	4,	2
(2)	Travers	(305439)	4/5/02	B.	5,	1,	3,	2,	4
(3)	Tayler	(818134)	7/5/03	C.	1,	5,	3,	2,	4
(4)	Travers	(305349)	5/6/05	D.	1,	5,	4,	2,	3
(5)	Ridgeway	(623089)	10/9/06						

45.   45.____

(1)	Jaffe	(384737)	2/19/06	A.	3,	5,	2,	4,	1
(2)	Inez	(859176)	8/8/07	B.	3,	5,	2,	1,	4
(3)	Ingrahm	(946460)	8/6/04	C.	2,	3,	5,	1,	4
(4)	Karp	(256146)	5/5/05	D.	2,	3,	5,	4,	1
(5)	Ingrahm	(946460)	6/4/05						

46.   46.____

(1)	Marrano	(369421)	7/24/04	A.	1,	5,	3,	4,	2
(2)	Marks	(652910)	2/23/06	B.	3,	5,	4,	2,	1
(3)	Netto	(556772)	3/10/07	C.	2,	4,	1,	5,	3
(4)	Marks	(652901)	2/17/07	D.	4,	2,	1,	5,	3
(5)	Netto	(556772)	6/17/05						

47.   47.____

(1)	Abernathy	(712467)	6/23/05	A.	5,	3,	1,	2,	4
(2)	Acevedo	(680262)	6/23/03	B.	5,	4,	2,	3,	1
(3)	Aaron	(967647)	1/17/04	C.	1,	3,	5,	2,	4
(4)	Acevedo	(680622)	5/14/02	D.	2,	4,	1,	5,	3
(5)	Aaron	(967647)	4/1/00						

48.   48.____

(1)	Simon	(645219)	8/19/05	A.	4,	1,	2,	5,	3
(2)	Simon	(645219)	9/2/03	B.	4,	5,	2,	1,	3
(3)	Simons	(645218)	7/7/05	C.	3,	5,	2,	1,	4
(4)	Simms	(646439)	10/12/06	D.	5,	1,	2,	3,	4
(5)	Simon	(645219)	10/16/02						

49.   49.____

(1)	Rappaport	(312230)	6/11/06	A.	4,	3,	1,	2,	5
(2)	Rascio	(777510)	2/9/05	B.	4,	3,	1,	5,	2
(3)	Rappaport	(312230)	7/3/02	C.	3,	4,	1,	5,	2
(4)	Rapaport	(312330)	9/6/05	D.	5,	2,	4,	3,	1
(5)	Rascio	(777501)	7/7/05						

50.

(1)	Johnson	(843250)	6/8/02	A.	1,	3,	2,	4,	5
(2)	Johnson	(843205)	4/3/05	B.	1,	3,	2,	5,	4
(3)	Johnson	(843205)	8/6/02	C.	3,	2,	1,	4,	5
(4)	Johnson	(843602)	3/8/06	D.	3,	2,	1,	5,	4
(5)	Johnson	(843602)	8/3/05						

50._____

_____

KEY (CORRECT ANSWERS)

1.	D	11.	B	21.	C	31.	B	41.	C
2.	A	12.	A	22.	A	32.	B	42.	D
3.	C	13.	C	23.	D	33.	A	43.	C
4.	C	14.	C	24.	B	34.	C	44.	A
5.	C	15.	A	25.	D	35.	B	45.	C
6.	A	16.	D	26.	C	36.	A	46.	D
7.	B	17.	A	27.	B	37.	C	47.	A
8.	C	18.	C	28.	C	38.	B	48.	B
9.	D	19.	D	29.	A	39.	B	49.	B
10.	A	20.	B	30.	C	40.	B	50.	D

_____

EXAMINATION SECTION
TEST 1

DIRECTIONS: Each question or incomplete statement is followed by several suggested
answers or completions. Select the one that BEST answers the question or
completes the statement. *PRINT THE LETTER OF THE CORRECT ANSWER
IN THE SPACE AT THE RIGHT.*

1. A certain system for handling office supplies requires that supplies be issued to the vari-   1.____
    ous agency offices only on a bi-weekly basis and that all supply requisitions be autho-
    rized by the unit supervisor.
    The BEST reason for establishing this supplies system is to

    A. standardize ordering descriptions and stock identification codes
    B. prevent the disordering of stock shelves and cabinets by unauthorized persons
        searching for supplies
    C. ensure that unit supervisors properly exercise their right to make determinations
        on supply orders
    D. encourage proper utilization of supplies to control the workload

2. It is important that every office have a retention and disposal program for filing material.   2.____
    Suppose that you have been appointed administrative assistant in an office with a poorly
    organized records-retention program.
    In establishing a revised program for the transfer or disposal of records, the step which
    would logically be taken THIRD in the process is

    A. preparing a safe and inexpensive storage area and setting up an indexing system
        for records already in storage
    B. determining what papers to retain and for how long a period
    C. taking an inventory of what is filed, where it is filed, how much is filed, and how
        often it is used
    D. moving records from active to inactive files and destroying useless records

3. In the effective design of office forms, the FIRST step to take is to   3.____

    A. decide what information should be included
    B. decide the purpose for which the form will be used
    C. identify the form by name and number
    D. identify the employees who will be using the form

4. Some designers of office forms prefer to locate the instructions on how to fill out the form   4.____
    at the bottom of it. The MOST logical objection to placing such instructions at the bottom
    of the form is that

    A. instructions at the bottom require an excess of space
    B. all form instructions should be outlined with a separate paragraph
    C. the form may be partly filled out before the instructions are seen
    D. the bottom of the form should be reserved only for authorization and signature

5. A formal business report may consist of many parts, including the following: 5.___
      I.   Table of contents
     II.   List of references
    III.   Preface
    IV.   Index
     V.   List of tables
    VI.   Conclusions or recommendations
Of the following, in setting up a formal report, the PROPER order of the six parts listed is

  A. I, III, VI, V, II, IV   B. IV, III, II, V, VI, I
  C. III, I, V, VI, II, IV   D. II, V, III, I, IV, VI

6. Three of the basic functions of office management are considered to be planning, con- 6.___
trolling, and organizing. Of the following, the one which might BEST be considered
ORGANIZING activity is

  A. assigning personnel and materials to work units to achieve agreed-upon objectives
  B. determining future objectives and indicating conditions affecting the accomplish-
      ment of the goals
  C. evaluating accomplishments and applying necessary corrective measures to
      insure results
  D. motivating employees to perform their work in accordance with objectives

7. The following four statements relate to office layout. 7.___
      I.   Position supervisors' desks at the front of their work group so that they can
          easily be recognized as persons in authority
     II.   Arrange file cabinets and frequently used equipment near the employees
         who utilize them most often
    III.   Locate the receptionist's desk near the entrance of the office so that visitor
         traffic will not distract other workers
    IV.   Divide a large office area into many smaller offices by using stationary parti-
         tions so that all employees may have privacy and prestige
According to authorities in office management and administration, which of these
statements are GENERALLY recommended guides to effective office layout?

  A. I, II, III   B. II, III, IV
  C. II, III   D. All of the above

8. For which of the following purposes would a flow chart have the GREATEST applicabil- 8.___
ity?

  A. Training new employees in performance of routinized duties
  B. Determining adequacy of performance of employees
  C. Determining the accuracy of the organization chart
  D. Locating causes of delays in carrying out an operation

9. Office work management concerns tangible accomplishment or production. It has to do 9.___
with results; it does not deal with the amount of energy expended by the individual who
produces the results.
According to this statement, the production in which of the following kinds of jobs
would be MOST difficult to measure accurately? A(n)

A. file clerk
B. secretary
C. computer operator
D. office administrator

10. The FIRST step in the statistical analysis of a great mass of data secured from a survey   10.____
is to

    A. scan the data to determine which is atypical of the survey
    B. determine the number of deviations from the average
    C. arrange the data into groups on the basis of likenesses and differences
    D. plot the data on a graph to determine trends

11. Suppose that, as an administrative assistant in charge of an office, you are required to   11.____
change the layout of your office to accommodate expanding functions.
The LEAST important factor to be considered in planning the revised layout is the

    A. relative productivity of individuals in the office
    B. communication and work flow needs
    C. need for screening confidential activities from unauthorized persons
    D. areas of noise concentration

12. Suppose you have instructed a new employee to follow a standardized series of steps to   12.____
accomplish a job. He is to use a rubber stamp, then a red pencil on the first paper, and a
numbering machine on the second. Then, he is to staple the two sheets of paper together
and put them to one side. You observe, however, that he sometimes uses the red pencil
first, sometimes the numbering machine first. At other times, he does the stapling before
using the numbering machine.
For you as supervisor to suggest that the clerk use the standardized method when
doing this job would be

    A. *bad*, because the clerk should be given a chance to use his independent judgment
       on the best way to do his job
    B. *good*, because the clerk's sequence of actions results in a loss of efficiency
    C. *bad*, because it is not wise to interrupt the work habit the clerk has already devel-
       oped
    D. *good*, because the clerk should not be permitted to make unauthorized changes in
       standard office routines

13. Suppose study of the current records management system for students' transcripts   13.____
reveals needless recopying of transcript data throughout various offices within the university. On this basis, a recommendation is made that this unnecessary recopying of information be eliminated.
This decision to eliminate waste in material, time, and space is an application of the
office management principle of

    A. work simplification
    B. routing and scheduling
    C. job analysis
    D. cost and budgetary control

14. It is generally LEAST practical for an office manager to prepare for known peak work   14.____
periods by

    A. putting job procedures into writing so that they can be handled by more than one
       person
    B. arranging to make assignments of work on a short-interval scheduling basis

C. cleaning up as much work as possible ahead of known peak periods
D. rotating jobs and assignments among different employees to assure staff flexibility

15. The four statements below are about office manuals used for various purposes. 15.___
If you had the job of designing and controlling several kinds of office manuals to be used in your agency, which one of these statements would BEST apply as a general rule for you to follow?

A. Office manual content should be classified into main topics with proper subidivisions arranged in strict alphabetical order.
B. Manual additions and revisions should be distributed promptly to all holders of manuals for their approval, correction, and criticism.
C. The language used in office manuals should be simple, and charts and diagrams should be interspersed within the narrative material for further clarity.
D. Office manual content should be classified into main topics arranged in strict alphabetical order with subtopics in sequence according to importance.

16. Suppose that, as an administrative assistant, you have been assigned to plan the reorga- 16.___
nization of an office which has not been operating efficiently because of the uncoordi-
nated manner in which new functions have been assigned to it over the past year.
The FIRST thing you should do is

A. call a meeting of the office staff and explain the purposes of the planned reorganization
B. make a cost-value analysis of the present operations to determine what should be changed or eliminated
C. prepare a diagram of the flow of work as you think it should be
D. define carefully the current objectives to be achieved by this reorganization

17. Effective organization requires that specific actions be taken in proper sequence. 17.___
The following are four actions essential to effective organization:
    I. Group activities on the basis of human and material resources
    II. Coordinate functions and provide for good communications
    III. Formulate objectives, policies, and plans
    IV. Determine activities necessary to accomplish goals
The PROPER sequence of these four actions is:

A. III, II, IV, I   B. IV, III, I, II
C. III, IV, I, II   D. IV, I, III, II

18. For an administrative assistant to give each of his subordinates exactly the same type of 18.___
supervision is

A. *advisable,* because he will gain a reputation for being fair and impartial
B. *inadvisable,* because subordinates work more diligently when they think they are receiving preferential treatment
C. *advisable,* because most human problems can be classified into categories which make them easier to handle
D. *inadvisable,* because people differ and there is no one supervisory procedure that applies in every case to dealing with individuals

19. Suppose that, as an administrative assistant, you find that some of your subordinates are coming to you with complaints you think are trivial.
For you to hear them through is

    A. *poor practice*; subordinates should be trained to come to you only with major grievances
    B. *good practice*; major grievances sometimes are the underlying cause of minor complaints
    C. *poor practice*; you should delegate this kind of matter and spend your time on more important problems
    D. *good practice*; this will make you more popular with your subordinates

19.____

20. Suppose that a new departmental policy has just been established which you feel may be resented by your subordinates, but which they must understand and follow. Which would it be most advisable for you as their supervisor to do FIRST?

    A. Make clear to your subordinates that you are not responsible for making this policy.
    B. Tell your subordinates that you agree with the policy whether you do or not.
    C. Explain specifically to your subordinates the reasons for the policy and how it is going to affect them.
    D. Distribute a memo outlining the new policy and require your subordinates to read it.

20.____

21. An office assistant under your supervision tells you that she is reluctant to speak to one of her subordinates about poor work habits because this subordinate is strong-willed, and she does not want to antagonize her.
For you to refuse the office assistant's request that you speak to her subordinate about this matter is

    A. *inadvisable*, since you are in a position of greater authority
    B. *advisable*, since supervision of this subordinate is a basic responsibility of that office assistant
    C. *inadvisable*, since the office assistant must work more closely with her subordinate than you do
    D. *advisable*, since you should not risk antagonizing her subordinate yourself

21.____

22. The GREATEST advantage to a supervisor of using oral communications as compared to written is the

    A. opportunity provided for immediate feedback
    B. speed with which orders can be given and carried out
    C. reduction in amount of paper work
    D. establishment of an informal atmosphere

22.____

23. Of the following, the MOST important reason for an administrative assistant to have private, face-to-face discussions with subordinates about their performance is

    A. encourage a more competitive spirit among employees
    B. give special praise to employees who perform well
    C. discipline employees who perform poorly
    D. help employees improve their work

23.____

24. For a supervisor to keep records of reprimands to subordinates about violations of rules is   24.___

    A. *poor practice*; such records are evidence of the supervisor's inability to maintain discipline

    B. *good practice*; these records are valuable to support disciplinary actions recommended or taken

    C. *poor practice*; the best way to prevent recurrences is to apply penalties without delay

    D. *good practice*; such records are evidence that the supervisor is doing a good job

25. As an administrative assistant supervising a small office, you decide to hold a staff meeting to try to find an acceptable solution to a problem that is causing serious conflicts within the group.   25.___
At this meeting, your role should be to present the problem and

    A. see that the group keeps the problem in focus and does not discuss irrelevant matters

    B. act as chairman of the meeting, but take no other part in the discussion

    C. see to it that each member of the group offers a suggestion for its solution

    D. state your views on the matter before any discussion gets under way

---

KEY (CORRECT ANSWERS)

1.	D	11.	A
2.	A	12.	B
3.	B	13.	A
4.	C	14.	B
5.	C	15.	C
6.	A	16.	D
7.	C	17.	C
8.	D	18.	D
9.	D	19.	B
10.	C	20.	C

21.	B
22.	A
23.	D
24.	B
25.	A

TEST 2

DIRECTIONS: Each question or incomplete statement is followed by several suggested answers or completions. Select the one that BEST answers the question or completes the statement. *PRINT THE LETTER OF THE CORRECT ANSWER IN THE SPACE AT THE RIGHT.*

1. Suppose that one of your subordinates who supervises two young office assistants has been late for work a number of times and you have decided to talk to him about it. In your discussion, it would be MOST constructive for you to emphasize that   1.____

    A. personal problems cannot be used as an excuse for these latenesses
    B. the department suffers financially when he is late
    C. you will be forced to give him a less desirable assignment if his latenesses continue
    D. his latenesses set a bad example to those he supervises

2. Suppose that, as a newly-appointed administrative assistant, you are in charge of a small but very busy office. Your four subordinates are often required to make quick decisions on a wide range of matters while answering telephone or in-person inquiries. You can MOST efficiently help your subordinates meet such situations by   2.____

    A. delegating authority to make such decisions to only one or two trusted subordinates
    B. training each subordinate in the proper response for each kind of inquiry that might be made
    C. making certain that subordinates understand clearly the basic policies that affect these decisions
    D. making each subordinate an expert in one area

3. Of the following, the MOST recent development in methods of training supervisors that involves the human relations approach is   3.____

    A. conference training   B. the lecture method
    C. the case method   D. sensitivity training

4. Which of the following is MOST likely to result in failure as a supervisor?   4.____

    A. Showing permissiveness in relations with subordinates
    B. Avoiding delegation of tasks to subordinates
    C. Setting high performance standards for subordinates
    D. Using discipline only when necessary

5. The MOST important long-range benefit to an organization of proper delegation of work by supervisors is *generally* that   5.____

    A. subordinates will be developed to assume greater responsibilities
    B. subordinates will perform the work as their supervisors would
    C. errors in delegated work will be eliminated
    D. more efficient communication among organizational components will result

6. Which of the following duties would it be LEAST appropriate for an administrative assis-   6.___
tant in charge of an office to delegate to an immediate subordinate?

    A. Checking of figures to be used in a report to the head of the department
    B. On-the-job training of newly appointed college office assistants
    C. Reorganization of assignments for higher level office staff
    D. Contacting other school offices for needed information

7. Decisions should be delegated to the lowest point in the organization at which they can   7.___
be made effectively.
The one of the following which is MOST likely to be a result of the application of this
accepted management principle is that

    A. upward communications will be facilitated
    B. potential for more rapid decisions and implementation is increased
    C. coordination of decisions that are made will be simplified
    D. no important factors will be overlooked in making decisions

8. The lecture-demonstration method would be LEAST desirable in a training program set   8.___
up for

    A. changing the attitudes of long-term employees
    B. informing subordinates about new procedures
    C. explaining how a new office machine works
    D. orientation of new employees

9. Which one of the following conditions would be LEAST likely to indicate a need for   9.___
employee training?

    A. Large number of employee suggestions
    B. Large amount of overtime
    C. High number of chronic latenesses
    D. Low employee morale

10. An administrative assistant is planning to make a recommendation to change a proce-   10.___
dure which would substantially affect the work of his subordinates.
For this supervisor to consult with his subordinates about the recommendation before
sending it through would be

    A. *undesirable*; subordinates may lose respect for a supervisor who evidences such
indecisiveness
    B. *desirable;* since the change in procedure would affect their work, subordinates
should decide whether the change should be made
    C. *undesirable;* since subordinates would not receive credit if the procedure were
changed, their morale would be lowered
    D. *desirable;* the subordinates may have some worthwhile suggestions concerning
the recommendation

11. The BEST way to measure improvement in a selected group of office assistants who   11.___
have undergone a training course in the use of specific techniques is to

    A. have the trainees fill out questionnaires at the completion of the course as to what
they have learned and giving their opinions as to the value of the course

B. compare the performance of the trainees who completed the course with the performance of office assistants who did not take the course
C. compare the performance of the trainees in these techniques before and after the training course
D. compare the degree of success on the next promotion examination of trainees and non-trainees

12. When an administrative assistant finds it necessary to call in a subordinate for a disciplinary interview, his MAIN objective should be to   12.____

A. use techniques which can penetrate any deception and get at the truth
B. stress correction of, rather than punishment for, past errors
C. maintain a reputation for being an understanding superior
D. decide on disciplinary action that is consistent with penalties applied for similar infractions

13. Suppose that a newly promoted office assistant does satisfactory work during the first   13.____
five months of her probationary period. However, her supervisor notices shortly after this time that her performance is falling below acceptable standards. The supervisor decides to keep records of this employee's performance, and if there is no significant improvement by the end of 11 months, to recommend that this employee not be given tenure in the higher title.
This, as the sole course of action, is

A. *justified;* employees who do not perform satisfactorily should not be promoted
B. *unjustified;* the supervisor should attempt to determine the cause of the poor performance as soon as possible
C. *justified;* the supervisor will have given the subordinate the full probationary period to improve herself
D. *unjustified;* the subordinate should be demoted to her previous title as soon as her work becomes unsatisfactory

14. Suppose that you are conducting a conference-style training course for a group of 12   14.____
office assistants. Miss Jones is the only conferee who has not become involved in the discussion.
The BEST method of getting Miss Jones to participate is to

A. ask her to comment on remarks made by the best-informed participant
B. ask her to give a brief talk at the next session on a topic that interests her
C. set up a role-play situation and assign her to take a part
D. ask her a direct question which you know she can answer

15. Which of the following is NOT part of the *control* function of office management?   15.____

A. Deciding on alternative courses of action
B. Reporting periodically on productivity
C. Evaluating performance against the standards
D. Correcting deviations when required

16. Which of the following is NOT a principal aspect of the process of delegation?   16.____

A. Developing improvements in methods used to carry out assignments
B. Granting of permission to do what is necessary to carry out assignments

29

C. Assignment of duties by a supervisor to an immediate subordinate
D. Obligation on the part of a subordinate to carry out his assignment

17. Reluctance of a supervisor to delegate work effectively may be due to any or all of the following EXCEPT the supervisor's   17.___

    A. unwillingness to take calculated risks
    B. lack of confidence in subordinates
    C. inability to give proper directions as to what he wants done
    D. retention of ultimate responsibility for delegated work

18. A man cannot serve two masters.   18.___
    This statement emphasizes the importance in an organization of following the principle of

    A. specialization of work
    B. unity of command
    C. uniformity of assignment
    D. span of control

19. In general, the number of subordinates an administrative assistant can supervise effectively tends to vary   19.___

    A. *directly* with both similarity and complexity of their duties
    B. *directly* with similarity of their duties and *inversely* with complexity of their duties
    C. *inversely* with both similarity and complexity of their duties
    D. *inversely* with similarity of their duties and *directly* with complexity of their duties

20. When an administrative assistant practices *general* rather than *close* supervision, which one of the following is MOST likely to happen?   20.___

    A. His subordinates will not be as well-trained as employees who are supervised more closely.
    B. Standards are likely to be lowered because subordinates will be under fewer pressures and will not be motivated to work toward set goals.
    C. He will give fewer specific orders and spend more time on planning and coordinating than those supervisors who practice close supervision.
    D. This supervisor will spend more time checking and correcting mistakes made by subordinates than would one who supervises closely.

Questions 21-25.

DIRECTIONS: Questions 21 to 25 are to be answered SOLELY on the basis of the information contained in the following paragraph.
    Since an organization chart is pictorial in nature, there is a tendency for it to be drawn in an artistically balanced and appealing fashion, regardless of the realities of actual organizational structure. In addition to being subject to this distortion, there is the difficulty of communicating in any organization chart the relative importance or the relative size of various component parts of an organizational structure. Furthermore, because of the need for simplicity of design, an organization chart can never indicate the full extent of the interrelationships among the component parts of an organization. These interrelationships are often just as vital as the specifications which an organization chart endeavors to indicate. Yet, if an organization chart were to be drawn with all the wide variety of criss-crossing communication

and cooperation networks existent within a typical organization, the chart would probably be much more confusing than informative. It is also obvious that no organization chart as such can 'prove' or 'disprove' that the organizational structure it represents is effective in realizing the objectives of the organization. At best, an organization chart can only illustrate some of the various factors to be taken into consideration in understanding, devising, or altering organizational arrangements.

21. According to the above paragraph, an organization chart can be expected to portray the   21.____

    A. structure of the organization along somewhat ideal lines
    B. relative size of the organizational units quite accurately
    C. channels of information distribution within the organization graphically
    D. extent of the obligation of each unit to meet the organizational objectives

22. According to the above paragraph, those aspects of internal functioning which are NOT   22.____
shown on an organization chart

    A. can be considered to have little practical application in the operations of the organization
    B. might well be considered to be as important as the structural relationships which a chart does present
    C. could be the cause of considerable confusion in the operation of an organization which is quite large
    D. would be most likely to provide the information needed to determine the overall effectiveness of an organization

23. In the above paragraph, the one of the following conditions which is NOT implied as   23.____
being a defect of an organization chart is that an organization chart may

    A. present a picture of the organizational structure which is different from the structure that actually exists
    B. fail to indicate the comparative size of various organizational units
    C. be limited in its ability to convey some of the meaningful aspects of organizational relationships
    D. become less useful over a period of time during which the organizational facts which it illustrated have changed

24. The one of the following which is the MOST suitable title for the above paragraph is   24.____

    A. The Design and Construction of an Organization Chart
    B. The Informal Aspects of an Organization Chart
    C. The Inherent Deficiencies of an Organization Chart
    D. The Utilization of a Typical Organization Chart

25. It can be INFERRED from the above paragraph that the function of an organization chart   25.____
is to

    A. contribute to the comprehension of the organization form and arrangements
    B. establish the capabilities of the organization to operate effectively
    C. provide a balanced picture of the operations of the organization
    D. eliminate the need for complexity in the organization's structure

———

KEY (CORRECT ANSWERS)

1.	D		11.	C
2.	C		12.	B
3.	D		13.	B
4.	B		14.	D
5.	A		15.	A
6.	C		16.	A
7.	B		17.	D
8.	A		18.	B
9.	A		19.	B
10.	D		20.	C

21.	A
22.	B
23.	D
24.	C
25.	A

TEST 3

DIRECTIONS: Each question or incomplete statement is followed by several suggested answers or completions. Select the one that BEST answers the question or completes the statement. *PRINT THE LETTER OF THE CORRECT ANSWER IN THE SPACE AT THE RIGHT.*

1. Of the following problems that might affect the conduct and outcome of an interview, the MOST troublesome and usually the MOST difficult for the interviewer to control is the   1._____

    A. tendency of the interviewee to anticipate the needs and preferences of the inter-viewer
    B. impulse to cut the interviewee off when he seems to have reached the end of an idea
    C. tendency of interviewee attitudes to bias the results
    D. tendency of the interviewer to do most of the talking

2. The administrative assistant MOST likely to be a good interviewer is one who   2._____

    A. is adept at manipulating people and circumstances toward his objectives
    B. is able to put himself in the position of the interviewee
    C. gets the more difficult questions out of the way at the beginning of the interview
    D. develops one style and technique that can be used in any type of interview

3. A good interviewer guards against the tendency to form an overall opinion about an inter-viewee on the basis of a single aspect of the interviewee's make-up.
   This statement refers to a well-known source of error in interviewing known as the   3._____

    A. assumption error   B. expectancy error
    C. extension effect   D. halo effect

4. In conducting an *exit interview* with an employee who is leaving voluntarily, the inter-viewer's MAIN objective should be to   4._____

    A. see that the employee leaves with a good opinion of the organization
    B. learn the true reasons for the employee's resignation
    C. find out if the employee would consider a transfer
    D. try to get the employee to remain on the job

5. During an interview, an interviewee unexpectedly discloses a relevant but embarrassing personal fact.
   It would be BEST for the interviewer to   5._____

    A. listen calmly, avoiding any gesture or facial expression that would suggest approval or disapproval of what is related
    B. change the subject, since further discussion in this area may reveal other embar-rassing, but irrelevant, personal facts
    C. apologize to the interviewee for having led him to reveal such a fact and promise not to do so again
    D. bring the interview to a close as quickly as possible in order to avoid a discussion which may be distressful to the interviewee

6. Suppose that while you are interviewing an applicant for a position in your office, you notice a contradiction in facts in two of his responses.
   For you to call the contradictions to his attention would be

   A. *inadvisable,* because it reduces the interviewee's level of participation
   B. *advisable,* because getting the facts is essential to a successful interview
   C. *inadvisable,* because the interviewer should use more subtle techniques to resolve any discrepancies
   D. *advisable,* because the interviewee should be impressed with the necessity for giving consistent answers

6.___

7. An interviewer should be aware that an undesirable result of including *leading questions* in an interview is to

   A. cause the interviewee to give *yes* or *no* answers with qualification or explanation
   B. encourage the interviewee to discuss irrelevant topics
   C. encourage the interviewee to give more meaningful information
   D. reduce the validity of the information obtained from the interviewee

7.___

8. The kind of interview which is PARTICULARLY helpful in getting an employee to tell about his complains and grievances is one in which

   A. a pattern has been worked out involving a sequence of exact questions to be asked
   B. the interviewee is expected to support his statements with specific evidence
   C. the interviewee is not made to answer specific questions but is encouraged to talk freely
   D. the interviewer has specific items on which he wishes to get or give information

8.___

9. Suppose you are scheduled to interview a student aide under your supervision concerning a health problem. You know that some of the questions you will be asking him will seem embarrassing to him, and that he may resist answering these questions.
   In general, to hold these questions for the last part of the interview would be

   A. *desirable;* the intervening time period gives the interviewer an opportunity to plan how to ask these sensitive questions
   B. *undesirable;* the student aide will probably feel that he has been tricked when he suddenly must answer embarrassing questions
   C. *desirable;* the student aide will probably have increased confidence in the interviewer and be more willing to answer these questions
   D. *undesirable;* questions that are important should not be deferred until the end of the interview

9.___

10. The House passed an amendment to delete from the omnibus higher education bill a section that would have prohibited coeducational colleges and universities from considering sex as a factor in their admissions policy.
    According to the above passage, consideration of sex as a factor in the admissions policy of coeducational colleges and universities would

    A. be permitted by the omnibus higher education bill if passed without further amendment
    B. be prohibited by the amendment to the omnibus higher education bill

10.___

C. have been prohibited by the deletion of a section from the omnibus higher education bill
D. have been permitted if the House had failed to pass the amendment

Questions 11-14.

DIRECTIONS: Answer Questions 11 to 14 only according to the information given in the passage below.

*The proposition that administrative activity is essentially the same in all organizations
appears to underlie some of the practices in the administration of private higher education.
Although the practice is unusual in public education, there are numerous instances of industrial, governmental, or military administrators being assigned to private institutions of higher
education and, to a lesser extent, of college and university presidents assuming administrative positions in other types of organizations. To test this theory that administrators are inter-
changeable, there is a need for systematic observation and classification. The myth that an
educational administrator must first have experience in the teaching profession is firmly
rooted in a long tradition that has historical prestige. The myth is bound up in the expectations
of the public and personnel surrounding the administrator. Since administrative success
depends significantly on how well an administrator meets the expectations others have of
him, the myth may be more powerful than the special experience in helping the administrator
attain organizational and educational objectives. Educational administrators who have risen
through the teaching profession have often expressed nostalgia for the life of a teacher or
scholar, but there is no evidence that this nostalgia contributes to administrative success.*

11. Which of the following statements as completed is MOST consistent with the above pas-   11._____
sage?
The greatest number of administrators has moved from

A. industry and the military to government and universities
B. government and universities to industry and the military
C. government, the armed forces, and industry to colleges and universities
D. colleges and universities to government, the armed forces, and industry

12. Of the following, the MOST reasonable inference from the above passage is that a spe-   12._____
cific area requiring further research is the

A. place of myth in the tradition and history of the educational profession
B. relative effectiveness of educational administrators from inside and outside the
teaching profession
C. performance of administrators in the administration of public colleges
D. degree of reality behind the nostalgia for scholarly pursuits often expressed by
educational administrators

13. According to the above passage, the value to an educational administrator of experience   13._____
in the teaching profession

A. lies in the firsthand knowledge he has acquired of immediate educational problems
B. may lie in the belief of his colleagues, subordinates, and the public that such experience is necessary

C. has been supported by evidence that the experience contributes to administrative success in educational fields
D. would be greater if the administrator were able to free himself from nostalgia for his former duties

14. Of the following, the MOST appropriate title for the above passage is 14._____

A. Educational Administration, Its Problems
B. The Experience Needed for Educational Administration
C. Administration in Higher Education
D. Evaluating Administrative Experience

Questions 15-20.

DIRECTIONS: Answer Questions 15 to 20 only according to the information contained in the following paragraph.

Methods of administration of office activities, much of which consists of providing information and 'know-how' needed to coordinate both activities within that particular office and other offices, have been among the last to come under the spotlight of management analysis. Progress has been rapid during the past decade, however, and is now accelerating at such a pace that an 'information revolution' in office management appears to be in the making. Although triggered by technological breakthroughs in electronic computers and other giant steps in mechanization, this information revolution must be attributed to underlying forces, such as the increased complexity of both governmental and private enterprise, and ever-keener competition. Size, diversification, specialization of function, and decentralization are among the forces which make coordination of activities both more imperative and more difficult. Increased competition, both domestic and international, leaves little margin for error in managerial decisions. Several developments during recent years indicate an evolving pattern. In 1960, the American Management Association expanded the scope of its activities and changed the name of its Office Management Division to Administrative Services Division. Also in 1960, the magazine Office Management merged with the magazine American Business, and this new publication was named Administrative Management.

15. A REASONABLE inference that can be made from the information in the above paragraph is that an important role of the office manager today is to 15._____

A. work toward specialization of functions performed by his subordinates
B. inform and train subordinates regarding any new developments in computer technology and mechanization
C. assist the professional management analysts with the management analysis work in the organization
D. supply information that can be used to help coordinate and manage the other activities of the organization

16. An IMPORTANT reason for the 'information revolution' that has been taking place in office management is the 16._____

A. advance made in management analysis in the past decade
B. technological breakthrough in electronic computers and mechanization
C. more competitive and complicated nature of private business and government
D. increased efficiency of office management techniques in the past ten years

17. According to the above paragraph, specialization of function in an organization is MOST   17.____
    likely to result in

    A. the elimination of errors in managerial decisions
    B. greater need to coordinate activities
    C. more competition with other organizations, both domestic and international
    D. a need for office managers with greater flexibility

18. The word *evolving,* as used in the third from last sentence in the above paragraph,   18.____
    means *most nearly*

    A. developing by gradual changes
    B. passing on to others
    C. occurring periodically
    D. breaking up into separate, constituent parts

19. Of the following, the MOST reasonable implication of the changes in names mentioned in   19.____
    the last part of the above paragraph is that these groups are attempting to

    A. professionalize the field of office management and the title of Office Manager
    B. combine two publications into one because of the increased costs of labor and
       materials
    C. adjust to the fact that the field of office management is broadening
    D. appeal to the top managerial people rather than the office management people in
       business and government

20. According to the above paragraph, intense competition among domestic and interna-   20.____
    tional enterprises makes it MOST important for an organization's managerial staff to

    A. coordinate and administer office activities with other activities in the organization
    B. make as few errors in decision-making as possible
    C. concentrate on decentralization and reduction of size of the individual divisions of
       the organization
    D. restrict decision-making only to top management officials

————

KEY (CORRECT ANSWERS)

1.	A	11.	C
2.	B	12.	B
3.	D	13.	B
4.	B	14.	B
5.	A	15.	D
6.	B	16.	C
7.	D	17.	B
8.	C	18.	A
9.	C	19.	C
10.	A	20.	B

EXAMINATION SECTION
TEST 1

DIRECTIONS: Each question or incomplete statement is followed by several suggested answers or completions. Select the one that BEST answers the question or completes the statement. *PRINT THE LETTER OF THE CORRECT ANSWER IN THE SPACE AT THE RIGHT.*

Questions 1–5.

DIRECTIONS: Questions 1 through 5 consist of sentences each of which contains one under- lined word whose meaning you are to identify by marking your answer either A, B, C, or D.

EXAMPLE

Public employees should avoid <u>unethical</u> conduct.
The word unethical, as used in the sentence, means, most nearly,
  A. fine   B. dishonest   C. polite   D. sleepy
The correct answer is dishonest (B). Therefore, you should mark your answer B.

1. Employees who can produce a <u>considerable</u> amount of good work are very valuable.   1.____
The word *considerable*, as used in the sentence, means, most nearly,

  A. large   B. potential   C. necessary   D. frequent

2. No person should <u>assume</u> that he knows more than anyone else.   2.____
The word *assume,* as used in the sentence, means, most nearly,

  A. verify   B. hope   C. suppose   D. argue

3. The parties decided to <u>negotiate</u> through the night.   3.____
The word *negotiate,* as used in the sentence, means, most nearly,

  A. suffer   B. play   C. think   D. bargain

4. Employees who have <u>severe</u> emotional problems may create problems at work.   4.____
The word *severe,* as used in the sentence, means, most nearly,

  A. serious   B. surprising   C. several   D. common

5. Supervisors should try to be as <u>objective</u> as possible when dealing with subordinates.   5.____
The word *objective,* as used in the sentence, means, most nearly,

  A. pleasant   B. courteous   C. fair   D. strict

Questions 6–10.

DIRECTIONS: In each of Questions 6 through 10, *one* word is wrongly used because it is *NOT* in keeping with the intended meaning of the statement. First, decide which word is wrongly used; then select as your answer the right word which really belongs in its place.

EXAMPLE

The employee told ill and requested permission to leave early.
  A. felt   B. considered   C. cried   D. spoke
The word *"told"* is clearly wrong and not in keeping with the intended meaning of the quota- tion.

The word *"felt"* (A), however, would clearly convey the intended meaning of the sentence. Option A is correct. Your answer space, therefore, would be marked A.

6. Only unwise supervisors would deliberately overload their subordinates in order to create themselves look good.   6.____

    A. delegate   B. make   C. reduce   D. produce

7. In a democratic organization each employee is seen as a special individual kind of fair treatment,   7.____

    A. granted   B. denial   C. perhaps   D. deserving

8. In order to function the work flow in an office you should begin by identifying each important procedure being performed in that office.   8.____

    A. uniformity   B. study   C. standards   D. reward

9. A wise supervisor tries to save employees' time by simplifying forms or adding forms where possible.   9.____

    A. taxing   B. supervising   C. eliminating   D. protecting

10. A public agency, whenever it changes its program, should give requirements to the need for retraining its employees.   10.____

    A. legislation   B. consideration   C. permission   D. advice

Questions 11-15.

DIRECTIONS: Answer each of Questions 11 through 15 ONLY on the basis of the reading passage preceding each question.

11. Things may not always be what they seem to be. Thus, the wise supervisor should analyze his problems and determine whether there is something there that does not meet the eye. For example, what may seem on the surface to be a personality clash between two subordinates may really be a problem of faulty organization, bad communication, or bad scheduling.   11.____
    Which one of the following statements BEST supports this passage?

    A.   The wise supervisor should avoid personality clashes.
    B.   The smart supervisor should figure out what really is going on.
    C.   Bad scheduling is the result of faulty organization.
    D.   The best supervisor is the one who communicates effectively.

12. Some supervisors, under the pressure of meeting deadlines, become harsh and dictato-   12.____
rial to their subordinates. However, the supervisor most likely to be effective in meeting
deadlines is one who absorbs or cushions pressures from above.
According to the passage, if a supervisor wishes to meet deadlines, it is MOST important that he

    A.   be informative to his superiors
    B.   encourage personal initiative among his subordinates
    C.   become harsh and dictatorial to his subordinates
    D.   protects his subordinates from pressures from above

13. When giving instructions, a supervisor must always make clear his meaning, leaving no   13.____
room for misunderstanding. For example, a supervisor who tells a subordinate to do a
task "*as soon as possible*" might legitimately be understood to mean either "*it's top priority*" or "*do it when you can.*"
Which of the following statements is BEST supported by the passage?

    A.   Subordinates will attempt to avoid work by deliberately distorting instructions.
    B.   Instructions should be short, since brief instructions are the clearest.
    C.   Less educated subordinates are more likely to honestly misunderstand instruc-
tions.
    D.   A supervisor should give precise instructions that cannot be misinterpreted.

14. Practical formulas are often suggested to simplify what a supervisor should know and   14.____
how he should behave, such as the four F's (be firm, fair, friendly, and factual). But such
simple formulas are really broad principles, not necessarily specific guides in a real situation.
According to the passage, simple formulas for supervisory behavior

    A.   are superior to complicated theories and principles
    B.   not always of practical use in actual situations
    C.   useful only if they are fair and factual
    D.   would be better understood if written in clear language

15. Many management decisions are made far removed from the actual place of operations.   15.____
Therefore, there is a great need for reliable reports and records and, the larger the organization, the greater is the need for such reports and records.
According to the passage, management decisions made far from the place of operations are

    A.   dependent to a great extent on reliable reports and records
    B.   sometimes in error because of the great distances involved
    C.   generally unreliable because of poor communications
    D.   generally more accurate than on–the–scene decisions

16. Assume that you have just been advanced to a supervisory administrative position and   16.___
have been assigned as supervisor to a new office with subordinates you do not know,
The BEST way for you to establish good relations with these new subordinates would be
to

    A. announce that all actions of the previous supervisor are now cancelled
    B. hold a meeting and warn them that you will not tolerate loafing on the job
    C. reassign all your subordinates to new tasks on the theory that a thorough shake–up is good for morale
    D. act fairly and show helpful interest in their work

17. One of your subordinates asks you to let her arrive at work 15 minutes later than usual   17.___
but leave for the day 15 minutes later than she usually does. This is temporarily necessary, your subordinate states, because of early morning medication she must give her
sick child.
Which of the following would be the *MOST* appropriate action for you to take?

    A. *Suggest* to your subordinate that she choose another family doctor
    B. *Warn* your subordinate that untruthful excuses are not acceptable
    C. *Tell* your subordinate that you will consider the request and let her know very shortly
    D. *Deny* the request since late arrival at work interferes with work performance

18. A young newly–hired employee asked his supervisor several times for advice on private   18.___
financial matters. The supervisor commented, in a friendly manner, that he considered it
undesirable to give such advice.
The supervisor's response was

    A. *unwise;* the supervisor missed an opportunity to advise the employee on an impor-tant matter
    B. *wise;* if the financial advice was wrong, it could damage the supervisor's relation-ship with the subordinate
    C. *unwise;* the subordinate will take up the matter with his fellow workers and proba-bly get poor advice
    D. *wise;* the supervisor should never advise subordinates on any matter

19. Which of the following is the MOST justified reason for a supervisor to pay any serious   19.___
attention to a subordinate's off–the–job behavior? The

    A. subordinate's life style is different from the supervisor's way of life
    B. subordinate has become well–known as a serious painter of fine art
    C. subordinate's work has become very poor as a result of his or her personal prob-lems
    D. subordinate is a reserved person who, at work, seldom speaks of personal matters

20. One of your subordinates complains to you that you assign him to the least pleasant jobs   20._____
more often than anyone else. You are disturbed by this complaint since you believe you
have always rotated such assignments on a fair basis.
Of the following, it would be BEST for you to tell the complaining subordinate that

    A. you will review your past assignment records and discuss the matter with him fur-
ther
    B. complaints to supervisors are not the wise way to get ahead on the job
    C. disciplinary action will follow if the complaint is not justified
    D. he may be correct, but you do not have sufficient time to verify the complaint

21. Assume that you have called one of your subordinates into your office to talk about the   21._____
increasing number of careless errors in her work. Until recently, this subordinate had
been doing good work, but this is no longer so. Your subordinate does not seem to
respond to your questions about the reason for her poor work.
In these circumstances, your *next* step should be to tell her

    A. that her continued silence will result in severe disciplinary action
    B. to request an immediate transfer from your unit
    C. to return when she is ready to respond
    D. to be more open with you so that her work problem can be identified

22. Assume that you are given a complicated assignment with a tight deadline set by your   22._____
superior. Shortly after you begin work you realize that, if you are to do a top quality job,
you cannot possibly meet the deadline.
In these circumstances, what should be your FIRST course of action?

    A. *Continue* working as rapidly as possible, hoping that you will meet the deadline
after all
    B. *Request* the assignment be given to an employee whom you believe works faster
    C. *Advise* your superior of the problem and see whether the deadline can be
extended
    D. *Advise* your superior that the deadline cannot be met and, therefore, you will not
start the job

23. Assume that a member of the public comes to you to complain about a long–standing   23._____
practice of your agency. The complaint seems to be justified.
Which one of the following is the BEST way for you to handle this situation?

    A. *Inform* the complainant that you will have the agency practice looked into and that
he will be advised of any action taken
    B. *Listen* politely, express sympathy, and state that you see no fault in the practice
    C. *Express* agreement with the practice on the ground that it has been in effect for
many years
    D. *Advise* the complainant that things will work out well in good time

24. One of your subordinates tells you that he sees no good reason for having departmental safety rules.
Which one of the following replies would be BEST for you to make?

    A. Rules are meant to be obeyed without question.
    B. All types of rules are equally important.
    C. Safety rules are meant to protect people from injury.
    D. If a person is careful enough, he doesn't have to observe safety rules.

24._____

25. Assume that a supervisor, when he issues instructions to his subordinates, usually names his superior as the source of these instructions.
This practice is, generally,

    A. *wise,* since if things go wrong, the subordinates will know whom to blame
    B. *unwise,* since it may give the subordinates the impression that the supervisor doesn't really support the instructions
    C. *wise,* since it clearly invites the subordinates to go to higher authority if they don't like the instructions
    D. *unwise,* since the subordinates may thereby be given too much information

25._____

KEY (CORRECT ANSWERS)

1. A		11. B
2. C		12. D
3. D		13. D
4. A		14. B
5. C		15. A
6. B		16. D
7. D		17. C
8. B		18. B
9. C		19. C
10. B		20. A

21. D
22. C
23. A
24. C
25. B

TEST 2

DIRECTIONS: Each question or incomplete statement is followed by several suggested answers or completions. Select the one that *BEST* answers the question or completes the statement. *PRINT THE LETTER OF THE CORRECT ANSWER IN THE SPACE AT THE RIGHT*

1. An office aide is assigned as a receptionist in a busy office. The office aide often has stretches of idle time between visitors.
   In this situation, the supervisor should

   A. *give* the receptionist non–urgent clerical jobs which can quickly be done at the reception desk
   B. *offer* all office aides an opportunity to volunteer for this assignment
   C. *eliminate* the receptionist assignment
   D. *continue* the arrangement unchanged, because receptionist duties are so important nothing should interfere with them

1.____

2. A supervisor can MOST correctly assume that an employee is not performing up to his usual standard when the employee does not handle a task as skillfully as

   A. do other employees who have received less training
   B. do similar employees having comparable work experience
   C. he has handled it in several recent instances
   D. the supervisor himself could handle it

2.____

3. Assume that you receive a suggestion that you direct all the typists in a typing pool to complete the identical quantity of work each day.
   For you to adopt this suggestion would be

   A. *advisable;* it will demonstrate the absence of supervisory favoritism
   B. *advisable;* all employees in a given title should be treated identically
   C. *inadvisable;* a supervisor should decide on work standards without interference from others
   D. *inadvisable;* it ignores variations in specific assignments and individual skills

3.____

4. A certain supervisor encouraged her subordinates to tell her if they become aware of possible job problems.
   This practice is *good* MAINLY because

   A. early awareness of job problems allows more time for seeking solutions
   B. such expected job problems may not develop
   C. the supervisor will be able to solve the job problem without consulting other people
   D. the supervisor will be able to place responsibility for poor work

4.____

5. Some supervisors will discuss with a subordinate how he is doing on the job only when indicating his mistakes or faults.
   Which of the following is the MOST likely result of such a practice?

   A. The subordinate will become discouraged and frustrated.
   B. Management will set work standards too low.
   C. The subordinate will be favorably impressed by the supervisor's frankness.
   D. Supervisors will avoid creating any impression of favoritism.

5.____

6. A supervisor calls in a subordinate he supervises to discuss the subordinate's annual work performance, indicating his work deficiencies and also praising his job strengths. The subordinate nods his head as if in agreement with his supervisor's comments on both his strengths and weaknesses, but actually says nothing, even after the supervisor has completed his comments. At this point, the supervisor should

6.____

A. end the session and assume that the subordinate agrees completely with the evaluation
B. end the session, since all the subordinate's good and bad points have been identified
C. ask the subordinate whether the criticism is justified, and, if so, what he, the supervisor, can do to help
D. thank the subordinate for being so fair–minded in accepting the criticism in a positive manner

7. The successful supervisor is often one who gives serious attention to his subordinates' needs for job satisfaction. A supervisor who believes this statement is MOST likely to

7.____

A. treat all subordinates in an identical manner, irrespective of individual differences
B. permit each subordinate to perform his work as he wishes, within reasonable limits
C. give all subordinates both criticism and praise in equal measure
D. provide each subordinate with as much direct supervision as possible

8. Assume that you are supervising seven subordinates and have been asked by your superior to prepare an especially complex report due today. Its completion will take the rest of the day. You break down the assignment into simple parts and give a different part to each subordinate.
If you were to explain the work of each subordinate to more than one subordinate, your decision would be

8.____

A. *wise;* this would prevent boredom
B. *unwise;* valuable time would be lost
C. *wise;* your subordinates would become well–rounded
D. *unwise;* your subordinates would lose their competitive spirit

9. Suppose that an office associate whom you supervise has given you a well–researched report on a problem in an area in which he is expert. However, the report lacks solutions or recommendations. You know this office associate to be fearful of stating his opinions. In these circumstances, you should tell him that

9.____

A. you will seek recommendations on the problem from other, even if less expert, office associates
B. his work is unsatisfactory, in hope of arousing him to greater assertiveness
C. you need his advise and expertise, to help you reach a decision on the problem
D. his uncooperative behavior leaves you no choice but to speak to your superior

10. If a supervisor wishes to have the work of his unit completed on schedule, it is usually   10.____
MOST important to

    A. avoid listening to employees' complaints, thereby discouraging dissatisfaction
    B. perform much of the work himself, since he is generally more capable
    C. observe employees continuously, so they do not slacken their efforts
    D. set up the work carefully, then stay informed as to how it is moving

11. Of the following agencies, the one MOST likely to work out a proposed budget close to its   11.____
real needs is

    A. a newly–created agency staffed by inexperienced administrators
    B. funded with a considerable amount of money
    C. an existing agency which intends to install new, experimental systems for doing its
       work
    D. an existing agency which can base its estimate on its experience during the past
       few years

12. Assume that you are asked to prepare a report on the expected costs and benefits of a   12.____
proposed:new program to be installed in your office. However, you are aware that certain
factors are not really measurable in dollars and cents.
As a result, you should

    A. *identify* the non–measurable factors and state why they are important
    B. *assign* a fixed money value to all factors that are not really measurable
    C. *recommend* that programs containing non–measurable factors should be dropped
    D. *assume* that the non–measurable factors are really unimportant

13. Assume that you are asked for your opinion as to the necessity for hiring more employ-   13.____
ees to perform certain revenue–producing work in your office.
The information that you will MOST likely need in giving an informed opinion is

    A. whether public opinion would favor hiring additional employees
    B. an estimate of the probable additional revenue compared with the additional per-
       sonnel costs
    C. the total cots of all city operations in contrast to all city revenues
    D. the method by which present employees would be selected for promotion in an
       expanded operation

14. The *most* reasonable number of subordinates for a supervisor to have is BEST deter-   14.____
mined by the

    A. average number of subordinates other supervisors have
    B. particular responsibilities given to the supervisor
    C. supervisor's educational background
    D. personalities of the subordinates assigned to the supervisor

15. Most subordinates would need less supervision if they knew what they were supposed to do.
An ESSENTIAL first step in fixing in subordinates' minds exactly what is required of them is to

    A. *require* that supervisors be firm in their supervision of subordinates
    B. *encourage* subordinates to determine their own work standards
    C. *encourage* subordinates to submit suggestions to improve procedures
    D. *standardize* and simplify procedures and logically schedule activities

15.____

16. Assume that you have been asked to recommend an appropriate office layout to correspond with a just completed office reorganization.
Which of the following is it MOST advisable to recommend?

    A. *Allocate* most of the space for traffic flow
    B. *Use* the center area only for traffic flow
    C. *situate* close to each other those units whose work is closely related
    D. *Group* in an out–of–the–way corner the supply and file cabinets

16.____

17. Although an organization chart will illustrate the formal structure of an agency, it will seldom show a true picture of its actual workings.
Which of the following BEST explains this statement? Organization charts

    A. are often prepared by employees who may exaggerate their own importance
    B. usually show titles and sometimes names rather than the actual contacts and movements between employees
    C. are likely to discourage the use of official titles, and in so doing promote greater freedom in human relations
    D. usually show the informal arrangements and dealings between employees

17.____

18. Assume that a supervisor of a large unit has a variety of tasks to perform, and that he gives each of his subordinates just one set of tasks to do. He never rotates subordinates from one set of tasks to another.
Which one of the following is the *MOST* likely *advantage* to be gained by this practice?

    A. Each subordinate will get to know all the tasks of the unit.
    B. The subordinate will be encouraged to learn all they can about all the unit's tasks.
    C. Each subordinate will become an expert in his particular set of tasks.
    D. The subordinates will improve their opportunities for promotion.

18.____

19. Listed below are four steps commonly used in trying to solve administrative problems. These four steps are not listed in the order in which they normally would be taken. If they were listed in the proper order, which step should be taken *FIRST*?
    I. Choosing the most practical solution to the problem
    II. Analyzing the essential facts about the problem
    III. Correctly identifying the problem
    IV. Following up to see if the solution chosen really works
The CORRECT answer is:

    A. III   B. I   C. II   D. IV

19.____

20. Assume that another agency informally tells you that most of your agency's reports are coming to them with careless errors made by many of your office aides.
Which one of the following is MOST likely to solve this problem?   20.____

    A.   *Require* careful review of all outgoing reports by the supervisors of the office aides
    B.   *Request* the other agency to make necessary corrections whenever such errors come to their attention
    C.   *Ask* the other agency to submit a written report on this situation
    D.   *Establish* a small unit to review all reports received from other agencies

21. Assume that you supervise an office which gets two kinds of work. One kind is high–priority and must be done within two days. The other kind of work must be done within two weeks.
Which one of the following instructions would be MOST reasonable for you to give to your subordinates in this office?   21.____

    A.   If a backlog builds up during the day, clean the backlog up first, regardless of priority
    B.   Spend half the day doing priority work and the other half doing non–priority work
    C.   Generally do the priority work first as soon as it is received
    D.   Usually do the work in the order in which it comes in, priority or non–priority

22. An experienced supervisor should do advance planning of his subordinates' work assignments and schedules.
Which one of the following is the BEST reason for such advance planning? It   22.____

    A.   enables the supervisor to do less supervision
    B.   will assure the assignment of varied duties
    C.   will make certain a high degree of discipline among subordinates
    D.   helps make certain that essential operations are adequately covered

23. Agencies are required to evaluate the performance of their employees.
Which one of the following would generally be POOR evaluation practice by an agency rater? The rater   23.____

    A.   regularly observes the performance of the employee being rated
    B.   in evaluating the employee, acquaints himself with the employee's job
    C.   uses objective standards in evaluating the employee being rated
    D.   uses different standards in evaluating men and women

24. A good supervisor should have a clear idea of the quantity and quality of his subordinates' work.
Which one of the following sources would normally provide a supervisor with the LEAST reliable information about a subordinate's work performance?   24.____

    A.   Discussion with a friend of the subordinate
    B.   Comments by other supervisors who have worked recently with the subordinate
    C.   Opinions of fellow workers who work closely with the subordinate on a daily basis
    D.   Comparison with work records of others doing similar work during the same period of time

25. In order to handle the ordinary work of an office, a, supervisor sets up standard work pro-   25.____
    cedures.
    The MOST likely benefit of this is to reduce the need to

    A. motivate employees to do superior work
    B. rethink what has to be done every time a routine matter comes up
    C. keep records and write reports
    D. change work procedures as new situations come up

    _____

KEY (CORRECT ANSWERS

1.	A	11.	D
2.	C	12.	A
3.	D	13.	B
4.	A	14.	B
5.	A	15.	D
6.	C	16.	C
7.	B	17.	B
8.	B	18.	C
9.	C	19.	A
10.	D	20.	A

21.	C
22.	D
23.	D
24.	A
25.	B

_____

Effectively Interacting with Agency Staff and Members of the Public

Test material will be presented in a multiple-choice question format.

Test Task: You will be presented with a variety of situations in which you must apply knowledge of how best to interact with other people.

SAMPLE QUESTION:

A person approaches you expressing anger about a recent action by your department. Which one of the following should be your first response to this person?

   A. Interrupt to say you cannot discuss the situation until he calms down.
   B. Say you are sorry that he has been negatively affected by your department's action.
   C. Listen and express understanding that he has been upset by your department's action.
   D. Give him an explanation of the reasons for your department's action.

The correct answer to this sample question is Choice C. Solution:

Choice A is not correct. It would be inappropriate to interrupt. In addition, saying that you cannot discuss the situation until the person calms down will likely aggravate the person further.

Choice B is not correct. Apologizing for your department's action implies that the action was improper.

Choice C is the correct answer to this question. By listening and expressing understanding that your department's action has upset the person, you demonstrate that you have heard and understand the person's feelings and point of view.

Choice D is not correct. While an explanation of the reasons for the action may be appropriate at a later time, at this moment the person is angry and would not be receptive to such an explanation.

EXAMINATION SECTION
TEST 1

DIRECTIONS: Each question or incomplete statement is followed by several suggested answers or completions. Select the one that BEST answers the question or completes the statement. *PRINT THE LETTER OF THE CORRECT ANSWER IN THE SPACE AT THE RIGHT.*

1. Good procedure in handling complaints from the public may be divided into the following four principal stages:
    I.   Investigation of the complaint
    II. Receipt of the complaint
    III. Assignment of responsibility for investigation and correction
    IV. Notification of correction
   The ORDER in which these stages ordinarily come is:

   A. III, II, I, IV   B. II, III, I, IV
   C. II, III, IV, I   D. II, IV, III, I   1.____

2. The department may expect the MOST severe public criticism if   2.____

   A. it asks for an increase in its annual budget
   B. it purchases new and costly street cleaning equipment
   C. sanitation officers and men are reclassified to higher salary grades
   D. there is delay in cleaning streets of snow

3. The MOST important function of public relations in the department should be to   3.____

   A. develop cooperation on the part of the public in keeping streets clean
   B. get stricter penalties enacted for health code violations
   C. recruit candidates for entrance positions who can be developed into supervisors
   D. train career personnel so that they can advance in the department

4. The one of the following which has MOST frequently elicited unfavorable public comment has been   4.____

   A. dirty sidewalks or streets
   B. dumping on lots
   C. failure to curb dogs
   D. overflowing garbage cans

5. It has been suggested that, as a public relations measure, sections hold *open house* for the public.
   The MOST effective time for this would be   5.____

   A. during the summer when children are not in school and can accompany their parents
   B. during the winter when snow is likely to fall and the public can see snow removal preparations
   C. immediately after a heavy snow storm when department snow removal operations are in full progress
   D. when street sanitation is receiving general attention as during *Keep City Clean* week

53

6. When a public agency conducts a public relations program, it is MOST likely to find that each recipient of its message will

    A. disagree with the basic purpose of the message if the officials are not well known to him
    B. accept the message if it is presented by someone perceived as having a definite intention to persuade
    C. ignore the message unless it is presented in a literate and clever manner
    D. give greater attention to certain portions of the message as a result of his individual and cultural differences

6._____

7. Following are three statements about public relations and communications:
    I. A person who seeks to influence public opinion can speed up a trend
    II. Mass communications is the exposure of a mass audience to an idea
    III. All media are equally effective in reaching opinion leaders
Which of the following choices CORRECTLY classifies the above statements into those which are correct and those which are not?

    A. I and II are correct, but III is not
    B. II and III are correct, but I is not
    C. I and III are correct, but II is not
    D. III is correct, but I and II are not

7._____

8. Public relations experts say that MAXIMUM effect for a message results from

    A. concentrating in one medium
    B. ignoring mass media and concentrating on *opinion makers*
    C. presenting only those factors which support a given position
    D. using a combination of two or more of the available media

8._____

9. To assure credibility and avoid hostility, the public relations man MUST

    A. make certain his message is truthful, not evasive or exaggerated
    B. make sure his message contains some dire consequence if ignored
    C. repeat the message often enough so that it cannot be ignored
    D. try to reach as many people and groups as possible

9._____

10. The public relations man MUST be prepared to assume that members of his audience

    A. may have developed attitudes toward his proposals --favorable, neutral, or unfavorable
    B. will be immediately hostile
    C. will consider his proposals with an open mind
    D. will invariably need an introduction to his subject

10._____

11. The one of the following statements that is CORRECT is:

    A. When a stupid question is asked of you by the public, it should be disregarded
    B. If you insist on formality between you and the public, the public will not be able to ask stupid questions that cannot be answered
    C. The public should be treated courteously, regardless of how stupid their questions may be
    D. You should explain to the public how stupid their questions are

11._____

12. With regard to public relations, the MOST important item which should be emphasized in   12.____
an employee training program is that

    A. each inspector is a public relations agent
    B. an inspector should give the public all the information it asks for
    C. it is better to make mistakes and give erroneous information than to tell the public
       that you do not know the correct answer to their problem
    D. public relations is so specialized a field that only persons specially trained in it
       should consider it

13. Members of the public frequently ask about departmental procedures.   13.____
Of the following, it is BEST to

    A. advise the public to put the question in writing so ,that he can get a proper formal
       reply
    B. refuse to answer because this is a confidential matter
    C. explain the procedure as briefly as possible
    D. attempt to avoid the issue by discussing other matters

14. The effectiveness of a public relations program in a public agency such as the authority   14.____
is BEST indicated by the

    A. amount of mass media publicity favorable to the policies of the authority
    B. morale of those employees who directly serve the patrons of the authority
    C. public's understanding and support of the authority's program and policies
    D. number of complaints received by the authority from patrons using its facilities

15. In an attempt to improve public opinion about a certain idea, the BEST course of action   15.____
for an agency to take would be to present the

    A. clearest statements of the idea even though the language is somewhat technical
    B. idea as the result of long-term studies
    C. idea in association with something familiar to most people
    D. idea as the viewpoint of the majority leaders

16. The fundamental factor in any agency's community relations program is   16.____

    A. an outline of the objectives
    B. relations with the media
    C. the everyday actions of the employees
    D. a well-planned supervisory program

17. The FUNDAMENTAL factor in the success of a community relations program is   17.____

    A. true commitment by the community
    B. true commitment by the administration
    C. a well-planned, systematic approach
    D. the actions of individuals in their contacts with the public

18. The statement below which is LEAST correct is: 18.____

    A. Because of selection standards, the supervisor frequently encounters problems
       resulting from subordinates' inability to express themselves in the language of the
       profession

B. Distortion of the meaning of a communication is usually brought about by a failure to use language that has a precise meaning to others
C. The term *filtering* is the distortion or dilution of content of a communication that occurs as information is passed from individual to individual
D. The complexity of the *communications net* will directly affect

19. Consider the following three statements that may or may not be CORRECT:　　19._____
    I. In order to prevent the stifling of communications flow, supervisors should insist that employees use the formal communications network
    II. Two-way communications are faster and more accurate than one-way communications
    III. There is a direct correlation between the effectiveness of communications and the total setting in which they occur
    The choice below which MOST accurately describes the above statement is:

    A. All 3 are correct
    B. All 3 are incorrect
    C. More than one of the statements is correct
    D. Only one of the statements is correct

20. The statement below which is MOST inaccurate is:　　20._____

    A. The supervisor's most important tool in learning whether or not he is communicating well is feedback
    B. Follow-up is essential if useful feedback is to be obtained
    C. Subordinates are entitled, as a matter of right, to explanations from management concerning the reasons for orders or directives
    D. A skilled supervisor is often able to use the grapevine to good advantage

21. *Since concurrence by those affected is not sought, this kind of communication can be*　　21._____
    issued with relative ease. The kind of communication being referred to in this quotation is

    A. autocratic　　　B. democratic　　　C. directive　　　D. free-rein

22. The statement below which is LEAST correct is:　　22._____

    A. Clarity is more important in oral communicating than in written since the readers of a written communication can read it over again
    B. Excessive use of abbreviations in written communications should be avoided
    C. Short sentences with simple words are preferred over complex sentences and difficult words in a written communication
    D. The *newspaper* style of writing ordinarily simplifies expression and facilitates understanding

23. Which one of the following is the MOST important factor for the department to consider in　　23._____
    building a good public image?

    A. A good working relationship with the news media
    B. An efficient community relations program
    C. An efficient system for handling citizen complaints
    D. The proper maintenance of facilities and equipment
    E. The behavior of individuals in their contacts with the public

24. It has been said that the ability to communicate clearly and concisely is the MOST impor-   24.____
tant single skill of the supervisor.
Consider the following statements:
   I. The adage, *Actions speak louder than words,* has NO application in superior/
subordinate communications since good communications are accomplished
with words
   II. The environment in which a communication takes place will *rarely* determine
its effect
   III. Words are symbolic representations which must be associated with past
experience or else they are meaningless
The choice below which MOST accurately describes the above statements is:

  A. I, II and III are correct
  B. I and II are correct, but III is not
  C. I and III are correct, but II is not
  D. III is correct, but I and II are not
  E. I, II, and III are incorrect

25. According to expert opinion, the effectiveness of an organization is very dependent upon   25.____
good upward, downward, and lateral communications. Lateral communications are most
important to the activity of coordinating the efforts of organizational units. Before real
communication can take place at any level, barriers to communication must be recognized, understood, and removed. Consider the following three statements:
   I. The *principal* barrier to good communications is a failure to establish empa-
thy between sender and receiver
   II. The difference in status or rank between the sender and receiver of a communication may be a communications barrier
   III. Communications are easier if they travel upward from subordinate to superior
The choice below which MOST accurately describes the above statements is:

  A. I, II and III are incorrect
  B. I and II are incorrect
  C. I, II, and III are correct
  D. I and II are correct
  E. I and III are incorrect

KEY (CORRECT ANSWERS)

1.	B	11.	C
2.	D	12.	A
3.	A	13.	C
4.	A	14.	C
5.	D	15.	C
6.	D	16.	C
7.	A	17.	D
8.	D	18.	A
9.	A	19.	D
10.	A	20.	C

21.	A
22.	A
23.	E
24.	D
25.	E

———

EXAMINATION SECTION
TEST 1

DIRECTIONS: Each question or incomplete statement is followed by several suggested answers or completions. Select the one that BEST answers the question or completes the statement. *PRINT THE LETTER OF THE CORRECT ANSWER IN THE SPACE AT THE RIGHT.*

1. Assume that you are a supervisor of a unit which is about to start work on an urgent job. One of your subordinates starts to talk to you about the urgent job but seems not to be saying what is really on his mind.
   What is the BEST thing for you to say under these circumstances?   1.____

   A. *I'm not sure I understand. Can you explain that?*
   B. *Please come to the point. We haven't got all day.*
   C. *What is it? Can't you see I'm busy?*
   D. *Haven't you got work to do? What do you want?*

2. Assume that you have recently been assigned a new subordinate. You have explained to this subordinate how to fill out certain forms which will constitute the major portion of her job. After the first day, you find that she has filled out the forms correctly but has not completed as many as most other workers normally complete in a day.
   Of the following, the MOST appropriate action for you to take is to   2.____

   A. tell the subordinate how many forms she is expected to complete
   B. instruct the subordinate in the correct method of filling out the forms
   C. monitor the subordinate's production to see if she improves
   D. reassign the job of filling out the forms to a more experienced worker in the unit

3. One of the problems commonly met by the supervisor is the *touchy* employee who imagines slights when none are intended.
   Of the following, the BEST way to deal with such an employee is to   3.____

   A. ignore him, until he sees the error of his behavior
   B. frequently reassure him of his value as a person
   C. advise him that oversensitive people rarely get promoted
   D. issue written instructions to him to avoid misinterpretation

4. The understanding supervisor should recognize that a certain amount of anxiety is common to all newly-hired employees. If you are a supervisor of a unit and a newly-hired employee has been assigned to you, you can usually assume that the LEAST likely worry that the new employee has is worry about   4.____

   A. the job and the standards required in the job
   B. his acceptance by the other people in your unit
   C. the difficulty of advancing to top positions in the agency
   D. your fairness in evaluating his work

5. In assigning work to subordinates, it is often desirable for you to tell them the overall or   5.___
    ultimate objective of the assignment.
    Of the following, the BEST reason for telling them the objective is that it will

    A. assure them that you know what you are doing
    B. eliminate most of the possible complaints about the assignment
    C. give them confidence in their ability to do the assignment
    D. help them to make decisions consistent with the objective

6. Generally a supervisor wishes to increase the likelihood that instructions given to subor-   6.___
    dinates will be carried out properly.
    Of the following, the MOST important action for the supervisor to take to accomplish
    this objective when giving instructions to subordinates is to

    A. tailor the instructions to fit the interests of the subordinate
    B. use proper timing in giving the instruction
    C. make sure that the subordinates understand the instructions
    D. include only those instructions that are essential to the task at hand

7. Suppose that a supervisor, because of his heavy workload, has decided to delegate to   7.___
    his subordinates some of the duties that he has been performing.
    Of the following attitudes of the supervisor, the one that is LEAST conducive toward
    effective delegation is his belief that

    A. his subordinates will make some mistakes in performing these duties
    B. controls will be necessary to make sure the work is done
    C. performance of these duties may be slowed down temporarily
    D. much of his time will be spent supervising performance of these duties

8. In attempting to determine why one of his subordinates has frequently been coming to   8.___
    work late, a supervisor begins an interview with the subordinate by asking her whether
    everything is all right on the job and at home. The BEST of the following reasons for
    beginning the interview in this manner is that a question specifically about the reason for
    the lateness

    A. might indicate insecurity on the part of the supervisor
    B. might limit the responses of the subordinate
    C. will offend the subordinate
    D. might reveal the purpose of the interview

9. Of the following, the BEST use to which a supervisor should put his knowledge of human   9.___
    relations is to

    A. enhance his image among his subordinates
    B. improve interpersonal relationships with the organization
    C. prompt the organization to an awareness of mental health
    D. resolve technical differences of opinion among employees

10. Which of the following types of information would come tribute LEAST to a measure of the quality of working conditions for employees in various jobs?

    A. Data reflecting a view of working conditions as seen through the eyes of workers
    B. Objective data relating to problems in working conditions, such as occupational safety statistics
    C. The considered opinion of recognized specialists in relevant fields
    D. The impressionistic accounts of journalists in feature articles

10.____

Questions 11–15

DIRECTIONS: Questions 11 through 15 each consist of a sentence which may or may not be an example of good English usage. Consider grammar, punctuation, spelling, capitalization, verbosity, awkwardness, etc. Examine each sentence, and then choose the correct statement about it from the four choices below it. If the English usage in the sentence is better as given than with any of the changes suggested in options B, C, or D, choose option A. Do NOT choose an option that will change the meaning of the sentence.

11. The clerk could have completed the assignment on time if he knows where these materials were located.

    A. This is an example of acceptable writing.
    B. The word *knows* should be replaced by *had known*.
    C. The word *were* should be replaced by *had been*.
    D. The words *where these materials were located* should be replaced by *the location of these materials*.

11.____

12. All employees should be given safety training. Not just those who have accidents.

    A. This is an example of acceptable writing.
    B. The period after the word *training* should be changed to a colon.
    C. The period after the word *training* should be changed to a semicolon, and the first letter of the word *Not* should be changed to a small *n*.
    D. The period after the word *training* should be changed to a comma, and the first letter of the word *Not* should be changed to a small *n*.

12.____

13. This proposal is designed to promote employee awareness of the suggestion program, to encourage employee participation in the program, and to increase the number of suggestions submitted.

    A. This is an example of acceptable writing.
    B. The word *proposal* should be spelled *preposal*.
    C. the words *to increase the number of suggestions submitted* should be changed to *an increase in the number of suggestions is expected*.
    D. The word *promote* should be changed to *enhance* and the word *increase* should be changed to *add to*.

13.____

14. The introduction of inovative managerial techniques should be preceded by careful anal- 14.___
ysis of the specific circumstances and conditions in each department.

    A. This is an example of acceptable writing.
    B. The word *techniques* should be spelled *techneques*.
    C. The word *inovative* should be spelled *innovative*.
    D. A comma should be placed after the word *circumstance* and after the word *condi-tions*.

15. This occurrence indicates that such criticism embarrasses him. 15.___

    A. This is an example of acceptable writing.
    B. The word *occurrence* should be spelled *occurence*.
    C. The word *criticism* should be spelled *criticizm*.
    D. The word *embarrasses* should be spelled *embarasses*.

Questions 16–18.

DIRECTIONS: Questions 16 through 18 each consist of four sentences. Choose the one sentence in each set of four that would be BEST for a *formal* letter or report. Consider grammar and appropriate usage.

16. A. Most all the work he completed before he become ill. 16.___
    B. He completed most of the work before becoming ill.
    C. Prior to him becoming ill his work was mostly completed.
    D. Before he became ill most of the work he had completed.

17. A. Being that the report lacked a clearly worded recomendation, it did not matter that 17.___
       it contained enough information.
    B. There was enough information in the report, although it, including the recom-
       mendation, were not clearly worded.
    C. Although the report contained enough information, it did not have a clearly
       worded recommendation.
    D. Though the report did not have a recommendation that was clearly worded, and
       the information therein contained was enough.

18. A. Having already overlooked the important mistakes, the ones which she found were 18.___
       not as important toward the end of the letter.
    B. Toward the end of the letter she had already overlooked the important mistakes,
       so that which she had found were not as important.
    C. The mistakes which she had already overlooked were not as important as those
       which near the end of letter she had found.
    D. The mistakes which she found near the end of the letter were not as important
       as those which she had already overlooked.

19. Examine the following sentence, and then choose from below the words which should be 19.___
inserted in the blank spaces to produce the best sentence.
    The unit has exceeded _____ goals and the employees are satisfied
    with _____ accomplishments.

    A. their, it's   B. it's, it's
    C. its, there   D. its, their

20. Examine the following sentence, and then choose from below the words which should be   20._____
    inserted in the blank spaces to produce the best sentence.
        Research indicates that employees who _____ no opportunity for close social rela-
    tionships often find their work unsatisfying, and this _____ of satisfaction often
    reflects itself in low production.

    A. have, lack   B. have, excess
    C. has, lack   D. has, excess

    _____

KEY (CORRECT ANSWERS)

1.	A		11.	B
2.	C		12.	D
3.	B		13.	A
4.	C		14.	C
5.	D		15.	A
6.	C		16.	B
7.	D		17.	C
8.	B		18.	D
9.	B		19.	D
10.	D		20.	A

_____

TEST 2

DIRECTIONS: Each question or incomplete statement is followed by several suggested answers or completions. Select the one that BEST answers the question or completes the statement. *PRINT THE LETTER OF THE CORRECT ANSWER IN THE SPACE AT THE RIGHT.*

1. Of the following, the GREATEST *pitfall* in interviewing is that the result may be effected by the

    A. bias of the interviewee
    B. bias of the interviewer
    C. educational level of the interviewee
    D. educational level of the interviewer

1.___

2. Assume that you have been asked to interview each of several students who have been hired to work part-time. Which of the following could *ordinarily* be accomplished LEAST effectively in such an interview?

    A. Providing information about the organization or institution in which the students will be working
    B. Directing the students to report for work each afternoon at specified times
    C. Determining experience and background of the students so that appropriate assignments can be made
    D. Changing the attitudes of the students toward the importance of parental controls

2.___

3. Assume that someone you are interviewing is reluctant to give you certain information. He would *probably* be MORE responsive if you show him that

    A. all the other persons you interviewed provided you with the information
    B. it would serve his own best interests to give you the information
    C. the information is very important to you
    D. you are businesslike and take a no-nonsense approach

3.___

4. Taking notes while you are interviewing someone is *most likely* to

    A. arouse doubts as to your trustworthiness
    B. give the interviewee confidence in your ability
    C. insure that you record the facts you think are important
    D. make the responses of the interviewee unreliable

4.___

5. Assume that you have been asked to get all the pertinent information from an employee who claims that she witnessed a robbery.
Which of the following questions is LEAST likely to influence the witness's response?

    A. *Can you describe the robber's hair?*
    B. *Did the robber have a lot of hair?*
    C. *Was the robber's hair black or brown?*
    D. *Was the robber's hair very dark?*

5.___

6. If you are to interview several applicants for jobs and rate them on five different factors on a scale of 1 to 5, you should be MOST careful to *insure* that your   6.____

   A. rating on one factor does not influence your rating on another factor
   B. ratings on all factors are interrelated with a minimum of variation
   C. overall evaluation for employment exactly reflects the arithmetic average of your ratings
   D. overall evaluation for employment is unrelated to your individual ratings

7. In answering questions asked by students, faculty, and the public, it is MOST important that   7.____

   A. you indicate your source of information
   B. you are not held responsible for the answers
   C. the facts you give be accurate
   D. the answers cover every possible aspect of each question

8. One of the applicants for a menial job is a tall, stooped, husky individual with a low forehead, narrow eyes, a protruding chin, and a tendency to keep his mouth open.
   In interviewing him, you *should*   8.____

   A. check him more carefully than the other applicants regarding criminal background
   B. disregard any skills he might have for other jobs which are vacant
   C. make your vocabulary somewhat simpler than with the other applicants
   D. make no assumption regarding his ability on the basis of his appearance

9. Of the following, the BEST approach for you to use at the beginning of an interview with a job applicant is to   9.____

   A. caution him to use his time economically and to get to the point
   B. ask him how long he intends to remain on the job if hired
   C. make some pleasant remarks to put him at ease
   D. emphasize the importance of the interview in obtaining the job

10. Of the following, the BEST reason for conducting an *exit interview* with an employee is to   10.____

    A. make certain that he returns all identification cards and office keys
    B. find out why he is leaving
    C. provide a useful training device for the exit interviewer
    D. discover if his initial hiring was in error

11. Suppose that a visitor to an office asks a receptionist for a specific person by name. The person is available, but the visitor refuses to state the purpose of the visit, saying that it is *personal.*
    Which of the following is the MOST appropriate response for the receptionist to make?   11.____

    A. *Does M_____ know you?*
    B. *I'm sorry, M_____ is busy.*
    C. *M _____ won't be able to help you unless you're* more specific.
    D. *M_____ is not able to see you.*

65

12. When writing a reply to a letter you received, it is proper to mention the subject of the letter. 12.__
ter.
However, you should ordinarily NOT summarize the contents or repeat statements
made in the letter you received PRIMARILY because

    A. a letter writer answers people, not letters
    B. direct answers will help you avoid sounding pompous
    C. the response will thus be more confidential
    D. the sender usually knows what he or she wrote

13. Assume that you are a supervisor in an office which gets approximately equal quantities 13.__
of urgent work and work that is not urgent. The volume of work is high during some periods and low during others.
In order to level out the fluctuations in workload, it would be BEST for you to schedule
work so that

    A. urgent work which comes up in a period of high work volume can be handled expe-
       ditiously by the use of voluntary overtime
    B. urgent work is postponed for completion in periods of low volume
    C. work is completed as it comes into the office, except that when urgent work arises,
       other work is laid aside temporarily
    D. work is completed chronologically, that is, on the basis of *first in, first out*

14. Suppose that a supervisor sets up a pick-up and delivery messenger system to cover 14.__
several nearby buildings. Each building has at least one station for both pick-up and
delivery. Three messenger trips are scheduled for each day, and the messenger is
instructed to make pick-ups and deliveries at the same time.
In this situation, telling the messenger to visit each pick-up and delivery station even
though there is nothing to deliver to it is

    A. *advisable,* messengers are generally not capable of making decisions for them-
       selves
    B. *advisable,* there may be material for the messenger to pick up
    C. *inadvisable,* the system must be made flexible to meet variable workload condi-
       tions
    D. *inadvisable,* postponing the visit until there is something to deliver is more efficient

15. You, as a unit head, have been asked to submit budget estimates of staff, equipment and 15.__
supplies in terms of programs for your unit for the coming fiscal year. In addition to their
use in planning, such unit budget estimates can be BEST used to

    A. reveal excessive costs in operations
    B. justify increases in the debt limit
    C. analyze employee salary adjustments
    D. predict the success of future programs

Questions 16–21.

DIRECTIONS: Questions 16 through 21 involve calculations of annual grade averages for college students who have just completed their junior year. These averages are to be based on the following table showing the number of credit hours for each student during the year at each of the grade levels: A, B, C, D, and F. How these letter grades may be translated into numerical grades is indicated in the first column of the table.

Grade Value	Credit Hours – Junior Year					
	King	Lewis	Martin	Nonkin	Ottly	Perry
A=95	12	12	9	15	6	3
B=85	9	12	9	12	18	6
C=75	6	6	9	3	3	21
D=65	3	3	3	3	–	–
F=0	–	–	3	–	–	–

Calculating a grade average for an individual student is a 4-step process:
   I.   Multiply each grade value by the number of credit hours for which the student received that grade.
   II. Add these multiplication products for each student.
   III. Add the student's total credit hours.
   IV. Divide the multiplication product total by the total number of credit hours.
   V.   Round the result, if there is a decimal place, to the nearest whole number. A number ending in .5 would be rounded to the next higher number.

EXAMPLE
Using student King's grades as an example, his grade average can be calculated by going through the following four steps:

I.
95	x	12	=	1140
85	x	9	=	765
75	x	6	=	450
65	x	3	=	195
0	x	0	=	0

III.
12
9
6
3
0
30 total credit hours

II. Total   = 2550

IV. Divide 2550 by 30: $\frac{2550}{30} = 85$.

King's grade average is 85.
   Answer Questions 16 through 21 on the basis of the information given above.

16. The grade average of Lewis is   16.____

   A. 83   B. 84   C. 85   D. 86

17. The grade average of Martin is   17.____

   A. 72   B. 73   C. 74   D. 75

18. The grade average of Nonkin is   18.____

   A. 85   B. 86   C. 87   D. 88

19. Student Ottly must attain a grade average of 90 in each of his years in college to be   19.____
    accepted into the graduate school of his choice.
    If, in summer school during his junior year, he takes two 3–credit courses and
    receives a grade of 95 in each one, his grade average for his junior year will then be,
    most nearly,

    A. 87   B. 88   C. 89   D. 90

20. If Perry takes an additional 3–credit course during the year and receives a grade of 95,   20.____
    his grade average will be increased to approximately

    A. 79   B. 80   C. 81   D. 82

21. What has been the *effect* of automation in data processing on the planning of managerial   21.____
    objectives?

    A. Paperwork can be virtually eliminated from the planning process.
    B. The information on which such planning is based can be more precise and up-to-
        date.
    C. Planning must be done much more frequently because of the constantly changing
        nature of the objectives.
    D. Planning can be done much less frequently because of the increased stability of
        objectives.

22. Which of the following is the BEST reason for budgeting a new calculating machine for   22.____
    an office?

    A. The clerks in the office often make mistakes in adding.
    B. The machine would save time and money.
    C. It was budgeted last year but never received.
    D. All the other offices have calculating machines.

23. Which of the following is *most likely* to reduce the volume of paperwork in a unit respon-   23.____
    sible for preparing a large number of reports?

    A. Changing the office layout so that there will be a minimum of backtracking and
        delay.
    B. Acquiring additional adding and calculating machines.
    C. Consolidating some of the reports.
    D. Inaugurating a *records retention* policy to reduce the length of time office papers
        are retained.

24. With regard to typed correspondence received by most offices, which of the following is   24.____
    the GREATEST problem?

    A. Verbosity   B. Illegibility
    C. Improper folding   D. Excessive copies

25. Of the following, the GREATEST advantage of electronic typewriters over electric type-writers is that they *usually*   25._____

   A. are less expensive to repair
   B. are smaller and lighter
   C. produce better looking copy
   D. require less training for the typist

——————

KEY (CORRECT ANSWERS)

1.	B		11.	A
2.	D		12.	D
3.	B		13.	C
4.	C		14.	B
5.	A		15.	A
6.	A		16.	C
7.	C		17.	D
8.	D		18.	C
9.	C		19.	B
10.	B		20.	B

21.	B
22.	B
23.	C
24.	A
25.	C

——————

EXAMINATION SECTION
TEST 1

DIRECTIONS: Each question or incomplete statement is followed by several suggested answers or completions. Select the one that BEST answers the question or completes the statement. *PRINT THE LETTER OF THE CORRECT ANSWER IN THE SPACE AT THE RIGHT.*

Questions 1-6.

DIRECTIONS: Questions 1 through 6 each consist of four sentences. Choose the one sentence in each set of four that would be BEST for a formal letter or report. Consider grammar and appropriate usage.

1.   A. These statements can be depended on, for their truth has been guaranteed by reliable city employees.   1.____
   B. Reliable city employees guarantee the facts with regards to the truth of these statements.
   C. Most all these statements have been supported by city employees who are reliable and can be depended upon.
   D. The city employees which have guaranteed these statements are reliable.

2.   A. I believe the letter was addressed to either my associate or I.   2.____
   B. If properly addressed, the letter will reach my associate and I.
   C. My associate's name, as well as mine, was on the letter.
   D. The letter had been addressed to myself and my associate.

3.   A. The secretary would have corrected the errors if she knew that the supervisor would see the report.   3.____
   B. The supervisor reprimanded the secretary, whom she believed had made careless errors.
   C. Many errors were found in the report which she typed and could not disregard them.
   D. The errors in the typed report were so numerous that they could hardly be overlooked.

4.   A. His consultant was as pleased as he with the success of the project.   4.____
   B. The success of the project pleased both his consultant and he.
   C. he and also his consultant was pleased with the success of the project.
   D. Both his consultant and he was pleased with the success of the project.

5.   A. Since the letter did not contain the needed information, it was not real useful to him.   5.____
   B. Being that the letter lacked the needed information, he could not use it.
   C. Since the letter lacked the needed information, it was of no use to him.
   D. This letter was useless to him because there was no needed information in it.

6.   A.   Scarcely had the real estate tax increase been declared than the notices were   6.____
          sent out.
     B.   They had no sooner declared the real estate tax increases when they sent the
          notices to the owners.
     C.   The city had hardly declared the real estate tax increase till the notices were pre-
          pared for mailing.
     D.   No sooner had the real estate tax increase been declared than the notices were
          sent out.

Questions 7-14.

DIRECTIONS: Answer Questions 7 through 14 on the basis of the following passage.

        Important figures in education and in public affairs have recommended development of a
private organization sponsored in part by various private foundations which would offer
installment payment plans to full-time matriculated students in accredited colleges and universities in the United States and Canada. Contracts would be drawn to cover either tuition
and fees, or tuition, fees, room and board in college facilities, from one year up to and including six years. A special charge, which would vary with the length of the contract, would be
added to the gross repayable amount. This would be in addition to interest at a rate which
would vary with the income of the parents. There would be a 3% annual interest charge for
families with total income, before income taxes of $10,000 or less. The rate would increase by
1/10 of 1% for every $200 of additional net income in excess of $10,000 up to a maximum of
10% interest. Contracts would carry an insurance provision on the life of the parent or guardian who signs the contract; all contracts must have the signature of a parent or guardian. Payment would be scheduled in equal monthly installments.

7.   Which of the following students would be eligible for the payment plan described in the   7.____
     above passage?
     A

     A.   matriculated student taking 6 semester hours toward a graduate degree at CCNY
     B.   matriculated student taking 17 semester hours toward an undergraduate degree at
          Brooklyn College
     C.   CCNY graduate matriculated at the University of Mexico, taking 18 semester hours
          toward a graduate degree
     D.   student taking 18 semester hours in a special pre-matriculation program at Hunter
          College

8.   According to the above passage, the organization described would be sponsored in part   8.____
     by

     A.   private foundations
     B.   colleges and universities
     C.   persons in the field of education
     D.   persons in public life

9.   Which of the following expenses could NOT be covered by a contract with the organiza-   9.____
     tion described in the above passage?

     A.   Tuition amounting to $4,000 per year
     B.   Registration and laboratory fees

C. Meals at restaurants near the college
D. Rent for an apartment in a college dormitory

10. The total amount to be paid would include ONLY the   10.____

    A. principal
    B. principal and interest
    C. principal, interest, and special charge
    D. principal, interest, special charge, and fee

11. The contract would carry insurance on the   11.____

    A. life of the student
    B. life of the student's parents
    C. income of the parents of the student
    D. life of the parent who signed the contract

12. The interest rate for an annual loan of $5,000 from the organization described in the pas-   12.____
    sage for a student whose family's net income was $11,000 should be

    A. 3%   B. 3.5%   C. 4%   D. 4.5%

13. The interest rate for an annual loan of $7,000 from the organization described in the pas-   13.____
    sage for a student whose family's net income was $20,000 should be

    A. 5%   B. 8%   C. 9%   D. 10%

14. John Lee has submitted an application for the installment payment plan described in the   14.____
    passage. John's mother and father have a store which grossed $100,000 last year, but
    the income which the family received from the store was $18,000 before taxes. They also
    had $1,000 income from stock dividends. They paid $2,000 in income taxes.
    The amount of income upon which the interest should be based is

    A. $17,000   B. $18,000   C. $19,000   D. $21,000

15. One of the MOST important techniques for conducting good interviews is   15.____

    A. asking the applicant questions in rapid succession, thereby keeping the conversa-
       tion properly focused
    B. listening carefully to all that the applicant has to say, making mental notes of possi-
       ble areas for follow-up
    C. indicating to the applicant the criteria and standards on which you will base your
       judgment
    D. making sure that you are interrupted above five minutes before you wish to end so
       that you can keep on schedule

16. You are planning to conduct preliminary interviews of applicants for an important position   16.____
    in your department. Which of the following planning considerations is LEAST likely to
    contribute to successful interviews?

    A. Make provisions to conduct interviews in privacy
    B. Schedule your appointments so that interviews will be short
    C. Prepare a list of your objectives
    D. Learn as much as you can about the applicant before the interview.

17. In interviewing job applicants, which of the following usually does NOT have to be done   17.____
before the end of the interview?

    A. Making a decision to hire an applicant
    B. Securing information from applicants
    C. Giving information to applicants
    D. Establishing a friendly relationship with applicants

18. In the process of interviewing applicants for a position on your staff, the one of the follow-   18.____
ing which would be BEST is to

    A. make sure all applicants are introduced to the other members of your staff prior to
       the formal interview
    B. make sure the applicant does not ask questions about the job or the department
    C. avoid having the applicant talk with the staff under any circumstances
    D. introduce applicants to some of the staff at the conclusion of a successful interview

19. While interviewing a job applicant, you ask why the applicant left his last job. The appli-   19.____
cant does not answer immediately.
Of the following, the BEST action to take at that point is to

    A. wait until he answers
    B. ask another question
    C. repeat the question in a loud voice
    D. ask him why he does not answer

20. Which of the following actions would be LEAST desirable for you to take when you have   20.____
to conduct an interview?

    A. Set a relaxed and friendly atmosphere
    B. Plan your interview ahead of time
    C. Allow the person interviewed to structure the interview as he wishes
    D. Include some stock or standard question which you ask everyone

21. You know that a student applying for a job in your office has done well in college except   21.____
for two courses in science. However, when you ask him about his grades, his reply is
vague and general.
It would be BEST for you to

    A. lead the applicant to admitting doing poorly in science to be sure that the facts are
       correct
    B. judge the applicant's tact and skill in handling what may be for him a personally
       sensitive question
    C. immediately confront the applicant with the facts and ask for an explanation
    D. ignore the applicant's response since you have the transcript

22. A college student has applied for a position with your department. Prior to conducting an   22.____
interview of the job applicant, it would be LEAST helpful for you to have

    A. a personal resume   B. a job description
    C. references   D. hiring requirements

23. Job applicants tend to be nervous during interviews. Which of the following techniques is MOST likely to put such an applicant at ease?   23.____

   A. Try to establish rapport by asking general questions which are easily answered by the applicant
   B. Ask the applicant to describe his career objectives immediately, thus minimizing the anxiety caused by waiting
   C. Start the interview with another member of the staff present so that the applicant does not feel alone
   D. Proceed as rapidly as possible, since the emotional state of the applicant is none of your concern

24. Of the following abilities, the one which is LEAST important in conducting an interview is the ability to   24.____

   A. ask the interviewee pertinent questions
   B. evaluate the interviewee on the basis of appearance
   C. evaluate the responses of the interviewee
   D. gain the cooperation of the interviewee

25. One of the techniques of management often used by supervisors is performance appraisal.   25.____
   Which of the following is NOT one of the objectives of performance appraisal?

   A. Improve staff performance
   B. Determine individual training needs
   C. Improve organizational structure
   D. Set standards and performance criteria for employees

_____

KEY (CORRECT ANSWERS)

1.	A		11.	D
2.	C		12.	B
3.	D		13.	B
4.	A		14.	C
5.	C		15.	B
6.	D		16.	B
7.	B		17.	A
8.	A		18.	D
9.	C		19.	A
10.	C		20.	C

21. B
22. C
23. A
24. B
25. C

TEST 2

DIRECTIONS: Each question or incomplete statement is followed by several suggested answers or completions. Select the one that BEST answers the question or completes the statement. *PRINT THE LETTER OF THE CORRECT ANSWER IN THE SPACE AT THE RIGHT.*

1. Examine the following sentence, and then choose the BEST statement about it from the choices below.
   Clerks are expected to receive visitors, to answer telephones, and miscellaneous clerical work must be done.

   A. This sentence is an example of effective writing.
   B. This is a *run-on* sentence.
   C. The three ideas in this sentence are not parallel, and therefore they should be divided into separate sentences.
   D. The three ideas in this sentence are parallel, but they are not expressed in parallel form.

   1.____

2. Examine the following sentence, and then choose from below the word which should be inserted in the blank space.
   Mr. Luce is a top-notch interviewer, _____ he is very reliable.

   A. but   B. and   C. however   D. for

   2.____

3. Examine the following sentence, and then choose from below the words which should be inserted in the blank spaces.
   The committee _____ sent in _____ report.

   A. has; it's   B. has; their
   C. have; its   D. has; its

   3.____

4. Examine the following sentence, and then choose from below the words which should be inserted in the blank spaces.
   An organization usually contains more than just a few people; usually the membership is _____ enough so that close personal relationships among _____ impossible.

   A. large; are   B. large; found
   C. small; becomes   D. small; is

   4.____

5. Of the following, the BEST reference book to use to find a synonym for a common word is a(n)

   A. thesaurus   B. dictionary
   C. encyclopedia   D. catalog

   5.____

Questions 6-10.

DIRECTIONS: Questions 6 through 10 concern college students who have just completed their junior year for whom you must calculate grade averages for the year. These averages are to be based on the following table showing the number of credit hours for each student during the year at each of the grade levels: A, B, C, D, and F. How these letter grades may be translated into numerical grades is indicated in the first column of the table.

Grade Value	Credit Hours- Junior Year					
	King	Lewis	Martin	Nonkin	Ottly	Perry
A = 95	12	6	15	3	9	-
B = 85	9	15	6	12	9	3
C = 75	6	9	9	12	3	27
D = 65	3	-	3	3	6	-
F = 0	-	-	-	3	-	-

Calculating a grade average for an individual student is a 4-step process:

I. Multiply each grade value by the number of credit hours for which the student received that grade
II. Add these multiplication products for each student
III. Add the student's total credit hours
IV. Divide the multiplication product total by the total number of credit hours
V. Round the result, if there is a decimal place, to the nearest whole number. A number ending in .5 would be rounded to the next higher number

Example

Using student King's grades as an example, his grade average can be calculated by going through the following four steps:

I.
$$95 \times 12 = 1140$$
$$85 \times 9 = 765$$
$$75 \times 6 = 450$$
$$65 \times 3 = 195$$
$$0 \times 0 = 0$$

III.
12
9
6
3
0
30 TOTAL credit hours

II. Total $= 2550$

IV. Divide 2550 by 30: $\frac{2550}{30} = 85$

King's grade average is 85.

Answer Questions 6 through 10 on the basis of the information given above.

6. The grade average of Lewis is

   A. 83   B. 84   C. 85   D. 86   6.___

7. The grade average of Martin is

   A. 83   B. 84   C. 85   D. 86   7.___

8. The grade average of Nonkin is

   A. 72   B. 73   C. 79   D. 80   8.___

9. Student Ottly must attain a grade average of 85 in each of his years in college to be accepted into graduate school.
   If, in summer school during his junior year, he takes two 3-credit courses and receives a grade of 85 in one and 95 in the other, his grade average for his junior year will then be MOST NEARLY   9.___

   A. 82   B. 83   C. 84   D. 85

10. If Perry takes an additional 3-credit course during the year and receives a grade of 95,   10.____
his grade average will be increased to approximately

    A.   74   B.   76   C.   78   D.   80

11. You are in charge of verifying employees' qualifications. This involves telephoning previ-   11.____
ous employers and schools. One of the applications which you are reviewing contains
information which you are almost certain is correct on the basis of what the employee
has told you.
The BEST thing to do is to

    A.   check the information again with the employee
    B.   perform the required verification procedures
    C.   accept the information as valid
    D.   ask a superior to verify the information

12. The practice of immediately identifying oneself and one's place of employment when   12.____
contacting persons on the telephone is

    A.   *good,* because the receiver of the call can quickly identify the caller and establish a
frame of reference
    B.   *good,* because it helps to set the caller at ease with the other party
    C.   *poor,* because it is not necessary to divulge that information when making general
calls
    D.   *poor,* because it takes longer to arrive at the topic to be discussed

13. A supervisor, Miss Smith, meets with a group of subordinates and tells them how they   13.____
should perform certain tasks. The meeting is highly successful. She then attends a meeting to discuss common problems with a group of fellow supervisors with duties similar to
her own. When she tells them how their subordinates should perform the same tasks,
some of the other supervisors become angry.
Of the following, the MOST likely reason for this anger is that

    A.   tension is to be expected in situations in which supervisors deal with each other
    B.   the other supervisors are jealous of Miss Smith's knowledge
    C.   Miss Smith should not tell other supervisors what methods she uses
    D.   Miss Smith does not correctly perceive her role in relation to other supervisors

14. There is considerable rivalry among employees in a certain department over location of   14.____
desks. It is the practice of the supervisor to assign desks without any predetermined
plan. The supervisor is reconsidering his procedure.
In assigning desks, PRIMARY consideration should ordinarily be given to

    A.   past practices
    B.   flow of work
    C.   employee seniority
    D.   social relations among employees

15. Assume that, when you tell some of the typists under your supervision that the letters   15.___
they prepare have too many errors, they contend that the letters are readable and that
they obtain more satisfaction from their jobs if they do not have to be as concerned about
errors.
These typists are

    A.   *correct,* because the ultimate objective should be job satisfaction
    B.   *incorrect,* because every job should be performed perfectly
    C.   *correct,* because they do not compose the letters themselves
    D.   *incorrect,* because their satisfaction is not the only consideration

16. Which of the following possible conditions is LEAST likely to represent a hindrance to   16.___
effective communication?

    A.   The importance of a situation may not be apparent.
    B.   Words may mean different things to different people.
    C.   The recipient of a communication may respond to it, sometimes unfavorably.
    D.   Communications may affect the self-interest of those communicating.

17. You are revising the way in which your unit handles records.   17.___
One of the BEST ways to make sure that the change will be implemented with a mini-
mum of difficulty is to

    A.   allow everyone on the staff who is affected by the change to have an opportunity to
contribute their ideas to the new procedures
    B.   advise only the key members of your staff in advance so that they can help you
enforce the new method when it is implemented
    C.   give the assignment of implementation to the newest member of the unit
    D.   issue a memorandum announcing the change and stating that complaints will not
be tolerated

18. One of your assistants is quite obviously having personal problems that are affecting his   18.___
work performance.
As a supervisor, it would be MOST appropriate for you to

    A.   avoid any inquiry into the nature of the situation since this is not one of your
responsibilities
    B.   avoid any discussion of personal problems on the basis that there is nothing you
could do about them anyhow
    C.   help the employee obtain appropriate help with these problems
    D.   advise the employee that personal problems cannot be considered when evaluat-
ing work performance

19. The key to improving communication with your staff and other departments is the devel-   19.___
opment of an awareness of the importance of communication.
Which of the following is NOT a good suggestion for developing this awareness?

    A.   Be willing to look at your own attitude toward how you communicate.
    B.   Be sensitive and receptive to reactions to what you tell people.
    C.   Make sure all communication is in writing.
    D.   When giving your subordinates directions, try to put yourself in their place and see
if your instructions still make sense.

20. One of the assistants on your staff has neglected to complete an important assignment 　20.____
on schedule. You feel that a reprimand is necessary.
When speaking to the employee, it would usually be LEAST desirable to

    A. display your anger to show the employee how strongly you feel about the problem
    B. ask several questions about the reasons for failure to complete the assignment
    C. take the employee aside so that nobody else is present when you discuss the matter
    D. give the employee as much time as he needs to explain exactly what happened

---

KEY (CORRECT ANSWERS)

1.	D		11.	B
2.	B		12.	A
3.	D		13.	D
4.	A		14.	B
5.	A		15.	D
6.	B		16.	C
7.	C		17.	A
8.	B		18.	C
9.	C		19.	C
10.	C		20.	A

EXAMINATION SECTION
TEST 1

DIRECTIONS: Each question or incomplete statement is followed by several suggested answers or completions. Select the one that BEST answers the question or completes the statement. *PRINT THE LETTER OF THE CORRECT ANSWER IN THE SPACE AT THE RIGHT.*

1. If an inch on an office layout drawing equals 4 feet of actual floor dimension, then a room which actually measures 9 feet by 14 feet is represented on the drawing by measurements equalling _____ inches x _____ inches.

   A. 2 1/4; 3 1/2   B. 2 1/2; 3 1/2
   C. 2 1/4; 3 1/4   D. 2 1/2; 3 1/4

1.____

2. A cooperative education intern works from 1:30 p.m. to 5 p.m. on Mondays, Wednesdays and Fridays, and from 10 a.m. to 2:30 p.m. with no lunch hour on Tuesdays and Thursdays. He earns $7.15 an hour on this job. In addition, he has a Saturday job paying $8.40 an hour at which he works from 9 a.m. to 3 p.m. with a half hour off for lunch. The gross amount that the student earns each week is, MOST nearly,

   A. $160.95   B. $185.60   C. $192.30   D. $208.15

2.____

3. Thirty-five percent of the College Discovery students who entered community college in 2006 earned an associate degree. Of these students, 89% entered senior college of which 67% went on to earn baccalaureate degrees.
   If there were 529 College Discovery students who entered community college in 2006, then the number of those who went on to finally receive a baccalaureate degree is, MOST nearly,

   A. 354   B. 315   C. 124   D. 110

3.____

4. It takes 5 Office Assistants two days to type 125 letters. Each of the Assistants works at an equal rate of speed. How many days will it take 10 Office Assistants to type 200 letters? _____ day(s).

   A. 1   B. 1 3/5   C. 2   D. 2 1/5

4.____

5. The following are the grades and credits earned by Student X during the first two years in college

Grade	Credits		Weight	Quality Points
A	10	1/2	x 4	
B	24		x 3	
C	12		x 2	
D	4	1/2	x 1	
F, FW	5		x 0	

   To compute an index number:
   I.   Multiply the number of credits of each grade by the weight to get the number of *quality points.*
   II. Add the credits.
   III. Add the quality points.
   IV. Divide the total quality points by the total credits, and carry the division to two decimal places.

5.____

On the basis of the given information, the index number for Student X is

A. 2.54   B. 2.59   C. 2.64   D. 2.68

———————

KEY (CORRECT ANSWERS)

1. A
2. B
3. D
4. B
5. A

———————

TEST 2

DIRECTIONS: Each question or incomplete statement is followed by several suggested answers or completions. Select the one that BEST answers the question or completes the statement. *PRINT THE LETTER OF THE CORRECT ANSWER IN THE SPACE AT THE RIGHT.*

Questions 1-5.

DIRECTIONS: Answer questions 1 through 5 according to the information given in the graph and chart below.

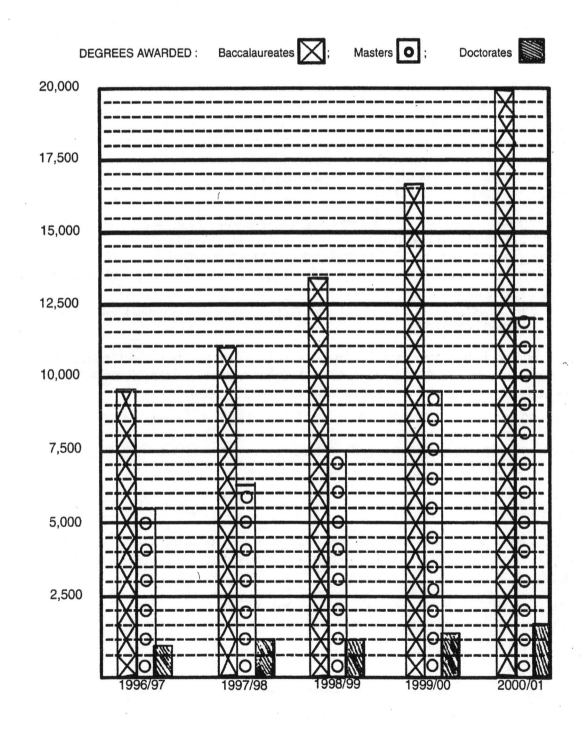

FRESHMAN ENROLLMENTS: BY FIELD

	1998/99		1999/00	
Field	Men	Women	Men	Women
Arts and Sciences	6,296	5,668	7,111	7,110
Engineering	2,098	28	2,370	35
Business	1,574	532	1,777	660
Agriculture	394	59	444	74
Education	1,192	2,272	1,150	2,660
Nursing	65	341	72	450
All Others	2,556	2,465	4,894	3,231
Totals	14,175	11,365	17,818	14,220

1. The data on freshman enrollments by field shows that the female enrollees outnumbered the male enrollees at a ratio of 25:4 in the field of   1.____

   A. Engineering in 1998/99
   B. Education in 1998/99
   C. Nursing in 1999/00
   D. Agriculture in 1999/00

2. In comparing the number of graduate degrees awarded during the five academic years shown, it is correct to state that   2.____

   A. the rise in the number of masters degrees awarded was greatest between the years 1999/00 and 2000/01
   B. a yearly average of 1,000 doctorate degrees were awarded
   C. the number of doctorates awarded in 1997/98 was 1/8 the number of masters degrees awarded that year
   D. the number of graduate degrees awarded in 2000/01 was double the number awarded in 1997/98

3. If the number of baccalaureate degrees awarded increases from 2000/01 to 2001/02 at the same rate as from 1999/00 to 2000/01, then the number of baccalaureate degrees awarded in the academic year 2001/02 would be MOST nearly,   3.____

   A. 20,500   B. 22,100   C. 23,800   D. 25,300

4. In which field of study did the overall freshman enrollment increase just 10% from 1998/99 to 1999/00?   4.____

   A. Agriculture
   B. Business
   C. Education
   D. Engineering

5. If the number of baccalaureate degrees awarded in 1999/00 is equal to 53% of the college entrants in 1996/97, then the number of college entrants in 1996/97 was, MOST nearly,   5.____

   A. 17,900   B. 20,210   C. 31,600   D. 35,640

KEY (CORRECT ANSWERS)

1. C
2. A
3. C
4. C
5. C

———

TEST 3

DIRECTIONS: Each question or incomplete statement is followed by several suggested answers or completions. Select the one that BEST answers the question or completes the statement. *PRINT THE LETTER OF THE CORRECT ANSWER IN THE SPACE AT THE RIGHT.*

Questions 1-5.

DIRECTIONS: Each of questions 1 through 5 consists of a quotation which contains one word that is incorrectly used because it is not in keeping with the meaning that the quotation is evidently intended to convey. Of the words underlined in each quotation, determine the word that is incorrectly used. Then select from among the words lettered A, B, C and D the word which, when substituted for the incorrectly used word, would best help to convey the meaning of the quotation. Indicate in the correspondingly numbered space at the right the letter preceding the word you have selected.

1. Insofar as an employee is permitted to *tell off* the boss in public and receives social approval from fellow employees who <u>derive</u> vicarious satisfaction from the employee's action, such <u>approval</u> may operate to <u>explain</u> the <u>effectiveness</u> of the boss's <u>authority.</u>

    A. diminish   B. feel
    C. power   D. attitude

1.____

2. The <u>demand</u> for practical education combined with the prestige <u>denied</u> to purely intellectual achievement has produced an educational system that tends to <u>insure</u> the <u>continuance</u> of education for both purposes.

    A. usefulness   B. accorded
    C. need   D. balance

2.____

3. Officials in college <u>placement</u> offices have often noted the contradiction which exists between the public <u>statements</u> of the company president who <u>questions</u> the value of a general liberal arts education in the business world and the practice of his recruiters who <u>seek</u> specialized training for particular jobs.

    A. praises   B. admissions
    C. reject   D. pronouncements

3.____

4. The <u>difference</u> between an organization as blueprinted and its actuality can be explained by <u>modifications</u> introduced by the people who do the <u>planning</u> of the <u>organization.</u>

    A. similarity   B. work
    C. behavior   D. blueprint

4.____

5. Students of educational administration have either <u>attempted</u> to accept and analyze the administrative process in their efforts to <u>produce</u> total improvement, or to look in two directions away from <u>education,</u> towards substantive educational activity and towards the community that <u>supports</u> the organization.

    A. change   B. failed
    C. administration   D. ignores

5.____

Questions 6-9.

DIRECTIONS: In questions 6 through 9 choose the sentence which is best from the point of view of English usuage suitable for a business letter or report.

6.   A.   Answering of veterans' inquiries, together with the receipt of fees, have been   6.____
            handled by the Bursar's Office since the new President came.
      B.   Since the new President's arrival, the handling of all veteran's inquiries has been
            turned over to the Bursar's Office.
      C.   In addition to the receipt of fees, the Bursar's Office has been handling veterans'
            inquiries since the new President came.
      D.   The principle change in the work of the Bursar's Office since the new President
            came is that it now handles veterans' inquires as well as the receipt of fees.

7.   A.   The current unrest about education undoubtedly stems in part from the fact that   7.____
            the people fear the basic purposes of the schools are being neglected or sup-
            planted by spurious ones.
      B.   The fears of people that the basic purposes of the schools are being neglected
            or supplanted by spurious ones contributes to the current unrest about educa-
            tion.
      C.   Undoubtedly some responsibility for the current unrest about education must be
            assigned to people's fears that the purpose and base of the school system is
            being neglected or supplanted.
      D.   From the fears of people that the basic purposes of the schools one being
            neglected or supplanted by spurious ones undoubtedly stem in part the current
            unrest about education.

8.   A.   The existence of administrative phenomena are clearly established, but their   8.____
            characteristics, relations and laws are obscure.
      B.   The obscurity of the characteristics, relations and laws of administrative phe-
            nomena do not preclude their existence.
      C.   Administrative phenomena clearly exists in spite of the obscurity of their charac-
            teristics, relations and laws.
      D.   The characteristics, relations and laws of administrative phenomena are obscure
            but the existence of the phenomena is clear.

9.   A.   Though deeply effected by the setback, the advice given by the admissions   9.____
            office began to seem more reasonable.
      B.   Although he was deeply effected by the setback, the advice given by the admis-
            sions office began to seem more reasonable.
      C.   Though the setback had affected him deeply, the advice given by the admissions
            office began to seem more reasonable.
      D.   Although he was deeply affected by the setback, the advice given by the admis-
            sions office began to seem more reasonable.

10. A. Returning to the administration building after attendance at a meeting, the door   10.____
        was locked despite an agreement that is would be left open.
     B. When he returned to the administration building after attending a meeting, he
        found the door locked, despite an agreement that it would be left open.
     C. After attending a meeting, the door to the administration building was locked,
        despite an agreement that it would be left open.
     D. When he returned to the administration building after attendance at a meeting,
        he found the door locked, despite an agreement that it would be left open.

———————

KEY (CORRECT ANSWERS)

1.	A	6.	C
2.	B	7.	A
3.	A	8.	D
4.	B	9.	D
5.	C	10.	B

———————

EXAMINATION SECTION

DIRECTIONS: Each question or incomplete statement is followed by several suggested answers or completions. Select the one that BEST answers the question or completes the statement. *PRINT THE LETTER OF THE CORRECT ANSWER IN THE SPACE AT THE RIGHT.*

Questions 1-5.

DIRECTIONS: Each of Questions 1 through 5 consists of a passage which contains one word that is incorrectly used because it is not in keeping with the meaning that the quotation is evidently intended to convey. Determine which word is incorrectly used. Select from the choices lettered A, B, C, and D the word which, when substituted for the incorrectly used word, would BEST help to convey the meaning of the quotation.

1. Whatever the method, the necessity to keep up with the dynamics of an organization is   1.____
   the point on which many classification plans go awry. The budgetary approach to "positions," for example, often leads to using for recruitment and pay purposes a position
   authorized many years earlier for quite a different purpose than currently contemplated –
   making perhaps the title, the class, and the qualifications required inappropriate to the
   current need. This happens because executives overlook the stability that takes place in
   job duties and fail to reread an initial description of the job before saying, as they scan a
   list of titles, "We should fill this position right away." Once a classification plan is adopted,
   it is pointless to do anything less than provide for continuous, painstaking maintenance
   on a current basis, else once different positions that have actually become similar to
   each other remain in different classes, and some former cognates that have become
   quite different continue in the same class. Such a program often seems expensive. But to
   stint too much on this out-of-pocket cost may create still higher hidden costs growing out
   of lowered morale, poor production, delayed operating programs, excessive pay for simple work, and low pay for responsible work (resulting in poorly qualified executives and
   professional men) – all normal concomitants of inadequate, hasty, or out-of-date classification.

   A. evolution   B. personnel
   C. disapproved   D. forward

2. At first sight, it may seem that there is little or no difference between the usableness of a   2.____
   manual and the degree of its use. But there is a difference. A manual may have all the
   qualities which make up the usable manual and still not be used. Take this instance as an
   example: Suppose you have a satisfactory manual but issue instructions from day to day
   through the avenue of bulletins, memorandums, and other informational releases. Which
   will the employee use, the manual or the bulletin which passes over his desk? He will, of
   course, use the latter, for some obsolete material will not be contained in this manual.
   Here we have a theoretically usable manual which is unused because of the other ave-
   nues by which procedural information may be issued.

   A. countermand   B. discard
   C. intentional   D. worthwhile

3. By reconcentrating control over its operations in a central headquarters, a firm is able to extend the influence of automation to many, if not all, of its functions – from inventory and payroll to production, sales, and personnel. In so doing, businesses freeze all the elements of the corporate function in their relationship to one another and to the overall objectives of the firm. From this total systems concept, companies learn that computers can accomplish much more than clerical and accounting jobs. Their capabilities can be tapped to perform the traditional applications (payroll processing, inventory control, accounts payable, and accounts receivable) as well as newer applications such as spotting deviations from planned programs (exception reporting), adjusting planning schedules, forecasting business trends, simulating market conditions, and solving production problems. Since the office manager is a manager of information and each of these applications revolves around the processing of data, he must take an active role in studying and improving the system under his care.

    3.____

    A. maintaining   B. inclusion
    C. limited   D. visualize

4. In addition to the formal and acceptance theories of the source of authority, although perhaps more closely related to the latter, is the belief that authority is generated by personal qualifies of technical competence. Under this heading is the individual who has made, in effect, subordinates of others through sheer force of personality, and the engineer or economist who exerts influence by furnishing answers or sound advice. These may have no actual organizational authority, yet their advice may be so eagerly sought and so unerringly followed that it appears to carry the weight of an order.
But, above all, one cannot discount the importance of formal authority with its institutional foundations. Buttressed by the qualities of leadership implicit in the acceptance theory, formal authority is basic to the managerial job. Once abrogated, it may be delegated or withheld, used or misused, and be effective in capable hands or be ineffective in inept hands.

    4.____

    A. selected   B. delegation
    C. limited   D. possessed

5. Since managerial operations in organizing, staffing, directing, and controlling are designed to support the accomplishment of enterprise objectives, planning logically precedes the execution of all other managerial functions. Although all the functions intermesh in practice, planning is unique in that it establishes the objectives necessary for all group effort. Besides, plans must be made to accomplish these objectives before the manager knows what kind of organization relationships and personal qualifications are needed, along which course subordinates are to be directed, and what kind of control is to be applied. And, of course, each of the other managerial functions must be planned if they are to be effective.
Planning and control are inseparable – the Siamese twins of management. Unplanned action cannot be controlled, for control involves keeping activities on course by correcting deviations from plans. Any attempt to control without plans would be meaningless, since there is no way anyone can tell whether he is going where he wants to go – the task of control – unless first he knows where he wants to go – the task of planning. Plans thus preclude the standards of control.

    5.____

    A. coordinating   B. individual
    C. furnish   D. follow

Questions 6-7.

DIRECTIONS: Answer Questions 6 and 7 SOLELY on the basis of information given in the fol-
              lowing paragraph.

*In-basket tests are often used to assess managerial potential. The exercise consists of a
set of papers that would be likely to be found in the in-basket of an administrator or manager
at any given time, and requires the individuals participating in the examination to indicate how
they would dispose of each item found in the in-basket. In order to handle the in-basket effectively, they must successfully manage their time, refer and assign some work to subordinates,
juggle potentially conflicting appointments and meetings, and arrange for follow-up of problems generated by the items in the in-basket. In other words, the in-basket test is attempting
to evaluate the participants' abilities to organize their work, set priorities, delegate, control,
and make decisions.*

6.   According to the above paragraph, to succeed in an in-basket test, an administrator must   6._____

     A.   be able to read very quickly
     B.   have a great deal of technical knowledge
     C.   know when to delegate work
     D.   arrange a lot of appointments and meetings

7.   According to the above paragraph, all of the following abilities are indications of manage-   7._____
     rial potential EXCEPT the ability to

     A.   organize and control   B.   manage time
     C.   write effective reports   D.   make appropriate decisions

Questions 8-9.

DIRECTIONS: Answer Questions 8 and 9 SOLELY on the basis of information given in the fol-
              lowing paragraph.

*One of the biggest mistakes of government executives with substantial supervisory
responsibility is failing to make careful appraisals of performance during employee probationary periods. Many a later headache could have been avoided by prompt and full appraisal
during the early months of an employee's assignment. There is not much more to say about
this except to emphasize the common prevalence of this oversight, and to underscore that for
its consequences, which are many and sad, the offending managers have no one to blame
but themselves.*

8.   According to the above passage, probationary periods are   8._____

     A.   a mistake, and should not be used by supervisors with large responsibilities
     B.   not used properly by government executives
     C.   used only for those with supervisory responsibility
     D.   the consequence of management mistakes

9. The one of the following conclusions that can MOST appropriately be drawn from the
    above passage is that   9.___

    A. management's failure to appraise employees during their probationary period is a
        common occurrence
    B. there is not much to say about probationary periods, because they are unimportant
    C. managers should blame employees for failing to use their probationary periods
        properly
    D. probationary periods are a headache to most managers

Questions 10-12.

DIRECTIONS: Answer Questions 10 through 12 SOLELY on the basis of information given in
              the following paragraph.

*The common sense character of the merit system seems so natural to most Americans
that many people wonder why it should ever have been inoperative. After all, the American
economic system, the most phenomenal the world has ever known, is also founded on a rug-
ged selective process which emphasizes the personal qualities of capacity, industriousness,
and productivity. The criteria may not have always been appropriate and competition has not
always been fair, but competition there was, and the responsibilities and the rewards – with
exceptions, of course – have gone to those who could measure up in terms of intelligence,
knowledge, or perseverance. This has been true not only in the economic area, in the money-
making process, but also in achievement in the professions and other walks of life.*

10. According to the above paragraph, economic rewards in the United States have   10.___

    A. always been based on appropriate, fair criteria
    B. only recently been based on a competitive system
    C. not gone to people who compete too ruggedly
    D. usually gone to those people with intelligence, knowledge, and perseverance

11. According to the above passage, a merit system is   11.___

    A. an unfair criterion on which to base rewards
    B. unnatural to anyone who is not American
    C. based only on common sense
    D. based on the same principles as the American economic system

12. According to the above passage, it is MOST accurate to say that   12.___

    A. the United States has always had a civil service merit system
    B. civil service employees are very rugged
    C. the American economic system has always been based on a merit objective
    D. competition is unique to the American way of life

Questions 13-15.

DIRECTIONS: The management study of employee absence due to sickness is an effective tool in planning. Answer Questions 13 through 15 SOLELY on the data given below.

Number of days absent per worker (sickness)	1	2	3	4	5	6	7	8 or Over
Number of workers	76	23	6	3	1	0	1	0

Total Number of Workers: 400
Period Covered: January 1 - December 31

13. The total number of man days lost due to illness was   13.____

    A. 110   B. 137   C. 144   D. 164

14. What percent of the workers had 4 or more days absence due to sickness?   14.____

    A. .25%   B. 2.5%   C. 1.25%   D. 12.5%

15. Of the 400 workers studied, the number who lost no days due to sickness was   15.____

    A. 190   B. 236   C. 290   D. 346

Questions 16-18.

DIRECTIONS: In the graph below, the lines labeled "A" and "B" represent the cumulative progress in the work of two file clerks, each of whom was given 500 consecutively numbered applications to file in the proper cabinets over a five-day work week. Answer Questions 16 through 18 SOLELY upon the data provided in the graph.

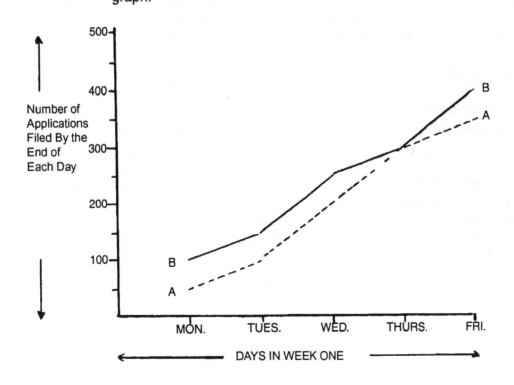

16. The day during which the LARGEST number of applications was filed by both clerks was   16.____

    A. Monday   B. Tuesday   C. Wednesday   D. Friday

17. At the end of the second day, the percentage of applications STILL to be filed was   17.____

    A. 25%   B. 50%   C. 66%   D. 75%

18. Assuming that the production pattern is the same the following week as the week shown   18.____
    in the chart, the day on which the file clerks will FINISH this assignment will be

    A. Monday   B. Tuesday   C. Wednesday   D. Friday

Questions 19-21.

DIRECTIONS: The following chart shows the differences between the rates of production of
employees in Department D in 1996 and 2006. Answer Questions 19 through
21 SOLELY on the basis of the information given in the chart.

Number of Employees Producing Work-Units Within Range in 1996	Number of Work-Units Produced	Number of Employees Producing Work-Units Within Range in 2006
7	500 - 1000	4
14	1001 - 1500	11
26	1501 - 2000	28
22	2001 - 2500	36
17	2501 - 3000	39
10	3001 - 3500	23
4	3501 - 4000	9

19. Assuming that within each range of work-units produced the average production was at   19.____
    the mid-point at that range (e.g., category 500 - 1000 = 750), then the AVERAGE number
    of work-units produced per employee in 1996 fell into the range

    A. 1001 - 1500   B. 1501 - 2000
    C. 2001 - 2500   D. 2501 - 3000

20. The ratio of the number of employees producing more than 2000 work-units in 1996 to   20.____
    the number of employees producing more than 2000 work-units in 2006 is *most nearly*

    A. 1:2   B. 2:3   C. 3:4   D. 4:5

21. In Department D, which of the following were GREATER in 2006 than in 1996?   21.____
        I.   Total number of employees
        II. Total number of work-units produced
        III. Number of employees producing 2000 or fewer work-units
    The CORRECT answer is:

    A. I, II, III   B. I, II
    C. I, III   D. II, III

22. Unit S's production fluctuated substantially from one year to another. In 2004, Unit S's production was 100% greater than in 2003. In 2005, production decreased by 25% from 2004. In 2006, Unit S's production was 10% greater than in 2005.
On the basis of this information, it is CORRECT to conclude that Unit S's production in 2006 exceeded Unit S's production in 2003 by

22.____

    A. 65%   B. 85%   C. 95%   D. 135%

23. Agency "X" is moving into a new building. It has 1500 employees presently on its staff and does not contemplate much variance from this level. The new building contains 100 available offices, each with a maximum capacity of 30 employees. It has been decided that only 2/3 of the maximum capacity of each office will be utilized. The TOTAL number of offices that will be occupied by Agency "X" is

23.____

    A. 30   B. 66   C. 75   D. 90

24. One typist completes a form letter every 5 minutes and another typist completes one every 6 minutes.
If the two typists start together, they will again start typing new letters simultaneously _____ minutes later and will have completed ____ letters by that time.

24.____

    A. 11; 30   B. 12; 24   C. 24; 12   D. 30; 11

25. During one week, a machine operator produces 10 fewer pages per hour of work than he usually does. If it ordinarily takes him six hours to produce a 300-page report, it will take him____hours LONGER to produce that same 300-page report during the week when he produces MORE slowly.

25.____

    A. $1\frac{1}{2}$ B. $1\frac{2}{3}$ C. 2   D. $2\frac{3}{4}$

KEY (CORRECT ANSWERS)

		Incorrect Words
1.	A	stability
2.	D	obsolete
3.	D	freeze
4.	D	abrogated
5.	C	preclude

6.	C	16.	C
7.	C	17.	D
8.	B	18.	B
9.	A	19.	C
10.	D	20.	A
11.	D	21.	B
12.	C	22.	A
13.	D	23.	C
14.	C	24.	D
15.	C	25.	A

———

Evaluating Conclusions in Light of Known Facts

EXAMINATION SECTION
TEST 1

DIRECTIONS: Each question or incomplete statement is followed by several suggested answers or completions. Select the one that BEST answers the question or completes the statement. *PRINT THE LETTER OF THE CORRECT ANSWER IN THE SPACE AT THE RIGHT.*

Questions 1-9.

DIRECTIONS: In questions 1-9, you will read a set of facts and a conclusion drawn from them. The conclusion may be valid or invalid, based on the facts—it's your task to determine the validity of the conclusion.

For each question, select the letter before the statement that BEST expresses the relationship between the given facts and the conclusion that has been drawn from them. Your choices are:
A. The facts prove the conclusion
B. The facts disprove the conclusion; or
C. The facts neither prove nor disprove the conclusion.

1. FACTS: If the supervisor retires, James, the assistant supervisor, will not be transferred to another department. James will be promoted to supervisor if he is not transferred. The supervisor retired.

    CONCLUSION: James will be promoted to supervisor.

    A. The facts prove the conclusion.
    B. The facts disprove the conclusion.
    C. The facts neither prove nor disprove the conclusion.

    1.____

2. FACTS: In the town of Luray, every player on the softball team works at Luray National Bank. In addition, every player on the Luray softball team wears glasses.

    CONCLUSION: At least some of the people who work at Luray National Bank wear glasses.

    A. The facts prove the conclusion.
    B. The facts disprove the conclusion.
    C. The facts neither prove nor disprove the conclusion.

    2.____

3. FACTS: The only time Henry and June go out to dinner is on an evening when they have childbirth classes. Their childbirth classes meet on Tuesdays and Thursdays.

    CONCLUSION: Henry and June never go out to dinner on Friday or Saturday.

    A. The facts prove the conclusion.
    B. The facts disprove the conclusion.
    C. The facts neither prove nor disprove the conclusion.

    3.____

4. FACTS: Every player on the field hockey team has at least one bruise. Everyone on the field hockey team also has scarred knees.

4.____

CONCLUSION: Most people with both bruises and scarred knees are field hockey players.

   A. The facts prove the conclusion.
   B. The facts disprove the conclusion.
   C. The facts neither prove nor disprove the conclusion.

5. FACTS: In the chess tournament, Lance will win his match against Jane if Jane wins her match against Mathias. If Lance wins his match against Jane, Christine will not win her match against Jane.

5.____

CONCLUSION: Christine will not win her match against Jane if Jane wins her match against Mathias.

   A. The facts prove the conclusion.
   B. The facts disprove the conclusion.
   C. The facts neither prove nor disprove the conclusion.

6. FACTS: No green lights on the machine are indicators for the belt drive status. Not all of the lights on the machine's upper panel are green. Some lights on the machine's lower panel are green.

6.____

CONCLUSION: The green lights on the machine's lower panel may be indicators for the belt drive status.

   A. The facts prove the conclusion.
   B. The facts disprove the conclusion.
   C. The facts neither prove nor disprove the conclusion.

7. FACTS: At a small, one-room country school, there are eight students: Amy, Ben, Carla, Dan, Elliot, Francine, Greg, and Hannah. Each student is in either the 6th, 7th, or 8th grade. Either two or three students are in each grade. Amy, Dan, and Francine are all in different grades. Ben and Elliot are both in the 7th grade. Hannah and Carl are in the same grade.

7.____

CONCLUSION: Exactly three students are in the 7th grade.

   A. The facts prove the conclusion.
   B. The facts disprove the conclusion.
   C. The facts neither prove nor disprove the conclusion.

8. FACTS: Two married couples are having lunch together. Two of the four people are German and two are Russian, but in each couple the nationality of a spouse is not necessarily the same as the other's. One person in the group is a teacher, the other a lawyer, one an engineer, and the other a writer. The teacher is a Russian man. The writer is Russian, and her husband is an engineer. One of the people, Mr. Stern, is German.

8.____

CONCLUSION: Mr. Stern's wife is a writer.

A. The facts prove the conclusion.
B. The facts disprove the conclusion.
C. The facts neither prove nor disprove the conclusion.

9. FACTS: The flume ride at the county fair is open only to children who are at least 36   9.____
inches tall. Lisa is 30 inches tall. John is shorter than Henry, but more than 10 inches
taller than Lisa.

CONCLUSION: Lisa is the only one who can't ride the flume ride.

A. The facts prove the conclusion.
B. The facts disprove the conclusion.
C. The facts neither prove nor disprove the conclusion.

Questions 10-17.

DIRECTIONS: Questions 10-17 are based on the following reading passage. It is not your
knowledge of the particular topic that is being tested, but your ability to reason
based on what you have read. The passage is likely to detail several proposed
courses of action and factors affecting these proposals. The reading passage
is followed by a conclusion or outcome based on the facts in the passage, or a
description of a decision taken regarding the situation. The conclusion is followed by a number of statements that have a possible connection to the conclusion. For each statement, you are to determine whether:

A. The statement proves the conclusion.
B. The statement supports the conclusion but does not prove it.
C. The statement disproves the conclusion.
D. The statement weakens the conclusion but does not disprove it.
E. The statement has no relevance to the conclusion.

Remember that the conclusion after the passage is to be accepted as the outcome of
what actually happened, and that you are being asked to evaluate the impact each statement would have had on the conclusion.

PASSAGE:

The Grand Army of Foreign Wars, a national veteran's organization, is struggling to
maintain its National Home, where the widowed spouses and orphans of deceased members
are housed together in a small village-like community. The Home is open to spouses and children who are bereaved for any reason, regardless of whether the member's death was
related to military service, but a new global conflict has led to a dramatic surge in the number
of members' deaths: many veterans who re-enlisted for the conflict have been killed in action.

The Grand Army of Foreign Wars is considering several options for handling the
increased number of applications for housing at the National Home, which has been tradition-
ally supported by membership dues. At its national convention, it will choose only one of the
following:

The first idea is a one-time $50 tax on all members, above and beyond the dues they pay
already. Since the organization has more than a million members, this tax should be sufficient

for the construction and maintenance of new housing for applicants on the existing grounds of the National Home. The idea is opposed, however, by some older members who live on fixed incomes. These members object in principle to the taxation of Grand Army members. The Grand Army has never imposed a tax on its members.

The second idea is to launch a national fund-raising drive and public relations campaign that will attract donations for the National Home. Several national celebrities are members of the organization, and other celebrities could be attracted to the cause. Many Grand Army members are wary of this approach, however: in the past, the net receipts of some fund-raising efforts have been relatively insignificant, given the costs of staging them.

A third approach, suggested by many of the younger members, is to have new applicants share some of the costs of construction and maintenance. The spouses and children would pay an up-front "enrollment" fee, based on a sliding scale proportionate to their income and assets, and then a monthly fee adjusted similarly to contribute to maintenance costs. Many older members are strongly opposed to this idea, as it is in direct contradiction to the principles on which the organization was founded more than a century ago.

The fourth option is simply to maintain the status quo, focus the organization's efforts on supporting the families who already live at the National Home, and wait to accept new applicants based on attrition.

CONCLUSION: At its annual national convention, the Grand Army of Foreign Wars votes to impose a one-time tax of $10 on each member for the purpose of expanding and supporting the National Home to welcome a larger number of applicants. The tax is considered to be the solution most likely to produce the funds needed to accommodate the growing number of applicants.

10. Actuarial studies have shown that because the Grand Army's membership consists mostly of older veterans from earlier wars, the organization's membership will suffer a precipitous decline in numbers in about five years.

    10.____

    A.
    B.
    C.
    D.
    E.

11. After passage of the funding measure, a splinter group of older members appeals for the "sliding scale" provision to be applied to the tax, so that some members may be allowed to contribute less based on their income.

    11.____

    A.
    B.
    C.
    D.
    E.

12. The original charter of the Grand Army of Foreign Wars specifically states that the organization will not levy any taxes or duties on its members beyond its modest annual dues. It takes a super-majority of attending delegates at the national convention to make alterations to the charter.

12.____

    A.
    B.
    C.
    D.
    E.

13. Six months before Grand Army of Foreign Wars' national convention, the Internal Revenue Service rules that because it is an organization that engages in political lobbying, the Grand Army must no longer enjoy its own federal tax-exempt status.

13.____

    A.
    B.
    C.
    D.
    E.

14. Two months before the national convention, Dirk Rockwell, arguably the country's most famous film actor, announces in a nationally televised interview that he has been saddened to learn of the plight of the National Home, and that he is going to make it his own personal crusade to see that it is able to house and support a greater number of widowed spouses and orphans in the future.

14.____

    A.
    B.
    C.
    D.
    E.

15. The Grand Army's final estimate is that the cost of expanding the National Home to accommodate the increased number of applicants will be about $61 million.

15.____

    A.
    B.
    C.
    D.
    E.

16. Just before the national convention, the federal Department of Veterans Affairs announces steep cuts in the benefits package that is currently offered to the widowed spouses and orphans of veterans.

16.____

    A.
    B.
    C.
    D.

17. After the national convention, the Grand Army of Foreign Wars begins charging a modest   17.____
    "start-up" fee to all families who apply for residence at the national home.

    A.
    B.
    C.
    D.
    E.

Questions 18-25.

DIRECTIONS: Questions 18-25 each provide four factual statements and a conclusion based
               on these statements. After reading the entire question, you will decide
               whether:
               A.   The conclusion is proved by statements 1-4;
               B.   The conclusion is disproved by statements 1-4; or
               C.   The facts are not sufficient to prove or disprove the conclusion.

18. FACTUAL STATEMENTS: 18.____

     1. In the Field Day high jump competition, Martha jumped higher than Frank.
     2. Carl jumped higher than Ignacio.
     3. I gnacio jumped higher than Frank.
     4. Dan jumped higher than Carl.

     CONCLUSION: Frank finished last in the high jump competition.

         A.   The conclusion is proved by statements 1-4.
         B.   The conclusion is disproved by statements 1-4.
         C.   The facts are not sufficient to prove or disprove the conclusion.

19. FACTUAL STATEMENTS: 19.____

     1. The door to the hammer mill chamber is locked if light 6 is red.
     2. The door to the hammer mill chamber is locked only when the mill is operating.
     3. If the mill is not operating, light 6 is blue.
     4. Light 6 is blue.

     CONCLUSION: The door to the hammer mill chamber is locked.

         A.   The conclusion is proved by statements 1-4.
         B.   The conclusion is disproved by statements 1-4.
         C.   The facts are not sufficient to prove or disprove the conclusion.

20. FACTUAL STATEMENTS: 20.____

    1. Ziegfried, the lion tamer at the circus, has demanded ten additional minutes of perfor-
       mance time during each show.
    2. If Ziegfried is allowed his ten additional minutes per show, he will attempt to teach
       Kimba the tiger to shoot a basketball.
    3. If Kimba learns how to shoot a basketball, then Ziegfried was not given his ten addi-
       tional minutes.
    4. Ziegfried was given his ten additional minutes.

    CONCLUSION: Despite Ziegfried's efforts, Kimba did not learn how to shoot a basket-
    ball.

    A. The conclusion is proved by statements 1-4.
    B. The conclusion is disproved by statements 1-4.
    C. The facts are not sufficient to prove or disprove the conclusion.

21. FACTUAL STATEMENTS: 21.____

    1. If Stan goes to counseling, Sara won't divorce him.
    2. If Sara divorces Stan, she'll move back to Texas.
    3. If Sara doesn't divorce Stan, Irene will be disappointed.
    4. Stan goes to counseling.

    CONCLUSION: Irene will be disappointed.

    A. The conclusion is proved by statements 1-4.
    B. The conclusion is disproved by statements 1-4.
    C. The facts are not sufficient to prove or disprove the conclusion.

22. FACTUAL STATEMENTS: 22.____

    1. If Delia is promoted to district manager, Claudia will have to be promoted to team
       leader.
    2. Delia will be promoted to district manager unless she misses her fourth-quarter sales
       quota.
    3. If Claudia is promoted to team leader, Thomas will be promoted to assistant team
       leader.
    4. Delia meets her fourth-quarter sales quota.

    CONCLUSION: Thomas is promoted to assistant team leader.

    A. The conclusion is proved by statements 1-4.
    B. The conclusion is disproved by statements 1-4.
    C. The facts are not sufficient to prove or disprove the conclusion.

23. FACTUAL STATEMENTS: 23.____

   1. Clone D is identical to Clone B.
   2. Clone B is not identical to Clone A.
   3. Clone D is not identical to Clone C.
   4. Clone E is not identical to the clones that are identical to Clone B.

   CONCLUSION: Clone E is identical to Clone D.

   A. The conclusion is proved by statements 1-4.
   B. The conclusion is disproved by statements 1-4.
   C. The facts are not sufficient to prove or disprove the conclusion.

24. FACTUAL STATEMENTS: 24.____

   1. In the Stafford Tower, each floor is occupied by a single business.
   2. Big G Staffing is on a floor between CyberGraphics and MainEvent.
   3. Gasco is on the floor directly below CyberGraphics and three floors above Treehorn
      Audio.
   4. MainEvent is five floors below EZ Tax and four floors below Treehorn Audio.

   CONCLUSION: EZ Tax is on a floor between Gasco and MainEvent.

   A. The conclusion is proved by statements 1-4.
   B. The conclusion is disproved by statements 1-4.
   C. The facts are not sufficient to prove or disprove the conclusion.

25. FACTUAL STATEMENTS: 25.____

   1. Only county roads lead to Nicodemus.
   2. All the roads from Hill City to Graham County are federal highways.
   3. Some of the roads from Plainville lead to Nicodemus.
   4. Some of the roads running from Hill City lead to Strong City.

   CONCLUSION: Some of the roads from Plainville are county roads.

   A. The conclusion is proved by statements 1-4.
   B. The conclusion is disproved by statements 1-4.
   C. The facts are not sufficient to prove or disprove the conclusion.

KEY (CORRECT ANSWERS)

1.	A		11.	A
2.	A		12.	D
3.	A		13.	E
4.	C		14.	D
5.	A		15.	B
6.	B		16.	B
7.	A		17.	C
8.	A		18.	A
9.	A		19.	B
10.	E		20.	A

21.	A
22.	A
23.	B
24.	A
25.	A

———

SOLUTIONS TO PROBLEMS

1) (A) Given statement 3, we deduce that James will not be transferred to another department. By statement 2, we can conclude that James will be promoted.

2) (A) Since every player on the softball team wears glasses, these individuals compose some of the people who work at the bank. Although not every person who works at the bank plays softball, those bank employees who do play softball wear glasses.

3) (A) If Henry and June go out to dinner, we conclude that it must be on Tuesday or Thursday, which are the only two days when they have childbirth classes. This implies that if it is not Tuesday or Thursday, then this couple does not go out to dinner.

4) (C) We can only conclude that if a person plays on the field hockey team, then he or she has both bruises and scarred knees. But there are probably a great number of people who have both bruises and scarred knees but do not play on the field hockey team. The given conclusion can neither be proven or disproven.

5) (A) From statement 1, if Jane beats Mathias, then Lance will beat Jane. Using statement 2, we can then conclude that Christine will not win her match against Jane.

6) (B) Statement 1 tells us that no green light can be an indicator of the belt drive status. Thus, the given conclusion must be false.

7) (A) We already know that Ben and Elliot are in the 7th grade. Even though Hannah and Carl are in the same grade, it cannot be the 7th grade because we would then have at least four students in this 7th grade. This would contradict the third statement, which states that either two or three students are in each grade. Since Amy, Dan, and Francine are in different grades, exactly one of them must be in the 7th grade. Thus, Ben, Elliot and exactly one of Amy, Dan, and Francine are the three students in the 7th grade.

8) (A) One man is a teacher, who is Russian. We know that the writer is female and is Russian. Since her husband is an engineer, he cannot be the Russian teacher. Thus, her husband is of German descent, namely Mr. Stern. This means that Mr. Stern's wife is the writer. Note that one couple consists of a male Russian teacher and a female German lawyer. The other couple consists of a male German engineer and a female Russian writer.

9) (A) Since John is more than 10 inches taller than Lisa, his height is at least 46 inches. Also, John is shorter than Henry, so Henry's height must be greater than 46 inches. Thus, Lisa is the only one whose height is less than 36 inches. Therefore, she is the only one who is not allowed on the flume ride.

18) (A) Dan jumped higher than Carl, who jumped higher than Ignacio, who jumped higher than Frank. Since Martha jumped higher than Frank, every person jumped higher than Frank. Thus, Frank finished last.

19) (B) If the light is red, then the door is locked. If the door is locked, then the mill is operating. Reversing the logical sequence of these statements, if the mill is not operating, then the door is not locked, which means that the light is blue. Thus, the given conclusion is disproved.

20) (A) Using the contrapositive of statement 3, if Ziegfried was given his ten additional minutes, then Kimba did not learn how to shoot a basketball. Since statement 4 is factual, the conclusion is proved.

21) (A) From statements 4 and 1, we conclude that Sara doesn't divorce Stan. Then statement 3 reveals that Irene will be disappointed. Thus the conclusion is proved.

22) (A) Statement 2 can be rewritten as "Delia is promoted to district manager or she misses her sales quota." Furthermore, this statement is equivalent to "If Delia makes her sales quota, then she is promoted to district manager." From statement 1, we conclude that Claudia is promoted to team leader. Finally, by statement 3, Thomas is promoted to assistant team leader. The conclusion is proved.

23) (B) By statement 4, Clone E is not identical to any clones identical to clone B. Statement 1 tells us that clones B and D are identical. Therefore, clone E cannot be identical to clone D. The conclusion is disproved.

24) (A) Based on all four statements, CyberGraphics is somewhere below Main Event. Gasco is one floor below CyberGraphics. EZ Tax is two floors below Gasco. Treehorn Audio is one floor below EZ Tax. Main Event is four floors below Treehorn Audio. Thus, EZ Tax is two floors below Gasco and five floors above Main Event. The conclusion is proved.

25) (A) From statement 3, we know that some of the roads from Plainville lead to Nicodemus. But statement 1 tells us that only county roads lead to Nicodemus. Therefore, some of the roads from Plainville must be county roads. The conclusion is proved.

TEST 2

Questions 1-9.

DIRECTIONS: In questions 1-9, you will read a set of facts and a conclusion drawn from them. The conclusion may be valid or invalid, based on the facts-it's your task to determine the validity of the conclusion.

For each question, select the letter before the statement that BEST expresses the relationship between the given facts and the conclusion that has been drawn from them. Your choices are:
A. The facts prove the conclusion
B. The facts disprove the conclusion; or
C. The facts neither prove nor disprove the conclusion.

1. FACTS: Some employees in the testing department are statisticians. Most of the statisticians who work in the testing department are projection specialists. Tom Wilks works in the testing department.

   CONCLUSION: Tom Wilks is a statistician.

   A. The facts prove the conclusion.
   B. The facts disprove the conclusion.
   C. The facts neither prove nor disprove the conclusion.

   1.____

2. FACTS: Ten coins are split among Hank, Lawrence, and Gail. If Lawrence gives his coins to Hank, then Hank will have more coins than Gail. If Gail gives her coins to Lawrence, then Lawrence will have more coins than Hank.

   CONCLUSION: Hank has six coins.

   A. The facts prove the conclusion.
   B. The facts disprove the conclusion.
   C. The facts neither prove nor disprove the conclusion.

   2.____

3. FACTS: Nobody loves everybody. Janet loves Ken. Ken loves everybody who loves Janet.

   CONCLUSION: Everybody loves Janet.

   A. The facts prove the conclusion.
   B. The facts disprove the conclusion.
   C. The facts neither prove nor disprove the conclusion.

   3.____

4. FACTS: Most of the Torres family lives in East Los Angeles. Many people in East Los Angeles celebrate Cinco de Mayo. Joe is a member of the Torres family.

   4.____

   CONCLUSION: Joe lives in East Los Angeles.

   A. The facts prove the conclusion.
   B. The facts disprove the conclusion.
   C. The facts neither prove nor disprove the conclusion.

5. FACTS: Five professionals each occupy one story of a five-story office building. Dr. Kane's office is above Dr. Assad's. Dr. Johnson's office is between Dr. Kane's and Dr. Conlon's. Dr. Steen's office is between Dr. Conlon's and Dr. Assad's. Dr. Johnson is on the fourth story.

   5.____

   CONCLUSION: Dr. Kane occupies the top story.

   A. The facts prove the conclusion.
   B. The facts disprove the conclusion.
   C. The facts neither prove nor disprove the conclusion.

6. FACTS: To be eligible for membership in the Yukon Society, a person must be able to either tunnel through a snowbank while wearing only a T-shirt and shorts, or hold his breath for two minutes under water that is 50° F. Ray can only hold his breath for a minute and a half.

   6.____

   CONCLUSION: Ray can still become a member of the Yukon Society by tunneling through a snowbank while wearing a T-shirt and shorts.

   A. The facts prove the conclusion.
   B. The facts disprove the conclusion.
   C. The facts neither prove nor disprove the conclusion.

7. FACTS: A mark is worth five plunks. You can exchange four sharps for a tinplot. It takes eight marks to buy a sharp.

   7.____

   CONCLUSION: A sharp is the most valuable.

   A. The facts prove the conclusion.
   B. The facts disprove the conclusion.
   C. The facts neither prove nor disprove the conclusion.

8. FACTS: There are gibbons, as well as lemurs, who like to play in the trees at the monkey house. All those who like to play in the trees at the monkey house are fed lettuce and bananas.

   8.____

   CONCLUSION: Lemurs and gibbons are types of monkeys.

   A. The facts prove the conclusion.
   B. The facts disprove the conclusion.
   C. The facts neither prove nor disprove the conclusion.

9. FACTS: None of the Blackfoot tribes is a Salishan Indian tribe. Sal-ishan Indians came   9.____
from the northern Pacific Coast. All Salishan Indians live east of the Continental Divide.

CONCLUSION: No Blackfoot tribes live east of the Continental Divide.

   A. The facts prove the conclusion.
   B. The facts disprove the conclusion.
   C. The facts neither prove nor disprove the conclusion.

Questions 10-17.

DIRECTIONS: Questions 10-17 are based on the following reading passage. It is not your
knowledge of the particular topic that is being tested, but your ability to reason
based on what you have read. The passage is likely to detail several proposed
courses of action and factors affecting these proposals. The reading passage
is followed by a conclusion or outcome based on the facts in the passage, or a
description of a decision taken regarding the situation. The conclusion is followed by a number of statements that have a possible connection to the conclusion. For each statement, you are to determine whether:

   A. The statement proves the conclusion.
   B. The statement supports the conclusion but does not prove it.
   C. The statement disproves the conclusion.
   D. The statement weakens the conclusion but does not disprove it.
   E. The statement has no relevance to the conclusion.

Remember that the conclusion after the passage is to be accepted as the outcome of
what actually happened, and that you are being asked to evaluate the impact each statement would have had on the conclusion.

PASSAGE:

On August 12, Beverly Willey reported that she was in the elevator late on the previous
evening after leaving her office on the 16th floor of a large office building. In her report,
she states that a man got on the elevator at the 11th floor, pulled her off the elevator,
assaulted her, and stole her purse. Ms. Willey reported that she had seen the man in the
elevators and hallways of the building before. She believes that the man works in the
building. Her description of him is as follows: he is tall, unshaven, with wavy brown hair
and a scar on his left cheek. He walks with a pronounced limp, often dragging his left foot
behind his right.

CONCLUSION: After Beverly Willey makes her report, the police arrest a 43-year-man,
Barton Black, and charge him with her assault.

10. Barton Black is a former Marine who served in Vietnam, where he sustained shrapnel   10.____
wounds to the left side of his face and suffered nerve damage in his left leg.

   A.
   B.
   C.
   D.
   E.

11. When they arrived at his residence to question him, detectives were greeted at the door   11.____
by Barton Black, who was tall and clean-shaven.

    A.
    B.
    C.
    D.
    E.

12. Barton Black was booked into the county jail several days after Beverly Willey's assault.   12.____

    A.
    B.
    C.
    D.
    E.

13. Upon further investigation, detectives discover that Beverly Willey does not work at the   13.____
office building.

    A.
    B.
    C.
    D.
    E.

14. Upon further investigation, detectives discover that Barton Black does not work at the   14.____
office building.

    A.
    B.
    C.
    D.
    E.

15. In the spring of the following year, Barton Black is convicted of assaulting Beverly Willey   15.____
on August 11.

    A.
    B.
    C.
    D.
    E.

16. During their investigation of the assault, detectives determine that Beverly Willey was   16.____
assaulted on the 12th floor of the office building.

    A.
    B.
    C.
    D.
    E.

17. The day after Beverly Willey's assault, Barton Black fled the area and was never seen   17.___
    again.

    A.
    B.
    C.
    D.
    E.

Questions 18-25.

DIRECTIONS: Questions 18-25 each provide four factual statements and a conclusion based
              on these statements. After reading the entire question, you will decide
              whether:

              A.   The conclusion is proved by statements 1-4;
              B.   The conclusion is disproved by statements 1-4; or
              C.   The facts are not sufficient to prove or disprove the conclusion.

18. FACTUAL STATEMENTS: 18.___

    1. Among five spice jars on the shelf, the sage is to the right of the parsley.
    2. The pepper is to the left of the basil.
    3. The nutmeg is between the sage and the pepper.
    4. The pepper is the second spice from the left.

    CONCLUSION: The sage is the farthest to the right.

    A.   The conclusion is proved by statements 1-4.
    B.   The conclusion is disproved by statements 1-4.
    C.   The facts are not sufficient to prove or disprove the conclusion.

19. FACTUAL STATEMENTS: 19.___

    1. Gear X rotates in a clockwise direction if Switch C is in the OFF position
    2. Gear X will rotate in a counter-clockwise direction if Switch C is ON.
    3. If Gear X is rotating in a clockwise direction, then Gear Y will not be rotating at all.
    4. Switch C is ON.

    CONCLUSION: Gear X is rotating in a counter-clockwise direction.

    A.   The conclusion is proved by statements 1-4.
    B.   The conclusion is disproved by statements 1-4.
    C.   The facts are not sufficient to prove or disprove the conclusion.

20. FACTUAL STATEMENTS: 20.____
    1. Lane will leave for the Toronto meeting today only if Terence, Rourke, and Jackson all
       file their marketing reports by the end of the work day.
    2. Rourke will file her report on time only if Ganz submits last quarter's data.
    3. If Terence attends the security meeting, he will attend it with Jackson, and they will not
       file their marketing reports by the end of the work day.
    4. Ganz submits last quarter's data to Rourke.

    CONCLUSION: Lane will leave for the Toronto meeting today.

    A.   The conclusion is proved by statements 1-4.
    B.   The conclusion is disproved by statements 1-4.
    C.   The facts are not sufficient to prove or disprove the conclusion.

21. FACTUAL STATEMENTS: 21.____

    1. Bob is in second place in the Boston Marathon.
    2. Gregory is winning the Boston Marathon.
    3. There are four miles to go in the race, and Bob is gaining on Gregory at the rate of
       100 yards every minute.
    4. There are 1760 yards in a mile, and Gregory's usual pace during the Boston Mara-
       thon is one mile every six minutes.

    CONCLUSION: Bob wins the Boston Marathon.

    A.   The conclusion is proved by statements 1-4.
    B.   The conclusion is disproved by statements 1-4.
    C.   The facts are not sufficient to prove or disprove the conclusion.

22. FACTUAL STATEMENTS: 22.____

    1. Four brothers are named Earl, John, Gary, and Pete.
    2. Earl and Pete are unmarried.
    3. John is shorter than the youngest of the four.
    4. The oldest brother is married, and is also the tallest.

    CONCLUSION: Gary is the oldest brother.

    A.   The conclusion is proved by statements 1-4.
    B.   The conclusion is disproved by statements 1-4.
    C.   The facts are not sufficient to prove or disprove the conclusion.

23. FACTUAL STATEMENTS: 23.____

    1. Brigade X is ten miles from the demilitarized zone.
    2. If General Woundwort gives the order, Brigade X will advance to the demilitarized
       zone, but not quickly enough to reach the zone before the conflict begins.
    3. Brigade Y, five miles behind Brigade X, will not advance unless General Woundwort
       gives the order.
    4. Brigade Y advances.

    CONCLUSION: Brigade X reaches the demilitarized zone before the conflict begins.

A. The conclusion is proved by statements 1-4.
B. The conclusion is disproved by statements 1-4.
C. The facts are not sufficient to prove or disprove the conclusion.

24. FACTUAL STATEMENTS: 24.____

1. Jerry has decided to take a cab from Fullerton to Elverton.
2. Chubby Cab charges $5 plus $3 a mile.
3. Orange Cab charges $7.50 but gives free mileage for the first 5 miles.
4. After the first 5 miles, Orange Cab charges $2.50 a mile.

CONCLUSION: Orange Cab is the cheaper fare from Fullerton to Elverton.

A. The conclusion is proved by statements 1-4.
B. The conclusion is disproved by statements 1-4.
C. The facts are not sufficient to prove or disprove the conclusion.

25. FACTUAL STATEMENTS: 25.____

1. Dan is never in class when his friend Lucy is absent.
2. Lucy is never absent unless her mother is sick.
3. If Lucy is in class, Sergio is in class also
4. Sergio is never in class when Dalton is absent.

CONCLUSION: If Lucy is absent, Dalton may be in class.

A. The conclusion is proved by statements 1-4.
B. The conclusion is disproved by statements 1-4.
C. The facts are not sufficient to prove or disprove the conclusion.

KEY (CORRECT ANSWERS)

1.	C		11.	E
2.	B		12.	B
3.	B		13.	D
4.	C		14.	E
5.	A		15.	A
6.	A		16.	E
7.	B		17.	C
8.	C		18.	B
9.	C		19.	A
10.	B		20.	C

21.	C
22.	A
23.	B
24.	A
25.	B

SOLUTIONS TO PROBLEMS

1) (C) Statement 1 only tells us that some employees who work in the Testing Department are statisticians. This means that we need to allow the possibility that at least one person in this department is not a statistician. Thus, if a person works in the Testing Department, we cannot conclude whether or not this individual is a statistician.

2) (B) If Hank had six coins, then the total of Gails collection and Lawrence's collection would be four. Thus, if Gail gave all her coins to Lawrence, Lawrence would only have four coins. Thus, it would be impossible for Lawrence to have more coins than Hank.

3) (B) Statement 1 tells us that nobody loves everybody. If everybody loved Janet, then Statement 3 would imply that Ken loves everybody. This would contradict statement 1. The conclusion is disproved.

4) (C) Although most of the Torres family lives in East Los Angeles, we can assume that some members of this family do not live in East Los Angeles. Thus, we cannot prove or disprove that Joe, who is a member of the Torres family, lives in East Los Angeles.

5) (A) Since Dr. Johnson is on the 4th floor, either (a) Dr. Kane is on the 5th floor and Dr. Conlon is on the 3rd floor, or (b) Dr. Kane is on the 3rd floor and Dr. Conlon is on the 5th floor. If option (b) were correct, then since Dr. Assad would be on the 1st floor, it would be impossible for Dr. Steen's office to be between Dr. Conlon and Dr. Assad's office. Therefore, Dr. Kane's office must be on the 5th floor. The order of the doctors' offices, from 5th floor down to the 1st floor is: Dr. Kane, Dr. Johnson, Dr. Conlon, Dr. Steen, Dr. Assad.

6) (A) Ray does not satisfy the requirement of holding his breath for two minutes under water, since he can only hold his breath for one minute in that setting. But if he tunnels through a snowbank with just a T-shirt and shorts, he will satisfy the eligibility requirement. Note that the eligibility requirement contains the key word "or." So only one of the two clauses separated by "or" need to be fulfilled.

7) (B) Statement 2 says that four sharps is equivalent to one tinplot. This means that a tinplot is worth more than a sharp. The conclusion is disproved. We note that the order of these items, from most valuable to least valuable are: tinplot, sharp, mark, plunk.

8) (C) We can only conclude that gibbons and lemurs are fed lettuce and bananas. We can neither prove or disprove that these animals are types of monkeys.

9) (C) We know that all Salishan Indians live east of the Continental Divide. But some nonmembers of this tribe of Indians may also live east of the Continental Divide. Since none of the members of the Blackfoot tribe belong to the Salishan Indian tribe, we cannot draw any conclusion about the location of the Blackfoot tribe with respect to the Continental Divide.

18) (B) Since the pepper is second from the left and the nutmeg is between the sage and the pepper, the positions 2, 3, and 4 (from the left) are pepper, nutmeg, sage. By statement 2, the basil must be in position 5, which implies that the parsley is in position 1. Therefore, the basil, not the sage is farthest to the right. The conclusion disproved.

19) (A) Statement 2 assures us that if switch C is ON, then Gear X is rotating in a counterclockwise direction. The conclusion is proved.

20) (C) Based on Statement 4, followed by Statement 2, we conclude that Ganz and Rourke will file their reports on time. Statement 3 reveals that if Terence and Jackson attend the security meeting, they will fail to file their reports on time. We have no further information if Terence and Jackson attended the security meeting, so we are not able to either confirm or deny that their reports were filed on time. This implies that we cannot know for certain that Lane will leave for his meeting in Toronto.

21) (C) Although Bob is in second place behind Gregory, we cannot deduce how far behind Gregory he is running. At Gregory's current pace, he will cover four miles in 24 minutes. If Bob were only 100 yards behind Gregory, he would catch up to Gregory in one minute. But if Bob were very far behind Gregory, for example 5 miles, this is the equivalent of $(5)(1760) = 8800$ yards. Then Bob would need $8800/100 = 88$ minutes to catch up to Gregory. Thus, the given facts are not sufficient to draw a conclusion.

22) (A) Statement 2 tells us that neither Earl nor Pete could be the oldest; also, either John or Gary is married. Statement 4 reveals that the oldest brother is both married and the tallest. By statement 3, John cannot be the tallest. Since John is not the tallest, he is not the oldest. Thus, the oldest brother must be Gary. The conclusion is proved.

23) (B) By statements 3 and 4, General Woundwort must have given the order to advance. Statement 2 then tells us that Brigade X will advance to the demilitarized zone, but not soon enough before the conflict begins. Thus, the conclusion is disproved.

24) (A) If the distance is 5 miles or less, then the cost for the Orange Cab is only $7.50, whereas the cost for the Chubby Cab is $5 + 3x$, where x represents the number of miles traveled. For 1 to 5 miles, the cost of the Chubby Cab is between $8 and $20. This means that for a distance of 5 miles, the Orange Cab costs $7.50, whereas the Chubby Cab costs $20. After 5 miles, the cost per mile of the Chubby Cab exceeds the cost per mile of the Orange Cab. Thus, regardless of the actual distance between Fullerton and Elverton, the cost for the Orange Cab will be cheaper than that of the Chubby Cab.

25) (B) It looks like "Dalton" should be replaced by "Dan in the conclusion. Then by statement 1, if Lucy is absent, Dan is never in class. Thus, the conclusion is disproved.

READING COMPREHENSION
UNDERSTANDING AND INTERPRETING WRITTEN MATERIAL
EXAMINATION SECTION
TEST 1

DIRECTIONS: Each question or incomplete statement is followed by several suggested answers or completions. Select the one that BEST answers the question or completes the statement. *PRINT THE LETTER OF THE CORRECT ANSWER IN THE SPACE AT THE RIGHT.*

Questions 1-2.

DIRECTIONS: Questions 1 and 2 are to be answered SOLELY on the basis of the following passage.

The employees in a unit or division of a government agency may be referred to as a work group. Within a government agency which has existed for some time, the work groups will have evolved traditions of their own. The persons in these work groups acquire these traditions as part of the process of work adjustment within their groups. Usually, a work group in a large organization will contain *oldtimers*, *newcomers*, and *in-betweeners*. Like the supervisor of a group, who is not necessarily an oldtimer or the oldest member, oldtimers usually have great influence. They can recall events unknown to others and are a storehouse of information and advice about current problems in the light of past experience. They pass along the traditions of the group to the others who, in turn, become oldtimers themselves. Thus, the traditions of the group which have been honored and revered by long acceptance are continued.

1. According to the above passage, the traditions of a work group within a government agency are developed

    A. at the time the group is established
    B. over a considerable period of time
    C. in order to give recognition to oldtimers
    D. for the group before it is established

1.____

2. According to the above passage, the oldtimers within a work group

    A. are the means by which long accepted practices and customs are perpetuated
    B. would best be able to settle current problems that arise
    C. are honored because of the changes they have made in the traditions
    D. have demonstrated that they have learned to do their work well

2.____

Questions 3-4.

DIRECTIONS: Questions 3 and 4 are to be answered SOLELY on the basis of the following passage.

In public agencies, the success of a person assigned to perform first-line supervisory duties depends in large part upon the personal relations between him and his subordinate employees. The goal of supervising effort is something more than to obtain compliance with procedures established by some central office. The major objective is work accomplishment. In order for this goal to be attained, employees must want to attain it and must exercise initiative in their work. Only if employees are generally satisfied with the type of supervision which exists in an organization will they put forth their best efforts.

3. According to the above passage, in order for employees to try to do their work as well as they can, it is essential that

    A. they participate in determining their working conditions and rates of pay
    B. their supervisors support the employees' viewpoints in meetings with higher management
    C. they are content with the supervisory practices which are being used
    D. their supervisors make the changes in working procedures that the employees request

4. It can be inferred from the above passage that the goals of a unit in a public agency will not be reached unless the employees in the unit

    A. wish to reach them and are given the opportunity to make individual contributions to the work
    B. understand the relationship between the goals of the unit and goals of the agency
    C. have satisfactory personal relationships with employees of other units in the agency
    D. carefully follow the directions issued by higher authorities

Questions 5-9.

DIRECTIONS: Questions 5 through 9 are to be answered SOLELY on the basis of the following passage.

If an employee thinks he can save money, time, or material for the city or has an idea about how to do something better than it is being done, he shouldn't keep it to himself. He should send his ideas to the Employees' Suggestion Program, using the special form which is kept on hand in all departments. An employee may send in as many ideas as he wishes. To make sure that each idea is judged fairly, the name of the suggester is not made known until an award is made. The awards are certificates of merit or cash prizes ranging from $10 to $500.

5. According to the above passage, an employee who knows how to do a job in a better way should

    A. be sure it saves enough time to be worthwhile
    B. get paid the money he saves for the city
    C. keep it to himself to avoid being accused of causing a speed-up
    D. send his idea to the Employees' Suggestion Program

6. In order to send his idea to the Employees' Suggestion Program, an employee should   6.____

    A. ask the Department of Personnel for a special form
    B. get the special form in his own department
    C. mail the idea using Special Delivery
    D. send it on plain, white letter-size paper

7. An employee may send to the Employees' Suggestion Program   7.____

    A. as many ideas as he can think of
    B. no more than one idea each week
    C. no more than ten ideas in a month
    D. only one idea on each part of the job

8. The reason the name of an employee who makes a suggestion is not made known at first   8.____
is to

    A. give the employee a larger award
    B. help the judges give more awards
    C. insure fairness in judging
    D. only one idea on each part of the job

9. An employee whose suggestion receives an award may be given a   9.____

    A. bonus once a year   B. certificate for $10
    C. cash prize of up to $500   D. salary increase of $500

Questions 10-12.

DIRECTIONS: Questions 10 through 12 are to be answered SOLELY on the basis of the following passage.

According to the rules of the Department of Personnel, the work of every permanent city employee is reviewed and rated by his supervisor at least once a year. The civil service rating system gives the employee and his supervisor a chance to talk about the progress made during the past year as well as about those parts of the job in which the employee needs to do better. In order to receive a pay increase each year, the employee must have a satisfactory service rating. Service ratings also count toward an employee's final mark on a promotion examination.

10. According to the above passage, a permanent city employee is rated AT LEAST once   10.____

    A. before his work is reviewed
    B. every six months
    C. yearly by his supervisor
    D. yearly by the Department of Personnel

11. According to the above passage, under the rating system the supervisor and the   11.____
employee can discuss how

    A. much more work needs to be done next year
    B. the employee did his work last year

C. the work can be made easier next year
D. the work of the Department can be increased

12. According to the above passage, a permanent city employee will NOT receive a yearly   12._
pay increase

A. if he received a pay increase the year before
B. if he used his service rating for his mark on a promotion examination
C. if his service rating is unsatisfactory
D. unless he got some kind of a service rating

Questions 13-16.

DIRECTIONS: Questions 13 through 16 are to be answered SOLELY on the basis of the
following passage.

It is an accepted fact that the rank and file employee can frequently advance worthwhile
suggestions toward increasing efficiency. For this reason, an Employees' Suggestion System
has been developed and put into operation. Suitable means have been provided at each
departmental location for the confidential submission of suggestions. Numerous suggestions
have been received thus far and, after study, about five percent of the ideas submitted are
being translated into action. It is planned to set up, eventually, monetary awards for all worthwhile suggestions.

13. According to the above passage, a MAJOR reason why an Employees' Suggestion Sys-   13._
tem was established is that

A. an organized program of improvement is better than a haphazard one
B. employees can often give good suggestions to increase efficiency
C. once a fact is accepted, it is better to act on it than to do nothing
D. the suggestions of rank and file employees were being neglected

14. According to the above passage, under the Employees' Suggestion System,   14._

A. a file of worthwhile suggestions will eventually be set up at each departmental
location
B. it is possible for employees to turn in suggestions without fellow employees knowing of it
C. means have been provided for the regular and frequent collection of suggestions
submitted
D. provision has been made for the judging of worthwhile suggestions by an Employees' Suggestion Committee

15. According to the above passage, it is reasonable to assume that   15._

A. all suggestions must be turned in at a central office
B. employees who make worthwhile suggestions will be promoted
C. not all the prizes offered will be monetary ones
D. prizes of money will be given for the best suggestions

16. According to the above passage, of the many suggestions made,　　16.＿＿＿

    A. all are first tested
    B. a small part are put into use
    C. most are very worthwhile
    D. samples are studied

Questions 17-20.

DIRECTIONS:　Questions 17 through 20 are to be answered SOLELY on the basis of the following passage.

Employees may be granted leaves of absence without pay at the discretion of the Personnel Officer. Such a leave without pay shall begin on the first working day on which the employee does not report for duty and shall continue to the first day on which the employee returns to duty. The Personnel Division may vary the dates of the leave for the record so as to conform with payroll periods, but in no case shall an employee be off the payroll for a different number of calendar days than would have been the case if the actual dates mentioned above had been used. An employee who has vacation or overtime to his credit, which is available for normal use, may take time off immediately prior to beginning a leave of absence without pay, chargeable against all or part of such vacation or overtime.

17. According to the above passage, the Personnel Officer must　　17.＿＿＿

    A. decide if a leave of absence without pay should be granted
    B. require that a leave end on the last working day of a payroll period
    C. see to it that a leave of absence begins on the first working day of a pay period
    D. vary the dates of a leave of absence to conform with a payroll period

18. According to the above passage, the exact dates of a leave of absence without pay may be varied provided that the　　18.＿＿＿

    A. calendar days an employee is off the payroll equal the actual leave granted
    B. leave conforms to an even number of payroll periods
    C. leave when granted made provision for variance to simplify payroll records
    D. Personnel Officer approves the variation

19. According to the above passage, a leave of absence without pay must extend from the　　19.＿＿＿

    A. first day of a calendar period to the first day the employee resumes work
    B. first day of a payroll period to the last calendar day of the leave
    C. first working day missed to the first day on which the employee resumes work
    D. last day on which an employee works through the first day he returns to work

20. According to the above passage, an employee may take extra time off just before the start of a leave of absence without pay if　　20.＿＿＿

    A. he charges this extra time against his leave
    B. he has a favorable balance of vacation or overtime which has been frozen
    C. the vacation or overtime that he would normally use for a leave without pay has not been charged in this way before
    D. there is time to his credit which he may use

Question 21.

DIRECTIONS: Question 21 is to be answered SOLELY on the basis of the following passage.

In considering those things which are motivators and incentives to work, it might be just as erroneous not to give sufficient weight to money as an incentive as it is to give too much weight. It is not a problem of establishing a rank-order of importance, but one of knowing that motivation is a blend or mixture rather than a pure element. It is simple to say that cultural factors count more than financial considerations, but this leads only to the conclusion that our society is financial-oriented.

21.   Based on the above passage, in our society, cultural and social motivations to work are   21.___

    A.   things which cannot be avoided
    B.   melded to financial incentives
    C.   of less consideration than high pay
    D.   not balanced equally with economic or financial considerations

Question 22.

DIRECTIONS: Question 22 is to be answered SOLELY on the basis of the following passage.

A general principle of training and learning with respect to people is that they learn more readily if they receive *feedback*. Essential to maintaining proper motivational levels is knowledge of results which indicate level of progress. Feedback also assists the learning process by identifying mistakes. If this kind of information were not given to the learner, then improper or inappropriate job performance may be instilled.

22.   Based on the above passage, which of the following is MOST accurate?   22.___

    A.   Learning will not take place without feedback.
    B.   In the absence of feedback, improper or inappropriate job performance will be learned.
    C.   To properly motivate a learner, the learner must have his progress made known to him.
    D.   Trainees should be told exactly what to do if they are to learn properly.

Question 23.

DIRECTIONS: Question 23 is to be answered SOLELY on the basis of the following passage.

In a democracy, the obligation of public officials is twofold. They must not only do an efficient and satisfactory job of administration, but also they must persuade the public that it is an efficient and satisfactory job. It is a burden which, if properly assumed, will make democracy work and perpetuate reform government.

23.   The above passage means that   23.___

    A.   public officials should try to please everybody
    B.   public opinion is instrumental in determining the policy of public officials

C. satisfactory performance of the job of administration will eliminate opposition to its work
D. frank and open procedure in a public agency will aid in maintaining progressive government

Question 24.

DIRECTIONS: Question 24 is to be answered SOLELY on the basis of the following passage.

Upon retirement for service, a member shall receive a retirement allowance which shall consist of an annuity which shall be the actuarial equivalent of his accumulated deductions at the time of his retirement and a pension, in addition to his annuity, which shall be equal to one service-fraction of his final compensation, multiplied by the number of years of service since he last became a member credited to him, and a pension which is the actuarial equivalent of the reserve-for-increased-take-home-pay to which he may then be entitled, if any.

24. According to the above passage, a retirement allowance shall consist of a(n)   24.____

   A. annuity, plus a pension, plus an actuarial equivalent
   B. annuity, plus a pension, plus reserve-for-increased-take-home-pay, if any
   C. annuity, plus reserve-for-increased-take-home-pay, if any, plus final compensation
   D. pension, plus reserve-for-increased-take-home-pay, if any, plus accumulated deductions

Question 25.

DIRECTIONS: Question 25 is to be answered SOLELY on the basis of the following passage.

Membership in the retirement system shall cease upon the occurrence of any one of the following conditions: when the time out of service of any member who has total service of less than 25 years, shall aggregate more than 5 years; when the time out of service of any member who has total service of 25 years or more, shall aggregate more than 10 years; when any member shall have withdrawn more than 50% of his accumulated deductions; or when any member shall have withdrawn the cash benefit provided by Section B3-35.0 of the Administrative Code.

25. According to the information in the above passage, membership in the retirement system   25.____
    shall cease when an employee

   A. with 17 years of service has been on a leave of absence for 3 years
   B. withdraws 50% of his accumulated deductions
   C. with 28 years of service has been out of service for 10 years
   D. withdraws his cash benefits

─────

KEY (CORRECT ANSWERS)

1.	B		11.	B
2.	A		12.	C
3.	C		13.	B
4.	A		14.	B
5.	D		15.	D
6.	B		16.	B
7.	A		17.	A
8.	C		18.	A
9.	B		19.	C
10.	C		20.	D

21. B
22. C
23. D
24. B
25. D

TEST 2

DIRECTIONS: Each question or incomplete statement is followed by several suggested answers or completions. Select the one that BEST answers the question or completes the statement. *PRINT THE LETTER OF THE CORRECT ANSWER IN THE SPACE AT THE RIGHT.*

Questions 1-6.

DIRECTIONS: Questions 1 through 6 are to be answered SOLELY on the basis of the following passage from an old office manual.

Since almost every office has some contact with data-processed records, a stenographer should have some understanding of the basic operations of data processing. Data processing systems now handle about one-third of all office paperwork. On punched cards, magnetic tape, or on other mediums, data are recorded before being fed into the computer for processing. A machine such as the keypunch is used to convert the data written on the source document into the coded symbols on punched cards or tapes. After data has been converted, it must be verified to guarantee absolute accuracy of conversion. In this manner, data becomes a permanent record which can be read by electronic computers that compare, store, compute, and otherwise process data at high speeds.

One key person in a computer installation is a programmer, the man or woman who puts business and scientific problems into special symbolic languages that can be read by the computer. Jobs done by the computer range all the way from payroll operations to chemical process control, but most computer applications are directed toward management data. About half of the programmers employed by business come to their positions with college degrees; the remaining half are promoted to their positions from within the organization on the basis of demonstrated ability without regard to education.

1. Of the following, the BEST title for the above passage is   1.____

    A. THE STENOGRAPHER AS DATA PROCESSOR
    B. THE RELATION OF KEYPUNCHING TO STENOGRAPHY
    C. UNDERSTANDING DATA PROCESSING
    D. PERMANENT OFFICE RECORDS

2. According to the above passage, a stenographer should understand the basic operations   2.____
   of data processing because

    A. almost every office today has contact with data processed by computer
    B. any office worker may be asked to verify the accuracy of data
    C. most offices are involved in the production of permanent records
    D. data may be converted into computer language by typing on a keypunch

3. According to the above passage, the data which the computer understands is MOST   3.____
   often expressed as

    A. a scientific programming language
    B. records or symbols punched on tape, cards, or other mediums
    C. records on cards
    D. records on tape

4. According to the above passage, computers are used MOST often to handle   4._

   A. management data
   B. problems of higher education
   C. the control of chemical processes
   D. payroll operations

5. Computer programming is taught in many colleges and business schools.   5._
   The above passage implies that programmers in industry

   A. must have professional training
   B. need professional training to advance
   C. must have at least a college education to do adequate programming tasks
   D. do not need college education to do programming work

6. According to the above passage, data to be processed by computer should be   6._

   A. recent   B. basic
   C. complete   D. verified

Questions 7-10.

DIRECTIONS: Questions 7 through 10 are to be answered SOLELY on the basis of the follow-
               ing passage.

   There is nothing that will take the place of good sense on the part of the stenographer.
You may be perfect in transcribing exactly what the dictator says and your speed may be adequate, but without an understanding of the dictator's intent as well as his words, you are likely
to be a mediocre secretary.

   A serious error that is made when taking dictation is putting down something that does
not make sense. Most people who dictate material would rather be asked to repeat and
explain than to receive transcribed material which has errors due to inattention or doubt.
Many dictators request that their grammar be corrected by their secretaries, but unless specifically asked to do so, secretaries should not do it without first checking with the dictator.
Secretaries should be aware that, in some cases, dictators may use incorrect grammar or
slang expressions to create a particular effect.

   Some people dictate commas, periods, and paragraphs, while others expect the stenographer to know when, where, and how to punctuate. A well-trained secretary should be able
to indicate the proper punctuation by listening to the pauses and tones of the dictator's voice.

   A stenographer who has taken dictation from the same person for a period of time should
be able to understand him under most conditions, By increasing her tact, alertness, and efficiency, a secretary can become more competent.

7. According to the above passage, which of the following statements concerning the dicta-   7._
   tion of punctuation is CORRECT?

   A. Dictator may use incorrect punctuation to create a desired style
   B. Dictator should indicate all punctuation
   C. Stenographer should know how to punctuate based on the pauses and tones of
      the dictator
   D. Stenographer should not type any punctuation if it has not been dictated to her

8. According to the above passage, how should secretaries handle grammatical errors in a dictation? Secretaries should

    A. *not correct* grammatical errors unless the dictator is aware that this is being done
    B. *correct* grammatical errors by having the dictator repeat the line with proper pauses
    C. *correct* grammatical errors if they have checked the correctness in a grammar book
    D. *correct* grammatical errors based on their own good sense

8.____

9. If a stenographer is confused about the method of spacing and indenting of a report which has just been dictated to her, she GENERALLY should

    A. do the best she can
    B. ask the dictator to explain what she should do
    C. try to improve her ability to understand dictated material
    D. accept the fact that her stenographic ability is not adequate

9.____

10. In the last line of the first paragraph, the word *mediocre* means MOST NEARLY

    A. superior   B. respected
    C. disregarded   D. second-rate

10.____

Questions 11-12.

DIRECTIONS: Questions 11 and 12 are to be answered SOLELY on the basis of the following passage.

The number of legible carbon copies required to be produced determines the weight of the carbon paper to be used. When only one copy is made, heavy carbon paper is satisfactory. Most typists, however, use medium-weight carbon paper and find it serviceable for up to three or four copies. If five or more copies are to be made, it is wise to use light carbon paper. On the other hand, the finish of carbon paper to be used depends largely on the stroke of the typist and, in lesser degree, on the number of copies to be made and on whether the typewriter has pica or elite type. A soft-finish carbon paper should be used if the typist's touch is light or if a noiseless machine is used. It is desirable for the average typist to use medium-finish carbon paper for ordinary work, when only a few carbon copies are required. Elite type requires a harder carbon finish than pica type for the same number of copies.

11. According to the above passage, the lighter the carbon paper used,

    A. the softer the finish of the carbon paper will be
    B. the greater the number of legible carbon copies that can be made
    C. the greater the number of times the carbon paper can be used
    D. the lighter the typist's touch should be

11.____

12. According to the above passage, the MOST important factor which determines whether the finish of carbon paper to be used in typing should be hard, medium, or soft is

    A. the touch of the typist
    B. the number of carbon copies required
    C. whether the type in the typewriter is pica or elite
    D. whether a machine with pica type will produce the same number of carbon copies as a machine with elite type

12.____

Questions 13-16.

DIRECTIONS: Questions 13 through 16 are to be answered SOLELY on the basis of the following passage.

Modern office methods, geared to ever higher speeds and aimed at ever greater efficiency, are largely the result of the typewriter. The typewriter is a substitute for handwriting and, in the hands of a skilled typist, not only turns out letters and other documents at least three times faster than a penman can do the work, but turns out the greater volume more uniformly and legibly. With the use of carbon paper and onionskin paper, identical copies can be made at the same time.

The typewriter, besides its effect on the conduct of business and government, has had a very important effect on the position of women. The typewriter has done much to bring women into business and government, and today there are vastly more women than men typists. Many women have used the keys of the typewriter to climb the ladder to responsible managerial positions.

The typewriter, as its name implies, employs type to make an ink impression on paper. For many years, the manual typewriter was the standard machine used. Today, the electric typewriter is dominant, and completely automatic electronic typewriters are coming into wider use.

The mechanism of the office manual typewriter includes a set of keys arranged systematically in rows; a semicircular frame of type, connected to the keys by levers; the carriage, or paper carrier; a rubber roller, called a platen, against which the type strikes; and an inked ribbon which make the impression of the type character when the key strikes it.

13. The above passage mentions a number of good features of the combination of a skilled typist and a typewriter. Of the following, the feature which is NOT mentioned in the passage is   13.___

    A. speed   B. reliability
    C. uniformity   D. legibility

14. According to the above passage, a skilled typist can   14.___

    A. turn out at least five carbon copies of typed matter
    B. type at least three times faster than a penman can write
    C. type more than 80 words a minute
    D. readily move into a managerial position

15. According to the above passage, which of the following is NOT part of the mechanism of a manual typewriter?   15.___

    A. Carbon paper   B. Platen
    C. Paper carrier   D. Inked ribbon

16. According to the above passage, the typewriter has helped   16.___

    A. men more than women in business
    B. women in career advancement into management
    C. men and women equally, but women have taken better advantage of it
    D. more women than men, because men generally dislike routine typing work

Questions 17-21.

DIRECTIONS: Questions 17 through 21 are to be answered SOLELY on the basis of the following passage.

The recipient gains an impression of a typewritten letter before he begins to read the message. Factors which provide for a good first impression include margins and spacing that are visually pleasing, formal parts of the letter which are correctly placed according to the style of the letter, copy which is free of obvious erasures and over-strikes, and transcript that is even and clear. The problem for the typist is that of how to produce that first, positive impression of her work.

There are several general rules which a typist can follow when she wishes to prepare a properly spaced letter on a sheet of letterhead. Ordinarily, the width of a letter should not be less than four inches nor more than six inches. The side margins should also have a desirable relation to the bottom margin and the space between the letterhead and the body of the letter. Usually the most appealing arrangement is when the side margins are even and the bottom margin is slightly wider than the side margins. In some offices, however, standard line length is used for all business letters, and the secretary then varies the spacing between the date line and the inside address according to the length of the letter.

17. The BEST title for the above passage would be

    A. WRITING OFFICE LETTERS
    B. MAKING GOOD FIRST IMPRESSIONS
    C. JUDGING WELL-TYPED LETTERS
    D. GOOD PLACING AND SPACING FOR OFFICE LETTERS

17.____

18. According to the above passage, which of the following might be considered the way in which people very quickly judge the quality of work which has been typed? By

    A. measuring the margins to see if they are correct
    B. looking at the spacing and cleanliness of the typescript
    C. scanning the body of the letter for meaning
    D. reading the date line and address for errors

18.____

19. What, according to the above passage, would be definitely UNDESIRABLE as the average line length of a typed letter?

    A. 4"   B. 6"
    C. 5"   D. 7"

19.____

20. According to the above passage, when the line length is kept standard, the secretary

    A. does not have to vary the spacing at all since this also is standard
    B. adjusts the spacing between the date line and inside address for different lengths of letters
    C. uses the longest line as a guideline for spacing between the date line and inside address
    D. varies-the number of spaces between the lines

20.____

21. According to the above passage, side margins are MOST pleasing when they   21._

   A.   are even and somewhat smaller than the bottom margin
   B.   are slightly wider than the bottom margin
   C.   vary with the length of the letter
   D.   are figured independently from the letterhead and the body of the letter

Questions 22-25.

DIRECTIONS: Questions 22 through 25 are to be answered SOLELY on the basis of the fol-
              lowing passage.

Typed pages can reflect the simplicity of modern art in a machine age. Lightness and
evenness can be achieved by proper layout and balance of typed lines and white space.
Instead of solid, cramped masses of uneven, crowded typing, there should be a pleasing balance up and down as well as horizontal.

To have real balance, your page must have a center. The eyes see the center of the
sheet slightly above the real center. This is the way both you and the reader see it. Try imag-
ining a line down the center of the page that divides the paper in equal halves. On either side
of your paper, white space and blocks of typing need to be similar in size and shape.
Although left and right margins should be equal, top and bottom margins need not be as
exact. It looks better to hold a bottom border wider than a top margin, so that your typing rests
upon a cushion of white space. To add interest to the appearance of the page, try making one
paragraph between one-half and two-thirds the size of an adjacent paragraph.

Thus, by taking full advantage of your typewriter, the pages that you type will not only be
accurate but will also be attractive.

22. It can be inferred from the above passage that the basic importance of proper balancing   22._
    on a typed page is that proper balancing

   A.   makes a typed page a work of modern art
   B.   provides exercise in proper positioning of a typewriter
   C.   increases the amount of typed copy on the paper
   D.   draws greater attention and interest to the page

23. A reader will tend to see the center of a typed page   23._

   A.   somewhat higher than the true center
   B.   somewhat lower than the true center
   C.   on either side of the true center
   D.   about two-thirds of an inch above the true center

24. Which of the following suggestions is NOT given by the above passage?   24._

   A.   Bottom margins may be wider than top borders.
   B.   Keep all paragraphs approximately the same size.
   C.   Divide your page with an imaginary line down the middle.
   D.   Side margins should be equalized.

25. Of the following, the BEST title for the above passage is   25.____

    A.   INCREASING THE ACCURACY OF THE TYPED PAGE
    B.   DETERMINATION OF MARGINS FOR TYPED COPY
    C.   LAYOUT AND BALANCE OF THE TYPED PAGE
    D.   HOW TO TAKE FULL ADVANTAGE OF THE TYPEWRITER

KEY (CORRECT ANSWERS)

1.	C		11.	B
2.	A		12.	A
3.	B		13.	C
4.	A		14.	B
5.	D		15.	A
6.	D		16.	B
7.	C		17.	D
8.	A		18.	B
9.	B		19.	D
10.	D		20.	B

21.	A
22.	D
23.	A
24.	B
25.	C

TEST 3

Questions 1-5.

DIRECTIONS: Questions 1 through 5 are to be answered SOLELY on the basis of the following passage.

A written report is a communication of information from one person to another. It is an account of some matter especially investigated, however routine that matter may be. The ultimate basis of any good written report is facts, which become known through observation and verification. Good written reports may seem to be no more than general ideas and opinions. However, in such cases, the facts leading to these opinions were gathered, verified, and reported earlier, and the opinions are dependent upon these facts. Good style, proper form, and emphasis cannot make a good written report out of unreliable information and bad judgment; but on the other hand, solid investigation and brilliant thinking are not likely to become very useful until they are effectively communicated to others. If a person's work calls for written reports, then his work is often no better than his written reports.

1. Based on the information in the above passage, it can be concluded that opinions expressed in a report should be

   A. based on facts which are gathered and reported
   B. emphasized repeatedly when they result from a special investigation
   C. kept to a minimum
   D. separated from the body of the report

1.___

2. In the above passage, the one of the following which is mentioned as a way of establishing facts is

   A. authority   B. reporting
   C. communication   D. verification

2.___

3. According to the above passage, the characteristic shared by ALL written reports is that they are

   A. accounts of routine matters   B. transmissions of information
   C. reliable and logical   D. written in proper form

3.___

4. Which of the following conclusions can logically be drawn from the information given in the above passage?

   A. Brilliant thinking can make up for unreliable information in a report.
   B. One method of judging an individual's work is the quality of the written reports he is required to submit.
   C. Proper form and emphasis can make a good report out of unreliable information.
   D. Good written reports that seem to be no more than general ideas should be rewritten.

4

5. Which of the following suggested titles would be MOST appropriate for the above pas-   5.___
   sage?

   A. GATHERING AND ORGANIZING FACTS
   B. TECHNIQUES OF OBSERVATION
   C. NATURE AND PURPOSE OF REPORTS
   D. REPORTS AND OPINIONS: DIFFERENCES AND SIMILARITIES

Questions 6-8.

DIRECTIONS: Questions 6 through 8 are to be answered SOLELY on the basis of the follow-
               ing passage.

The most important unit of the mimeograph machine is a perforated metal drum over
which is stretched a cloth ink pad. A reservoir inside the drum contains the ink which flows
through the perforations and saturates the ink pad. To operate the machine, the operator first
removes from the machine the protective sheet, which keeps the ink from drying while the
machine is not in use. He then hooks the stencil face down on the drum, draws the stencil
smoothly over the drum, and fastens the stencil at the bottom. The speed with which the
drum turns determines the blackness of the copies printed. Slow turning gives heavy, black
copies; fast turning gives light, clear-cut reproductions. If reproductions are run on other than
porous paper, slip-sheeting is necessary to prevent smearing. Often, the printed copy fails to
drop readily as it comes from the machine. This may be due to static electricity. To remedy
this difficulty, the operator fastens a strip of tinsel from side to side near the impression roller
so that the printed copy just touches the soft stems of the tinsel as it is ejected from the
machine, thus grounding the static electricity to the frame of the machine.

6. According to the above passage,   6.___

   A. turning the drum fast produces light copies
   B. stencils should be placed face up on the drum
   C. ink pads should be changed daily
   D. slip-sheeting is necessary when porous paper is being used

7. According to the above passage, when a mimeograph machine is not in use,   7.___

   A. the ink should be drained from the drum
   B. the ink pad should be removed
   C. the machine should be covered with a protective sheet
   D. the counter should be set at zero

8. According to the above passage, static electricity is grounded to the frame of the mimeo-   8.___
   graph machine by means of

   A. a slip-sheeting device
   B. a strip of tinsel
   C. an impression roller
   D. hooks located at the top of the drum

Questions 9-10.

DIRECTIONS: Questions 9 and 10 are to be answered SOLELY on the basis of the following passage.

The proofreading of material typed from copy is performed more accurately and more speedily when two persons perform this work as a team. The person who did not do the typing should read aloud the original copy while the person who did the typing should check the reading against the typed copy. The reader should speak very slowly and repeat the figures, using a different grouping of numbers when repeating the figures. For example, in reading 1967, the reader may say *one-nine-six-seven* on first reading the figure and *nineteen-sixty-seven* on repeating the figure. The reader should read all punctuation marks, taking nothing for granted. Since mistakes can occur anywhere, everything typed should be proofread. To avoid confusion, the proofreading team should use the standard proofreading marks, which are given in most dictionaries.

9.   According to the above passage, the   9.__

    A.   person who holds the typed copy is called the reader
    B.   two members of a proofreading team should take turns in reading the typed copy aloud
    C.   typed copy should be checked by the person who did the typing
    D.   person who did not do the typing should read aloud from the typed copy

10.   According to the above passage,   10.__

    A.   it is unnecessary to read the period at the end of a sentence
    B.   typographical errors should be noted on the original copy
    C.   each person should develop his own set of proofreading marks
    D.   figures should be read twice

Questions 11-16.

DIRECTIONS: Questions 11 through 16 are to be answered SOLELY on the basis of the above passage.

Basic to every office is the need for proper lighting. Inadequate lighting is a familiar cause of fatigue and serves to create a somewhat dismal atmosphere in the office. One requirement of proper lighting is that it be of an appropriate intensity. Intensity is measured in foot candles. According to the Illuminating Engineering Society of New York, for casual seeing tasks such as in reception rooms, inactive file rooms, and other service areas, it is recommended that the amount of light be 30 foot-candles. For ordinary seeing tasks such as reading, work in active file rooms, and in mailrooms, the recommended lighting is 100 foot-candles. For very difficult seeing tasks such as accounting, transcribing, and business machine use, the recommended lighting is 150 foot-candles.

Lighting intensity is only one requirement. Shadows and glare are to be avoided. For example, the larger the proportion of a ceiling filled with lighting units, the more glare-free and comfortable the lighting will be. Natural lighting from windows is not too dependable because on dark wintry days, windows yield little usable light, and on sunny summer afternoons, the glare from windows may be very distracting. Desks should not face the windows. Finally, the main lighting source ought to be overhead and to the left of the user,

11. According to the above passage, insufficient light in the office may cause   11.____

   A. glare   B. tiredness
   C. shadows   D. distraction

12. Based on the above passage, which of the following must be considered when planning   12.____
    lighting arrangements? The

   A. amount of natural light present
   B. amount of work to be done
   C. level of difficulty of work to be done
   D. type of activity to be carried out

13. It can be inferred from the above passage that a well-coordinated lighting scheme is   13.____
    LIKELY to result in

   A. greater employee productivity
   B. elimination of light reflection
   C. lower lighting cost
   D. more use of natural light

14. Of the following, the BEST title for the above passage is   14.____

   A. CHARACTERISTICS OF LIGHT
   B. LIGHT MEASUREMENT DEVICES
   C. FACTORS TO CONSIDER WHEN PLANNING LIGHTING SYSTEMS
   D. COMFORT VS. COST WHEN DEVISING LIGHTING ARRANGEMENTS

15. According to the above passage, a foot-candle is a measurement of the   15.____

   A. number of bulbs used
   B. strength of the light
   C. contrast between glare and shadow
   D. proportion of the ceiling filled with lighting units

16. According to the above passage, the number of foot-candles of light that would be   16.____
    needed to copy figures onto a payroll is _____ foot-candles.

   A. less than 30   B. 100
   C. 30   D. 150

Questions 17-23.

DIRECTIONS: Questions 17 through 23 are to be answered SOLELY on the basis of the fol-
            lowing passage, which is the Fee Schedule of a hypothetical college.

FEE SCHEDULE

A. A candidate for any baccalaureate degree is not required to pay tuition fees for undergraduate courses until he exceeds 128 credits, Candidates exceeding 128 credits in undergraduate courses are charged at the rate of $100 a credit for each credit of undergraduate course work in excess of 128. Candidates for a baccalaureate degree who are taking graduate courses must pay the same fee as any other student taking graduate courses

B. Non-degree students and college graduates are charged tuition fees for courses, whether undergraduate or graduate, at the rate of $180 a credit. For such students, there is an additional charge of $150 for each class hour per week in excess of the number of course credits. For example, if a three-credit course meets five hours a week, there is an additional charge for the extra two hours. Graduate courses are shown with a (G) before the course number.

C. All students are required to pay the laboratory fees indicated after the number of credits given for that course.

D. All students must pay a $250 general fee each semester.

E. Candidates for a baccalaureate degree are charged a $150 medical insurance fee for each semester. All other students are charged a $100 medical insurance fee each semester.

17. Miss Burton is not a candidate for a degree. She registers for the following courses in the spring semester: Economics 12, 4 hours a week, 3 credits; History (G) 23, 4 hours a week, 3 credits; English 1, 2 hours a week, 2 credits. The TOTAL amount in fees that Miss Burton must pay is

    17.__

    A. less than $2000
    B. at least $2000 but less than $2100
    C. at least $2100 but less than $2200
    D. $2200 or over

18. Miss Gray is not a candidate for a degree. She registers for the following courses in the fall semester: History 3, 3 hours a week, 3 credits; English 5, 3 hours a week, 2 credits; Physics 5, 6 hours a week, 3 credits, laboratory fee $ 60; Mathematics 7, 4 hours a week, 3 credits. The TOTAL amount in fees that Miss Gray must pay is

    18.__

    A. less than $3150
    B. at least $3150 but less than $3250
    C. at least $3250 but less than $3350
    D. $3350 or over

19. Mr. Wall is a candidate for the Bachelor of Arts degree and has completed 126 credits. He registers for the following courses in the spring semester, his final semester at college: French 4, 3 hours a week, 3 credits; Physics (G) 15, 6 hours a week, 3 credits, laboratory fee $80; History (G) 33, 4 hours a week, 3 credits. The TOTAL amount in fees that this candidate must pay is

    19.__

    A. less than $2100
    B. at least $2100 but less than $2300
    C. at least $2300 but less than $2500
    D. $2500

20. Mr. Tindall, a candidate for the B.A. degree, has completed 122 credits of undergraduate courses. He registers for the following courses in his final semester: English 31, 3 hours a week, 3 credits; Philosophy 12, 4 hours a week, 4 credits; Anthropology 15, 3 hours a week, 3 credits; Economics (G) 68, 3 hours a week, 3 credits. The TOTAL amount in fees that Mr. Tindall must pay in his final semester is

    20.__

    A. less than $1200
    B. at least $1200 but less than $1400
    C. at least $1400 but less than $1600
    D. $1600

21. Mr. Cantrell, who was graduated from the college a year ago, registers for graduate courses in the fall semester. Each course for which he registers carries the same number of credits as the number of hours a week it meets.
    If he pays a total of $1530; including a $100 laboratory fee, the number of credits for which he is registered is

    21.____

    A. 4   B. 5   C. 6   D. 7

22. Miss Jayson, who is not a candidate for a degree, has, registered for several courses including a lecture course in History. She withdraws from the course in History for which she had paid the required course fee of $690. The number of hours that this course is scheduled to meet is

    22.____

    A. 4   B. 5   C. 2   D. 3

23. Mr. Van Arsdale, a graduate of a college is Iowa, registers for the following courses in one semester: Chemistry 35, 5 hours a week, 3 credits; Biology 13, 4 hours a week, 3 credits, laboratory fee $150; Mathematics (G) 179, 3 hours a week, 3 credits.
    The TOTAL amount in fees that Mr. Van Arsdale must pay is

    23.____

    A. less than $2400
    B. at least $2400 but less than $2500
    C. at least $2500 but less than $2600
    D. at least $2600 or over

Questions 24-25.

DIRECTIONS: Questions 24 and 25 are to be answered SOLELY on the basis of the following passage.

A duplex envelope is an envelope composed of two sections securely fastened together so that they become one mailing piece. This type of envelope makes it possible for a first class letter to be delivered simultaneously with third or fourth class matter and yet not require payment of the much higher first class postage rate on the entire mailing. First class postage is paid only on the letter which goes in the small compartment, third or fourth class postage being paid on the contents of the larger compartment. The larger compartment generally has an ungummed flap or clasp for sealing. The first class or smaller compartment has a gummed flap for sealing. Postal regulations require that the exact amount of postage applicable to each compartment be separately attached to it.

24. On the basis of the above passage, it is MOST accurate to state that

    24.____

    A. the smaller compartment is placed inside the larger compartment before mailing
    B. the two compartments may be detached and mailed separately
    C. two classes of mailing matter may be mailed as a unit at two different postage rates
    D. the more expensive postage rate is paid on the matter in the larger compartment

25. When a duplex envelope is used, the 25.__

    A. first class compartment may be sealed with a clasp
    B. correct amount of postage must be placed on each compartment
    C. compartment containing third or fourth class mail requires a gummed flap for sealing
    D. full amount of postage for both compartments may be placed on the larger compartment

---

KEY (CORRECT ANSWERS)

1.	A		11.	C
2.	D		12.	D
3.	B		13.	A
4.	B		14.	C
5.	C		15.	B
6.	A		16.	D
7.	C		17.	B
8.	B		18.	A
9.	C		19.	B
10.	D		20.	B

21.	C
22.	A
23.	C
24.	C
25.	B

RECORD KEEPING
EXAMINATION SECTION
TEST 1

DIRECTIONS: Each question or incomplete statement is followed by several suggested answers or completions. Select the one that BEST answers the question or completes the statement. *PRINT THE LETTER OF THE CORRECT ANSWER IN THE SPACE AT THE RIGHT.*

Questions 1-7.

DIRECTIONS: In answering Questions 1 through 7, use the following master list. For each question, determine where the name would fit on the master list. Each answer choice indicates right before or after the name in the answer choice.

Aaron, Jane
Armstead, Brendan
Bailey, Charles
Dent, Ricardo
Grant, Mark
Mars, Justin
Methieu, Justine
Parker, Cathy
Sampson, Suzy
Thomas, Heather

1. Schmidt, William   1.____
   A. Right before Cathy Parker   B. Right after Heather Thomas
   C. Right after Suzy Sampson   D. Right before Ricardo Dent

2. Asanti, Kendall   2.____
   A. Right before Jane Aaron   B. Right after Charles Bailey
   C. Right before Justine Methieu   D. Right after Brendan Armstead

3. O'Brien, Daniel   3.____
   A. Right after Justine Methieu   B. Right before Jane Aaron
   C. Right after Mark Grant   D. Right before Suzy Sampson

4. Marrow, Alison   4.____
   A. Right before Cathy Parker   B. Right before Justin Mars
   C. Right after Mark Grant   D. Right after Heather Thomas

5. Grantt, Marissa   5.____
   A. Right before Mark Grant   B. Right after Mark Grant
   C. Right after Justin Mars   D. Right before Suzy Sampson

6. Thompson, Heath   6._____
   A. Right after Justin Mars   B. Right before Suzy Sampson
   C. Right after Heather Thomas   D. Right before Cathy Parker

DIRECTIONS: Before answering Question 7, add in all of the names from Questions 1 through 6. Then fit the name in alphabetical order based on the new list.

7. Francisco, Mildred   7._____
   A. Right before Mark Grant   B. Right after Marissa Grantt
   C. Right before Alison Marrow   D. Right after Kendall Asanti

Questions 8-10.

DIRECTIONS: In answering Questions 8 through 10, compare each pair of names and addresses. Indicate whether they are the same or different in any way.

8. William H. Pratt, J.D.   William H. Pratt, J.D.   8._____
   Attourney at Law   Attorney at Law
   A. No differences   B. 1 difference
   C. 2 differences   D. 3 differences

9. 1303 Theater Drive,; Apt. 3-B   1330 Theatre Drive,; Apt. 3-B   9._____
   A. No differences   B. 1 difference
   C. 2 differences   D. 3 differences

10. Petersdorff, Briana and Mary   Petersdorff, Briana and Mary   10._____
   A. No differences   B. 1 difference
   C. 2 differences   D. 3 differences

11. Which of the following words, if any, are misspelled?   11._____
   A. Affordable   B. Circumstansial
   C. Legalese   D. None of the above

Questions 12-13.

DIRECTIONS: Questions 12 and 13 are to be answered on the basis of the following table.

Standardized Test Results for High School Students in District #1230

	English	Math	Science	Reading
High School 1	21	22	15	18
High School 2	12	16	13	15
High School 3	16	181	21	17
High School 4	19	14	15	16

The scores for each high school in the district were averaged out and listed for each subject tested. Scores of 0-10 are significantly below College Readiness Standards. 11-15 are below College Readiness, 16-20 meet College Readiness, and 21-25 are above College Readiness.

12. If the high schools need to meet or exceed in at least half the categories in order to NOT be considered "at risk," which schools are considered "at risk"?   12.____
    A. High School 2   B. High School 3
    C. High School 4   D. Both A and C

13. What percentage of subjects did the district as a whole meet or exceed College Readiness standards?   13.____
    A. 25%   B. 50%   C. 75%   D. 100%

Questions 14-15.

DIRECTIONS: Questions 14 and 15 are to be answered on the basis of the following information.

You have seven employees working as a part of your team: Austin, Emily, Jeremy, Christina, Martin, Harriet, and Steve. You have just sent an e-mail informing them that there will be a mandatory training session next week. To ensure that work still gets done, you are offering the training twice during the week: once on Tuesday and also on Thursday. This way half the employees will still be working while the other half attend the training. The only other issue is that Jeremy doesn't work on Tuesdays and Harriet doesn't work on Thursdays due to compressed work schedules.

14. Which of the following is a possible attendance roster for the first training session?   14.____
    A. Emily, Jeremy, Steve   B. Steve, Christina, Harriet
    C. Harriet, Jeremy, Austin   D. Steve, Martin, Jeremy

15. If Harriet, Christina, and Steve attend the training session on Tuesday, which of the following is a possible roster for Thursday's training session?   15.____
    A. Jeremy, Emily, and Austin   B. Emily, Martin, and Harriet
    C. Austin, Christina, and Emily   D. Jeremy, Emily, and Steve

Questions 16-20.

DIRECTIONS: In answering Questions 16 through 20, you will be given a word and will need to choose the answer choice that is MOST similar or different to the word.

16. Which word means the SAME as *annual*?   16.____
    A. Monthly   B. Usually   C. Yearly   D. Constantly

17. Which word means the SAME as *effort*?   17.____
    A. Energy   B. Equate   C. Cherish   D. Commence

18. Which word means the OPPOSITE of *forlorn*?   18.____
    A. Neglected   B. Lethargy   C. Optimistic   D. Astonished

19. Which word means the SAME as *risk*?   19.____
    A. Admire   B. Hazard   C. Limit   D. Hesitant

20. Which word means the OPPOSITE of *translucent*?
    A. Opaque   B. Transparent C. Luminous   D. Introverted

20.____

21. Last year, Jamie's annual salary was $50,000. Her boss called her today to inform her that she would receive a 20% raise for the upcoming year. How much more money will Jamie receive next year?
    A. $60,000   B. $10,000   C. $1,000   D. $51,000

21.____

22. You and a co-worker work for a temp hiring agency as part of their office staff. You both are given 6 days off per month. How many days off are you and your co-worker given in a year?
    A. 24   B. 72   C. 144   D. 48

22.____

23. If Margot makes $34,000 per year and she works 40 hours per week for all 52 weeks, what is her hourly rate?
    A. $16.34/hour   B. $17.00/hour C. $15.54/hour D. $13.23/hour

23.____

24. How many dimes are there in $175.00?
    A. 175   B. 1,750   C. 3,500   D. 17,500

24.____

25. If Janey is three times as old as Emily, and Emily is 3, how old is Janey?
    A. 6   B. 9   C. 12   D. 15

25.____

KEY (CORRECT ANSWERS)

1.	C		11.	B
2.	D		12.	A
3.	A		13.	D
4.	B		14.	B
5.	B		15.	A
6.	C		16.	C
7.	A		17.	A
8.	B		18.	C
9.	C		19.	B
10.	A		20.	A

21.	B
22.	C
23.	A
24.	B
25.	B

TEST 2

DIRECTIONS: Each question or incomplete statement is followed by several suggested answers or completions. Select the one that BEST answers the question or completes the statement. *PRINT THE LETTER OF THE CORRECT ANSWER IN THE SPACE AT THE RIGHT.*

Questions 1-6.

DIRECTIONS: Questions 1 through 6 are to be answered on the basis of the following information.

item	name of item to be ordered
quantity	minimum number that can be ordered
beginning amount	amount in stock at start of month
amount received	amount receiving during month
ending amount	amount in stock at end of month
amount used	amount used during month
amount to order	will need at least as much of each item as used in the previous month
unit price	cost of each unit of an item
total price	total price for the order

Item	Quantity	Beginning	Received	Ending	Amount Used	Amount to Order	Unit Price	Total Price
Pens	10	22	10	8	24	20	$0.11	$2.20
Spiral notebooks	8	30	13	12			$0.25	
Binder clips	2 boxes	3 boxes	1 box	1 box			$1.79	
Sticky notes	3 packs	12 packs	4 packs	2 packs			$14.29	
Dry erase markers	1 pack (dozen)	34 markers	8 markers	40 markers			$16.49	
Ink cartridges (printer)	1 cartridge	3 cartridges	1 cartridge	2 cartridges			$79.99	
Folders	10 folders	25 folders	15 folders	10 folders			$1.08	

1. How many packs of sticky notes were used during the month?   1.____
   A. 16   B. 10   C. 12   D. 14

2. How many folders need to be ordered for next month?   2.____
   A. 15   B. 20   C. 30   D. 40

3. What is the total price of notebooks that you will need to order?   3.____
   A. $6.00   B. $0.25   C. $4.50   D. $2.75

4. Which of the following will you spend the second most money on?   4.____
   A. Ink cartridges   B. Dry erase markers
   C. Sticky notes   D. Binder clips

5. How many packs of dry erase markers should you order?   5.____
   A. 1   B. 8   C. 12   D. 0

6. What will be the total price of the file folders you order?   6._____
    A. $20.16   B. $2.16   C. $1.08   D. $4.32

Questions 7-11.

DIRECTIONS: Questions 7 through 11 are to be answered on the basis of the following table.

Number of Car Accidents, By Location and Cause, for 2014						
	Location 1		Location 2		Location 3	
Cause	Number	Percent	Number	Percent	Number	Percent
Severe Weather	10		25		30	
Excessive Speeding	20	40	5		10	
Impaired Driving	15		15	25	8	
Miscellaneous	5		15		2	4
TOTALS	50	100	60	100	50	100

7. Which of the following is the third highest cause of accidents for all three   7._____
   locations?
    A. Severe Weather   B. Impaired Driving
    C. Miscellaneous   D. Excessive Speeding

8. The average number of Severe Weather accidents per week at Location 3   8._____
   for the year (52 weeks) was MOST NEARLY
    A. 0.57   B. 30   C. 1   D. 1.25

9. Which location had the LARGEST percentage of accidents caused by   9._____
   Impaired Driving?
    A. 1   B. 2   C. 3   D. Both A and B

10. If one-third of the accidents at all three locations resulted in at least one   10._____
   fatality, what is the LEAST amount of deaths caused by accidents last year?
    A. 60   B. 106   C. 66   D. 53

11. What is the percentage of accidents caused by miscellaneous means from   11._____
   all three locations in 2014?
    A. 5%   B. 10%   C. 13%   D. 25%

12. How many pairs of the following groups of letters are exactly alike?   12._____
    ACDOBJ   ACDBOJ
    HEWBWR   HEWRWB
    DEERVS   DEERVS
    BRFQSX   BRFQSX
    WEYRVB   WEYRVB
    SPQRZA   SQRPZA

    A. 2   B. 3   C. 4   D. 5

Questions 13-19.

DIRECTIONS: Questions 13 through 19 are to be answered on the basis of the following information.

In 2012, the most current information on the American population was finished. The population was compiled by 200 people from each of the 50 states. The territory of Puerto Rico, a sovereign of the United States, had 25 people assigned to compile data. In February of 2010, each state began collecting information. In Puerto Rico, data collection finished by January 31st, 2011, while the United States finished on June 30, 2012. Each volunteer gathered data on the population of each state or sovereign. When the information was compiled, each volunteer had to send their information to the nation's capital, Washington, D.C. Each worker worked 20 hours per month and put together 10 reports per month. After the data was compiled in total, 50 people reviewed the data and worked from January 2012 to December 2012.

13. How many reports were generated from February 2010 to April 2010 in Illinois and Ohio?
 A. 3,000　　　　B. 6,000　　　　C. 12,000　　　　D. 15,000　　　　13._____

14. How many workers in total were collecting data in January 2012?
 A. 200　　　　B. 25　　　　C. 225　　　　D. 0　　　　14._____

15. How many reports were put together in May 2012?
 A. 2,000　　　　B. 50,000　　　　C. 100,000　　　　D. 100,250　　　　15._____

16. How many hours did the Puerto Rican volunteers work in the fall (September-November)?
 A. 60　　　　B. 500　　　　C. 1,500　　　　D. 0　　　　16._____

17. How many workers were there in February 2011?
 A. 25　　　　B. 200　　　　C. 225　　　　D. 250　　　　17._____

18. What was the total amount of hours worked in July 2010?
 A. 500　　　　B. 4,000　　　　C. 4,500　　　　D. 5,000　　　　18._____

19. How many reviewers worked in January 2013?
 A. 75　　　　B. 50　　　　C. 0　　　　D. 25　　　　19._____

20. John has to file 10 documents per shelf. How many documents would it take for John to fill 40 shelves?
 A. 40　　　　B. 400　　　　C. 4,500　　　　D. 5,000　　　　20._____

21. Jill wants to travel from New York City to Los Angeles by bike, which is approximately 2,772 miles. How many miles per day would Jill need to average if she wanted to complete the trip in 4 weeks?
 A. 100　　　　B. 89　　　　C. 99　　　　D. 94　　　　21._____

22. If there are 24 CPU's and only 7 monitors, how many more monitors do you need to have the same amount of monitors as CPU's?
    A. Not enough information   B. 17
    C. 31   D. 0

22.____

23. If Gerry works 5 days a week and 8 hours each day, and John works 3 days a week and 10 hours each day, how many more hours per year will Gerry work than John?
    A. They work the same amount of hours.
    B. 450
    C. 520
    D. 832

23.____

24. Jimmy gets transferred to a new office. The new office has 25 employees, but only 16 are there due to a blizzard. How many coworkers was Jimmy able to meet on his first day?
    A. 16   B. 25   C. 9   D. 7

24.____

25. If you do a fundraiser for charities in your area and raise $500 total, how much would you give to each charity if you were donating equal amounts to 3 of them?
    A. $250.00   B. $167.77   C. $50.00   D. $111.11

25.____

KEY (CORRECT ANSWERS)

1.	D		11.	C
2.	B		12.	B
3.	A		13.	C
4.	C		14.	A
5.	D		15.	A
6.	B		16.	C
7.	D		17.	B
8.	A		18.	C
9.	A		19.	C
10.	D		20.	B

21.	C
22.	B
23.	C
24.	A
25.	B

TEST 3

Questions 1-3.

DIRECTIONS: In answering Questions 1 through 3, choose the correctly spelled word.

1. A. allusion   B. alusion   C. allusien   D. allution   1._____

2. A. altitude   B. alltitude   C. atlitude   D. altlitude   2._____

3. A. althogh   B. allthough   C. althrough   D. although   3._____

Questions 4-9.

DIRECTIONS: In answering Questions 4 through 9, choose the answer that BEST completes the analogy.

4. Odometer is to mileage as compass is to   4._____
    A. speed   B. needle   C. hiking   D. direction

5. Marathon is to race as hibernation is to   5._____
    A. winter   B. dream   C. sleep   D. bear

6. Cup is to coffee as bowl is to   6._____
    A. dish   B. spoon   C. food   D. soup

7. Flow is to river as stagnant is to   7._____
    A. pool   B. rain   C. stream   D. canal

8. paw is to cat as hoof is to   8._____
    A. lamb   B. horse   C. lion   D. elephant

9. Architect is to building as sculptor is to   9._____
    A. museum   B. chisel   C. stone   D. statue

Questions 10-14.

DIRECTIONS: Questions 10 through 14 are to be answered on the basis of the following graph.

Population of Carroll City Broken Down by Age and Gender (in Thousands)			
Age	Female	Male	Total
Under 15	60	60	120
15-23		22	
24-33		20	44
34-43	13	18	31
44-53	20		67
64 and Over	65	65	130
TOTAL	230	232	462

10. How many people in the city are between the ages of 15-23?
    A. 70   B. 46,000   C. 70,000   D. 225,000

11. Approximately what percentage of the total population of the city was female aged 24-33?
    A. 10%   B. 5%   C. 15%   D. 25%

12. If 33% of the males have a job and 55% of females don't have a job, which of the following statements is TRUE?
    A. Males have approximately 2,600 more jobs than females.
    B. Females have approximately 49,000 more jobs than males.
    C. Females have approximately 26,000 more jobs than males.
    D. None of the above statements are true.

13. How many females between the ages of 15-23 live in Carroll City?
    A. 67,000   B. 24,000   C. 48,000   D. 91,000

14. Assume all males 44-53 living in Carroll city are employed. If two-thirds of males age 44-53 work jobs outside of Carroll City, how many work within city limits?
    A. 31,333
    B. 15,667
    C. 47,000
    D. Cannot answer the question with the information provided

10.____

11.____

12.____

13.____

14.____

Questions 15-16.

DIRECTIONS: Questions 15 and 16 are labeled as shown. Alphabetize them for filing. Choose the answer that correctly shows the order.

15. (1) AED
    (2) OOS
    (3) FOA
    (4) DOM
    (5) COB

    A. 2-5-4-3-2   B. 1-4-5-2-3   C. 1-5-4-2-3   D. 1-5-4-3-2

15.____

16. Alphabetize the names of the people. Last names are given last.
    (1) Lindsey Jamestown
    (2) Jane Alberta
    (3) Ally Jamestown
    (4) Allison Johnston
    (5) Lyle Moreno

    A. 2-1-3-4-5   B. 3-4-2-1-5   C. 2-3-1-4-5   D. 4-3-2-1-5

16.____

17. Which of the following words is misspelled?
    A. disgust   B. whisper
    C. vocale   D. none of the above

17.____

Questions 18-21.

DIRECTIONS: Questions 18 through 21 are to be answered on the basis of the following list of employees.

Robertson, Aaron
Bacon, Gina
Jerimiah, Trace
Gillette, Stanley
Jacks, Sharon

18. Which employee name would come in third in alphabetized list?
    A. Robertson, Aaron   B. Jerimiah, Trace
    C. Gillette, Stanley   D. Jacks, Sharon

18.____

19. Which employee's first name starts with the letter in the alphabet that is five letters after the first letter of their last name?
    A. Jerimiah, Trace   B. Bacon, Gina
    C. Jacks, Sharon   D. Gillette, Stanley

19.____

20. How many employees have last names that are exactly five letters long?
    A. 1   B. 2   C. 3   D. 4

20.____

21. How many of the employees have either a first or last name that starts
    with the letter "G"?
    A. 1   B. 2   C. 4   D. 5   21.____

Questions 22-25.

DIRECTIONS: Questions 22 through 25 are to be answered on the basis of the following
              chart.

Bicycle Sales (Model #34JA32)							
Country	May	June	July	August	September	October	Total
Germany	34	47	45	54	56	60	296
Britain	40	44	36	47	47	46	260
Ireland	37	32	32	32	34	33	200
Portugal	14	14	14	16	17	14	89
Italy	29	29	28	31	29	31	177
Belgium	22	24	24	26	25	23	144
Total	176	198	179	206	208	207	1166

22. What percentage of the overall total was sold to the German importer?   22.____
    A. 25.3%   B. 22%   C. 24.1%   D. 23%

23. What percentage of the overall total was sold in September?   23.____
    A. 24.1%   B. 25.6%   C. 17.9%   D. 24.6%

24. What is the average number of units per month imported into Belgium over   24.____
    the first four months shown?
    A. 26   B. 20   C. 24   D. 31

25. If you look at the three smallest importers, what is their total import   25.____
    percentage?
    A. 35.1%   B. 37.1%   C. 40%   D. 28%

KEY (CORRECT ANSWERS)

1.	A		11.	B
2.	A		12.	C
3.	D		13.	C
4.	D		14.	B
5.	C		15.	D
6.	D		16.	C
7.	A		17.	D
8.	B		18.	D
9.	D		19.	B
10.	C		20.	B

21.	B
22.	A
23.	C
24.	C
25.	A

TEST 4

DIRECTIONS: Each question or incomplete statement is followed by several suggested answers or completions. Select the one that BEST answers the question or completes the statement. *PRINT THE LETTER OF THE CORRECT ANSWER IN THE SPACE AT THE RIGHT.*

Questions 1-6.

DIRECTIONS: In answering Questions 1 through 6, choose the sentence that represents the BEST example of English grammar.

1. A. Joey and me want to go on a vacation next week.   1.____
    B. Gary told Jim he would need to take some time off.
    C. If turning six years old, Jim's uncle would teach Spanish to him.
    D. Fax a copy of your resume to Ms. Perez and me.

2. A. Jerry stood in line for almost two hours.   2.____
    B. The reaction to my engagement was less exciting than I thought it would be.
    C. Carlos and me have done great work on this project.
    D. Two parts of the speech needs to be revised before tomorrow.

3. A. Arriving home, the alarm was tripped.   3.____
    B. Jonny is regarded as a stand up guy, a responsible parent, and he doesn't give up until a task is finished.
    C. Each employee must submit a drug test each month.
    D. One of the documents was incinerated in the explosion.

4. A. As soon as my parents get home, I told them I finished all of my chores.   4.____
    B. I asked my teacher to send me my missing work, check my absences, and how did I do on my test.
    C. Matt attempted to keep it concealed from Jenny and me.
    D. If Mary or him cannot get work done on time, I will have to split them up.

5. A. Driving to work, the traffic report warned him of an accident on Highway 47.   5.____
    B. Jimmy has performed well this season.
    C. Since finishing her degree, several job offers have been given to Cam.
    D. Our boss is creating unstable conditions for we employees.

6. A. The thief was described as a tall man with a wiry mustache weighing approximately 150 pounds.   6.____
    B. She gave Patrick and I some more time to finish our work.
    C. One of the books that he ordered was damaged in shipping.
    D. While talking on the rotary phone, the car Jim was driving skidded off the road.

Questions 7-9.

DIRECTIONS: Questions 7 through 9 are to be answered on the basis of the following graph.

Ice Lake Frozen Flight (2002-2013)		
Year	Number of Participants	Temperature (Fahrenheit)
2002	22	4°
2003	50	33°
2004	69	18°
2005	104	22°
2006	108	24°
2007	288	33°
2008	173	9°
2009	598	39°
2010	698	26°
2011	696	30°
2012	777	28°
2013	578	32°

7. Which two year span had the LARGEST difference between temperatures?   7.____
   A. 2002 and 2003   B. 2011 and 2012
   C. 2008 and 2009   D. 2003 and 2004

8. How many total people participated in the years after the temperature   8.____
   reached at least 29°?
   A. 2,295   B. 1,717   C. 2,210   D. 4,543

9. In 2007, the event saw 288 participants, while in 2008 that number   9.____
   dropped to 173. Which of the following reasons BEST explains the drop in
   participants?
   A. The event had not been going on that long and people didn't know about
       it.
   B. The lake water wasn't cold enough to have people jump in.
   C. The temperature was too cold for many people who would have normally
       participated.
   D. None of the above reasons explain the drop in participants.

10. In the following list of numbers, how many times does 4 come just after 2   10.____
   when 2 comes just after an odd number?
   23652476538986324885724863 92424
   A. 2   B. 3   C. 4   D. 5

11. Which choice below lists the letter that is as far after B as S is after N in   11.____
   the alphabet?
   A. G   B. H   C. I   D. J

Questions 12-15.

DIRECTIONS: Questions 12 through 15 are to be answered on the basis of the following directory and list of changes.

Directory		
Name	Emp. Type	Position
Julie Taylor	Warehouse	Packer
James King	Office	Administrative Assistant
John Williams	Office	Salesperson
Ray Moore	Warehouse	Maintenance
Kathleen Byrne	Warehouse	Supervisor
Amy Jones	Office	Salesperson
Paul Jonas	Office	Salesperson
Lisa Wong	Warehouse	Loader
Eugene Lee	Office	Accountant
Bruce Lavine	Office	Manager
Adam Gates	Warehouse	Packer
Will Suter	Warehouse	Packer
Gary Lorper	Office	Accountant
Jon Adams	Office	Salesperson
Susannah Harper	Office	Salesperson

Directory Updates:
- Employee e-mail address will adhere to the following guidelines: lastnamefirstname@apexindustries.com (ex. Susannah Harper is harpersusannah@apexindustries.com). Currently, employees in the warehouse share one e-mail, distribution@apexindustries.com.
- The "Loader" position was now be referred to as "Specialist I"
- Adam Gates has accepted a Supervisor position within the Warehouse and is no longer a Packer. All warehouses employees report to the two Supervisors and all office employees report to the Manager.

12. Amy Jones tried to send an e-mail to Adam Gates, but it wouldn't send.   12.____
     Which of the following offers the BEST explanation?
     A. Amy put Adam's first name first and then his last name.
     B. Adam doesn't check his e-mail, so he wouldn't know if he received the e-mail or not.
     C. Adam does not have his own e-mail.
     D. Office employees are not allowed to send e-mails to each other.

13. How many Packers currently work for Apex Industries?   13.____
        A. 2   B. 3   C. 4   D. 5

14. What position does Lisa Wong currently hold?   14.____
        A. Specialist I   B. Secretary
        C. Administrative Assistant   D. Loader

15. If an employee wanted to contact the office manager, which of the
    following e-mails should the e-mail be sent to?   15.____
    A. officemanager@apexindustries.com
    B. brucelavine@apexindustries.com
    C. lavinebruce@apexindustries.com
    D. distribution@apexindustries.com

Questions 16-19.

DIRECTIONS: In answering Questions 16 through 19, compare the three names, numbers or
              addresses.

16. Smiley Yarnell   Smiley Yarnel   Smily Yarnell   16.____
    A. All three are exactly alike.
    B. The first and second are exactly alike.
    C. The second and third are exactly alike.
    D. All three are different.

17. 1583 Theater Drive   1583 Theater Drive   1583 Theatre Drive   17.____
    A. All three are exactly alike.
    B. The first and second are exactly alike.
    C. The second and third are exactly alike.
    D. All three are different.

18. 3341893212   3341893212   3341893212   18.____
    A. All three are exactly alike.
    B. The first and second are exactly alike.
    C. The second and third are exactly alike.
    D. All three are different.

19. Douglass Watkins   Douglas Watkins   Douglass Watkins   19.____
    A. All three are exactly alike.
    B. The first and third are exactly alike.
    C. The second and third are exactly alike.
    D. All three are different.

Questions 20-24.

DIRECTIONS: In answering Questions 20 through 24, you will be presented with a word.
              Choose the synonym that BEST represents the word in question.

20. Flexible   20.____
    A. delicate   B. inflammable   C. strong   D. pliable

21. Alternative   21.____
    A. choice   B. moderate   C. lazy   D. value

22. Corroborate
    A. examine   B. explain   C. verify   D. explain   22.____

23. Respiration
    A. recovery   B. breathing   C. sweating   D. selfish   23.____

24. Negligent
    A. lazy   B. moderate   C. hopeless   D. lax   24.____

25. Plumber is to Wrench as Painter is to
    A. pipe   B. shop   C. hammer   D. brush   25.____

KEY (CORRECT ANSWERS)

1.	D		11.	A
2.	A		12.	C
3.	D		13.	A
4.	C		14.	A
5.	B		15.	C
6.	C		16.	D
7.	C		17.	B
8.	B		18.	A
9.	C		19.	B
10.	C		20.	D

21. A
22. C
23. B
24. D
25. D

REPORT WRITING
EXAMINATION SECTION
TEST 1

DIRECTIONS: Each question or incomplete statement is followed by several suggested answers or completions. Select the one that BEST answers the question or completes the statement. *PRINT THE LETTER OF THE CORRECT ANSWER IN THE SPACE AT THE RIGHT.*

Questions 1-4.

DIRECTIONS: Answer Questions 1 through 4 on the basis of the following report which was prepared by a supervisor for inclusion in his agency's annual report.

Line
#

1   On Oct. 13, I was assigned to study the salaries paid
2   to clerical employees in various titles by the city and by
3   private industry in the area.
4   In order to get the data I needed, I called Mr. Johnson at
5   the Bureau of the Budget and the payroll officers at X Corp. –
6   a brokerage house, Y Co. – an insurance company, and Z Inc. –
7   a publishing firm. None of them was available and I had to call
8   all of them again the next day.
9   When I finally got the information I needed, I drew up a
10 chart, which is attached. Note that not all of the companies I
11 contacted employed people at all the different levels used in the
12 city service.
13 The conclusions I draw from analyzing this information is
14 as follows: The city's entry-level salary is about average for
15 the region; middle-level salaries are generally higher in the
16 city government than in private industry; but salaries at the
17 highest levels in private industry are better than city em-
18 ployees' pay.

1. Which of the following criticisms about the style in which this report is written is *most*   1.____
    valid?

    A. It is too informal.   B. It is too concise.
    C. It is too choppy.   D. The syntax is too complex.

2. Judging from the statements made in the report, the method followed by this employee in   2.____
    performing his research was

    A. *good;* he contacted a representative sample of businesses in the area
    B. *poor;* he should have drawn more definite conclusions
    C. *good;* he was persistent in collecting information
    D. *poor;* he did not make a thorough study

3. One sentence in this report contains a grammatical error. This sentence *begins* on line number   3.__

   A. 4   B. 7   C. 10   D. 13

4. The type of information given in this report which should be presented in footnotes or in an appendix, is the   4.__

   A. purpose of the study
   B. specifics about the businesses contacted
   C. reference to the chart
   D. conclusions drawn by the author

5. The use of a graph to show statistical data in a report is *superior* to a table because it   5.__

   A. features approximations
   B. emphasizes facts and relationships more dramatically
   C. C. presents data more accurately
   D. is easily understood by the average reader

6. Of the following, the degree of formality required of a written report in tone is *most likely* to depend on the   6.__

   A. subject matter of the report
   B. frequency of its occurrence
   C. amount of time available for its preparation
   D. audience for whom the report is intended

7. Of the following, a distinguishing characteristic of a written report intended for the head of your agency as compared to a report prepared for a lower-echelon staff member, is that the report for the agency head should *usually* include   7.__

   A. considerably more detail, especially statistical data
   B. the essential details in an abbreviated form
   C. all available source material
   D. an annotated bibliography

8. Assume that you are asked to write a lengthy report for use by the administrator of your agency, the subject of which is "The Impact of Proposed New Data Processing Operations on Line Personnel" in your agency. You decide that the *most appropriate* type of report for you to prepare is an analytical report, including recommendations. The MAIN reason for your decision is that   8.__

   A. the subject of the report is extremely complex
   B. large sums of money are involved
   C. the report is being prepared for the administrator
   D. you intend to include charts and graphs

9. Assume that you are preparing a report based on a survey dealing with the attitudes of   9.____
    employees in Division X regarding proposed new changes in compensating employees
    for working overtime. Three per cent of the respondents to the survey voluntarily offer an
    unfavorable opinion on the method of assigning overtime work, a question not specifi-
    cally asked of the employees.
    On the basis of this information, the *most appropriate* and *significant* of the following
    comments for you to make in the report with regard to employees' attitudes on assign-
    ing overtime work, is that

    A. an insignificant percentage of employees dislike the method of assigning overtime
        work
    B. three per cent of the employees in Division X dislike the method of assigning over-
        time work
    C. three per cent of the sample selected for the survey voiced an unfavorable opinion
        on the method of assigning overtime work
    D. some employees voluntarily voiced negative feelings about the method of assign-
        ing overtime work, making it impossible to determine the extent of this attitude

10. A supervisor should be able to prepare a report that is well-written and unambiguous.   10.____
    Of the following sentences that might appear in a report, select the one which commu-
    nicates *most clearly* the intent of its author.

    A. When your subordinates speak to a group of people, they should be well-informed.
    B. When he asked him to leave, SanMan King told him that he would refuse the
        request.
    C. Because he is a good worker, Foreman Jefferson assigned Assistant Foreman
        D'Agostino to replace him.
    D. Each of us is responsible for the actions of our subordinates.

11. In some reports, especially longer ones, a list of the resources (books, papers, maga-   11.____
    zines, etc.) used to prepare it is included. This list is called the

    A. accreditation   B. bibliography
    C. summary   D. glossary

12. Reports are usually divided into several sections, some of which are more necessary   12.____
    than others.
    Of the following, the section which is ABSOLUTELY necessary to include in a report is

    A. a table of contents   B. the body
    C. an index   D. a bibliography

13. Suppose you are writing a report on an interview you have just completed with a particu-   13.____
    larly hostile applicant. Which of the following BEST describes what you should include in
    this report?

    A. What you think caused the applicant's hostile attitude during the interview
    B. Specific examples of the applicant's hostile remarks and behavior
    C. The relevant information uncovered during the interview
    D. A recommendation that the applicant's request be denied because of his hostility

14. When including recommendations in a report to your supervisor, which of the following is MOST important for you to do?

    14.__

    A. Provide several alternative courses of action for each recommendation
    B. First present the supporting evidence, then the recommendations
    C. First present the recommendations, then the supporting evidence
    D. Make sure the recommendations arise logically out of the information in the report

15. It is often necessary that the writer of a report present facts and sufficient arguments to gain acceptance of the points, conclusions, or recommendations set forth in the report. Of the following, the LEAST advisable step to take in organizing a report, when such argumentation is the important factor, is a(n)

    15.__

    A. elaborate expression of personal belief
    B. businesslike discussion of the problem as a whole
    C. orderly arrangement of convincing data
    D. reasonable explanation of the primary issues

16. In some types of reports, visual aids add interest, meaning, and support. They also provide an essential means of effectively communicating the message of the report. Of the following, the selection of the suitable visual aids to use with a report is LEAST dependent on the

    16.__

    A. nature and scope of the report
    B. way in which the aid is to be used
    C. aids used in other reports
    D. prospective readers of the report

17. Visual aids used in a report may be placed either in the text material or in the appendix. Deciding where to put a chart, table, or any such aid *should* depend on the

    17.__

    A. title of the report   B. purpose of the visual aid
    C. title of the visual aid   D. length of the report

18. A report is often revised several times before final preparation and distribution in an effort to make certain the report meets the needs of the situation for which it is designed. Which of the following is the BEST way for the author to be sure that a report covers the areas he intended?

    18.__

    A. Obtain a co-worker's opinion
    B. Compare it with a content checklist
    C. Test it on a subordinate
    D. Check his bibliography

19. In which of the following situations is an oral report preferable to a written report? When a(n)

    19.__

    A. recommendation is being made for a future plan of action
    B. department head requests immediate information
    C. long standing policy change is made
    D. analysis of complicated statistical data is involved

20. When an applicant is approved, the supervisor must fill in standard forms with certain information.
The GREATEST advantage of using standard forms in this situation rather than having the supervisor write the report as he sees fit, is that

    A. the report can be acted on quickly
    B. the report can be written without directions from a supervisor
    C. needed information is less likely to be left out of the report
    D. information that is written up this way is more likely to be verified

20.____

21. Assume that it is part of your job to prepare a monthly report for your unit head that eventually goes to the director. The report contains information on the number of applicants you have interviewed that have been approved and the number of applicants you have interviewed that have been turned down.
Errors on such reports are serious because

    A. you are expected to be able to prove how many applicants you have interviewed each month
    B. accurate statistics are needed for effective management of the department
    C. they may not be discovered before the report is transmitted to the director
    D. they may result in loss to the applicants left out of the report

21.____

22. The frequency with which job reports are submitted should depend MAINLY on

    A. how comprehensive the report has to be
    B. the amount of information in the report
    C. the availability of an experienced man to write the report
    D. the importance of changes in the information included in the report

22.____

23. The CHIEF purpose in preparing an outline for a report is *usually* to insure that

    A. the report will be grammatically correct
    B. every point will be given equal emphasis
    C. principal and secondary points will be properly integrated
    D. the language of the report will be of the same level and include the same technical terms

23.____

24. The MAIN reason for requiring written job reports is to

    A. avoid the necessity of oral orders
    B. develop better methods of doing the work
    C. provide a permanent record of what was done
    D. increase the amount of work that can be done

24.____

25. Assume you are recommending in a report to your supervisor that a radical change in a standard maintenance procedure should be adopted.
Of the following, the MOST important information to be included in this report is

    A. a list of the reasons for making this change
    B. the names of others who favor the change
    C. a complete description of the present procedure
    D. amount of training time needed for the new procedure

25.____

165

KEY (CORRECT ANSWERS)

1.	A		11.	B
2.	D		12.	B
3.	D		13.	C
4.	B		14.	D
5.	B		15.	A
6.	D		16.	C
7.	B		17.	B
8.	A		18.	B
9.	D		19.	B
10.	D		20.	C

21.	B
22.	D
23.	C
24.	C
25.	A

TEST 2

DIRECTIONS: Each question or incomplete statement is followed by several suggested answers or completions. Select the one that BEST answers the question or completes the statement. *PRINT THE LETTER OF THE CORRECT ANSWER IN THE SPACE AT THE RIGHT.*

1. It is often necessary that the writer of a report present facts and sufficient arguments to gain acceptance of the points, conclusions, or recommendations set forth in the report. Of the following, the LEAST advisable step to take in organizing a report, when such argumentation is the important factor, is a(n)

    A. elaborate expression of personal belief
    B. businesslike discussion of the problem as a whole
    C. orderly arrangement of convincing data
    D. reasonable explanation of the primary issues

    1.____

2. Of the following, the factor which is generally considered to be LEAST characteristic of a good control report is that it

    A. stresses performance that adheres to standard rather than emphasizing the exception
    B. supplies information intended to serve as the basis for corrective action
    C. provides feedback for the planning process
    D. includes data that reflect trends as well as current status

    2.____

3. An administrative assistant has been asked by his superior to write a concise, factual report with objective conclusions and recommendations based on facts assembled by other researchers.
    Of the following factors, the administrative assistant should give LEAST consideratio to

    A. the educational level of the person or persons for whom the report is being prepared
    B. the use to be made of the report
    C. the complexity of the problem
    D. his own feelings about the importance of the problem

    3.____

4. When making a written report, it is often recommended that the findings or conclusions be presented near the beginning of the report.
    Of the following, the MOST important reason for doing this is that it

    A. facilitates organizing the material clearly
    B. assures that all the topics will be covered
    C. avoids unnecessary repetition of ideas
    D. prepares the reader for the facts that will follow

    4.____

5. You have been asked to write a report on methods of hiring and training new employees. Your report is going to be about ten pages long.
    For the convenience of your readers, a brief summary of your findings *should*

    A. appear at the beginning of your report
    B. be appended to the report as a postscript
    C. be circulated in a separate memo
    D. be inserted in tabular form in the middle of your report

    5.____

6. In preparing a report, the MAIN reason for writing an outline is *usually* to   6.__

    A. help organize thoughts in a logical sequence
    B. provide a guide for the typing of the report
    C. allow the ultimate user to review the report in advance
    D. ensure that the report is being prepared on schedule

7. The one of the following which is *most appropriate* as a reason for including footnotes in   7.__
a report is to

    A. correct capitalization   B. delete passages
    C. improve punctuation   D. cite references

8. A completed formal report may contain all of the following EXCEPT   8.__

    A. a synopsis   B. a preface
    C. marginal notes   D. bibliographical references

9. Of the following, the MAIN use of proofreaders' marks is to   9.__

    A. explain corrections to be made
    B. indicate that a manuscript has been read and approved
    C. let the reader know who proofread the report
    D. indicate the format of the report

10. Informative, readable and concise reports have been found to observe the following   10.__
rules:
    Rule I.   Keep the report short and easy to understand.
    Rule II.   Vary the length of sentences.
    Rule III. Vary the style of sentences so that, for example, they are not all just sub
               ject-verb, subject-verb.
Consider this hospital laboratory report: The experiment was started in January. The
apparatus was put together in six weeks. At that time the synthesizing process was
begun. The synthetic chemicals were separated. Then they were used in tests on
patients.
Which one of the following choices MOST accurately classifies the above rules into
those which are *violated* by this report and those which are *not*?

    A. II is violated, but I and III are not.
    B. III is violated, but I and II are not.
    C. II and III are violated, but I is not.
    D. I, II, and III are violated.

Questions 11-13.

DIRECTIONS: Questions 11 through 13 are based on the following example of a report. The
report consists of eight numbered sentences, some of which are not consistent with the principles of good report writing.

(1) I interviewed Mrs. Loretta Crawford in Room 424 of County Hospital. (2) She had collapsed on the street and been brought into emergency. (3) She is an attractive woman with many friends judging by the cards she had received. (4) She did not know what her husband's last job had been, or what their present income was. (5) The first thing that Mrs. Crawford said was that she had never worked and that her husband was presently unemployed. (6) She did not know if they had any medical coverage or if they could pay the bill. (7) She said that her husband could not be reached by telephone but that he would be in to see her that afternoon. (8) I left word at the nursing station to be called when he arrived.

11. A good report should be arranged in logical order. Which of the following sentences from the report does NOT appear in its proper sequence in the report? Sentence

11.____

    A. 1   B. 4   C. 7   D. 8

12. Only material that is relevant to the main thought of a report should be included. Which of the following sentences from the report contains material which is LEAST relevant to this report? Sentence

12.____

    A. 3   B. 4   C. 6   D. 8

13. Reports should include all essential information.
    Of the following, the MOST important fact that is *missing* from this report is:

13.____

    A. Who was involved in the interview
    B. What was discovered at the interview
    C. When the interview took place
    D. Where the interview took place

Questions 14-15.

DIRECTIONS: Each of Questions 14 and 15 consists of four numbered sentences which constitute a paragraph in a report. They are not in the right order. Choose the numbered arrangement appearing after letter A, B, C, or D which is MOST logical and which BEST expresses the thought of the paragraph.

14.   I.   Congress made the commitment explicit in the Housing Act of 1949, establishing as a national goal the realization of a decent home and suitable environment for every American family.

14.____

     II.   The result has been that the goal of decent home and suitable environment is still as far distant as ever for the disadvantaged urban family.
    III.   In spite of this action by Congress, federal housing programs have continued to be fragmented and grossly under-funded.
     IV.   The passage of the National Housing Act signaled a new federal commitment to provide housing for the nation's citizens.

    A. I, IV, III, II   B. IV, I, III, II
    C. IV, I, III, II   D. II, IV, I, III

15. I.   The greater expense does not necessarily involve "exploitation," but it is often per-   15.__
          ceived as exploitative and unfair by those who are aware of the price differences
          involved, but unaware of operating costs.
     II. Ghetto residents believe they are "exploited" by local merchants, and evidence
          substantiates some of these beliefs.
     III. However, stores in low-income areas were more likely to be small independents,
          which could not achieve the economies available to supermarket chains and
          were, therefore, more likely to charge higher prices, and the customers were
          more likely to buy smaller-sized packages which are more expensive per unit of
          measure.
     IV. A study conducted in one city showed that distinctly higher prices were charged
          for goods sold in ghetto stores than in other areas.

     A.   IV, II, I, III   B.   IV, I, III, II
     C.   II, IV, III, I   D.   II, III, IV, I

16. In organizing data to be presented in a formal report, the FIRST of the following steps   16.__
     should be

     A.   determining the conclusions to be drawn
     B.   establishing the time sequence of the data
     C.   sorting and arranging like data into groups
     D.   evaluating how consistently the data support the recommendations

17. All reports should be prepared with *at least* one copy so that   17.__

     A.   there is one copy for your file
     B.   there is a copy for your supervisor
     C.   the report can be sent to more than one person
     D.   the person getting the report can forward a copy to someone else

18. Before turning in a report of an investigation he has made, a supervisor discovers some   18.__
     additional information he did not include in this report.
     Whether he rewrites this report to include this additional information should PRIMA-
     RILY depend on the

     A.   importance of the report itself
     B.   number of people who will eventually review this report
     C.   established policy covering the subject matter of the report
     D.   bearing this new information has on the conclusions of the report

_____

KEY (CORRECT ANSWERS)

1.	A		11.	B
2.	A		12.	A
3.	D		13.	C
4.	D		14.	B
5.	A		15.	C
6.	A		16.	C
7.	D		17.	A
8.	C		18.	D
9.	A			
10.	C			

PREPARING WRITTEN MATERIALS

EXAMINATION SECTION
TEST 1

DIRECTIONS: Each of the two sentences in the following questions may contain errors in punctuation, capitalization, or grammar.
If there is an error in only Sentence I, mark your answer A. If there is an error in only Sentence II, mark your answer B.
If there is an error in both Sentence I and Sentence II, mark your answer C. If both Sentence I and Sentence II are correct, mark your answer D.

1. I. The task of typing these reports is to be divided equally between you and me.   1.____
    II. If I was he, I would use a different method for filing these records.

2. I. The new clerk is just as capable as some of the older employees, if not more capa-   2.____
        ble.
    II. Using his knowledge of arithmetic to check the calculations, the supervisor found
        no errors in the report.

3. I. A typist who does consistently superior work probably merits promotion.   3.____
    II. In its report on the stenographic unit, the committee pointed out that neither the
        stenographers nor the typists were adequately trained.

4. I. Entering the office, the desk was noticed immediately by the visitor.   4.____
    II. Arrangements have been made to give this training to whoever applies for it.

5. I. The office manager estimates that this assignment, which is to be handled by you   5.____
        and I, will require about two weeks for completion.
    II. One of the recommendations of the report is that these kind of forms be dis-
        carded because they are of no value.

6. I. The supervisor knew that the typist was a quiet, cooperative, efficient, employee.   6.____
    II. The duties of a stenographer are to take dictation notes at conferences and tran-
        scribing them.

7. I. The stenographer has learned that she, as well as two typists, is being assigned to   7.____
        the new unit.
    II. We do not know who you have designated to take charge of the new program.

8. I. He asked, "When do you expect to return?"   8.____
    II. I doubt whether this system will be successful here; it is not suitable for the work
        of our agency.

9. I. It is a policy of this agency to encourage punctuality as a good habit for we employ-   9.____
        ees to adopt.
    II. The successful completion of the task was due largely to them cooperating
        effectively with the supervisor.

10. I. Mr. Smith, who is a very competent executive has offered his services to our   10.____
        department.
    II. Every one of the stenographers who work in this office is considered trustworthy.

11. I.   It is very annoying to have a pencil sharpener, which is not in proper working order.   11.____
     II. The building watchman checked the door of Charlie's office and found that the lock has been jammed.

12. I.   Since he went on the New York City council a year ago, one of his primary concerns has been safety in the streets.   12.____
     II. After waiting in the doorway for about 15 minutes, a black sedan appeared.

13. I.   When you are studying a good textbook is important.   13.____
     II. He said he would divide the money equally between you and me.

14. I.   The question is, "How can a large number of envelopes be sealed rapidly without the use of a sealing machine?"   14.____
     II. The administrator assigned two stenographers, Mary and I, to the new bureau.

15. I.   A dictionary, in addition to the office management textbooks, were placed on his desk.   15.____
     II. The concensus of opinion is that none of the employees should be required to work overtime.

16. I.   Mr. Granger has demonstrated that he is as courageous, if not more courageous, than Mr. Brown.   16.____
     II. The successful completion of the project depends on the manager's accepting our advisory opinion.

17. I.   Mr. Ames was in favor of issuing a set of rules and regulations for all of us employees to follow.   17.____
     II. It is inconceivable that the new clerk knows how to deal with that kind of correspondence.

18. I.   The revised referrence manual is to be used by all of the employees.   18.____
     II. Mr. Johnson told Miss Kent and me to accumulate all the letters that we receive.

19. I.   The supervisor said, that before any changes would be made in the attendance report, there must be ample justification for them.   19.____
     II. Each of them was asked to amend their preliminary report.

20. I.   Mrs. Peters conferred with Mr. Roberts before she laid the papers on his desk.   20.____
     II. As far as this report is concerned, Mr. Williams always has and will be responsible for its preparation.

KEY (CORRECT ANSWERS)

1.	B	11.	C
2.	D	12.	C
3.	D	13.	A
4.	A	14.	B
5.	C	15.	C
6.	C	16.	A
7.	B	17.	B
8.	D	18.	A
9.	C	19.	C
10.	A	20.	B

———

TEST 2

DIRECTIONS: Each question or incomplete statement is followed by several suggested answers or completions. Select the one that BEST answers the question or completes the statement. *PRINT THE LETTER OF THE CORRECT ANSWER IN THE SPACE AT THE RIGHT.*

Questions 1-9.

DIRECTIONS: Questions 1 through 9 consist of pairs of sentences which may or may not contain errors in grammar, capitalization, or punctuation.
If both sentences are correct, mark your answer A.
If the first sentence only is correct, mark your answer B.
If the second sentence only is correct, mark your answer C.
If both sentences are incorrect, mark your answer D.
NOTE: Consider a sentence correct if it contains no errors, although there may be other correct ways of writing the sentence.

1. I. An unusual conference will be held today at George Washington high school.   1.____
    II. The principal of the school, Dr. Pace, described the meeting as "a unique opportunity for educators to exchange ideas."

2. I. Studio D, which they would ordinarily use, will be occupied at that time.   2.____
    II. Any other studio, which is properly equipped, may be used instead.

3. I. D.H. Lawrence's <u>Sons and Lovers</u> were discussed on today's program.   3.____
    II. Either Eliot's or Yeats's work is to be covered next week.

4. I. This program is on the air for three years now, and has a well-established audience.   4.____
    II. We have received many complimentary letters from listeners, and scarcely no critical ones.

5. I. Both Mr. Owen and Mr. Mitchell have addressed the group.   5.____
    II. As has Mr. Stone, whose talks have been especially well received.

6. I. The original program was different in several respects from the version that eventually went on the air.   6.____
    II. Each of the three announcers who Mr. Scott thought had had suitable experience was asked whether he would be willing to take on the special assignment.

7. I. A municipal broadcasting system provides extensive coverage of local events, but also reports national and international news.   7.____
    II. A detailed account of happenings in the South may be carried by a local station hundreds of miles away.

8. I. Jack Doe the announcer and I will be working on the program.   8.____
    II. The choice of musical selections has been left up to he and I.

9.   I.   Mr. Taylor assured us that "he did not anticipate any difficulty in making arrange-   9.____
             ments for the broadcast ."
    II. Although there had seemed at first to be certain problems; these had been
          solved.

Questions 10-14.

DIRECTIONS: Questions 10 through 14 consist of pairs of sentences which may contain
                errors in grammar, sentence structure, punctuation, or spelling, or both sen-
                tences may be correct. Consider a sentence correct if it contains no errors,
                although there may be other correct ways of writing the sentence.
                If only Sentence I contains an error, mark your answer A.
                If only Sentence II contains an error, mark your answer B.
                If both sentences contain errors, mark your answer C.
                If both sentences are correct, mark your answer D.

10.   I.   No employee considered to be indispensable will be assigned to the new office.   10.____
     II. The arrangement of the desks and chairs give the office a neat appearance.

11.   I.   The recommendation, accompanied by a report, was delivered this morning.   11.____
     II. Mr. Green thought the procedure would facilitate his work; he knows better now.

12.   I.   Limiting the term "property" to tangible property, in the criminal mischief setting,   12.____
        accords with prior case law holding that only tangible property came within the pur-
        view of the offense of malicious mischief.
     II. Thus, a person who intentionally destroys the property of another, but under an
        honest belief that he has title to such property, cannot be convicted of criminal
        mischief under the Revised Penal Law.

13.   I.   Very early in its history, New York enacted statutes from time to time punishing,   13.____
        either as a felony or as a misdemeanor, malicious injuries to various kinds of prop-
        erty: piers, booms, dams, bridges, etc.
     II. The application of the statute is necessarily restricted to trespassory takings with
        larcenous intent: namely with intent permanently or virtually permanently to
        "appropriate" property or "deprive" the owner of its use.

14.   I.   Since the former Penal Law did not define the instruments of forgery in a general   14.____
        fashion, its crime of forgery was held to be narrower than the common law offense
        in this respect and to embrace only those instruments explicitly specified in the
        substantive provisions.
     II. After entering the barn through an open door for the purpose of stealing, it was
        closed by the defendants.

Questions 15-20.

DIRECTIONS: Questions 15 through 20 consist of pairs of sentences which may or may not
                contain errors in grammar, capitalization, or punctuation.
                If both sentences are correct, mark your answer A.
                If the first sentence only is correct, mark your answer B.
                If the second sentence only is correct, mark your answer C.
                If both sentences are incorrect, mark your answer D.

NOTE: Consider a sentence correct if it contains no errors, although there may be other correct ways of writing the sentence.

15. I. The program, which is currently most popular, is a news broadcast.   15._____
     II. The engineer assured his supervisor that there was no question of his being late again.

16. I. The announcer recommended that the program originally scheduled for that time   16._____
         be cancelled.
     II. Copies of the script may be given to whoever is interested.

17. I. A few months ago it looked like we would be able to broadcast the concert live.   17._____
     II. The program manager, as well as the announcers, were enthusiastic about the plan.

18. I. No speaker on the subject of education is more interesting than he.   18._____
     II. If he would have had the time, we would have scheduled him for a regular weekly broadcast.

19. I. This quartet, in its increasingly complex variations on a simple theme, admirably   19._____
         illustrates Professor Baker's point.
     II. Listeners interested in these kind of ideas will find his recently published study of Haydn rewarding.

20. I. The Commissioner's resignation at the end of next month marks the end of a long   20._____
         public service career.
     II. Outstanding among his numerous achievements were his successful implementation of several revolutionary schemes to reorganize the agency.

KEY (CORRECT ANSWERS)

1.	C		11.	D
2.	B		12.	C
3.	C		13.	B
4.	D		14.	A
5.	B		15.	C
6.	A		16.	A
7.	A		17.	D
8.	D		18.	B
9.	D		19.	B
10.	B		20.	B

PREPARING WRITTEN MATERIAL

PARAGRAPH REARRANGEMENT
COMMENTARY

The sentences which follow are in scrambled order. You are to rearrange them in proper order and indicate the letter choice containing the correct answer at the space at the right.

Each group of sentences in this section is actually a paragraph presented in scrambled order. Each sentence in the group has a place in that paragraph; no sentence is to be left out. You are to read each group of sentences and decide upon the best order in which to put the sentences so as to form as well-organized paragraph.

The questions in this section measure the ability to solve a problem when all the facts relevant to its solution are not given.

More specifically, certain positions of responsibility and authority require the employee to discover connections between events sometimes, apparently, unrelated. In order to do this, the employee will find it necessary to correctly infer that unspecified events have probably occurred or are likely to occur. This ability becomes especially important when action must be taken on incomplete information.

Accordingly, these questions require competitors to choose among several suggested alternatives, each of which presents a different sequential arrangement of the events. Competitors must choose the MOST logical of the suggested sequences.

In order to do so, they may be required to draw on general knowledge to infer missing concepts or events that are essential to sequencing the given events. Competitors should be careful to infer only what is essential to the sequence. The plausibility of the wrong alternatives will always require the inclusion of unlikely events or of additional chains of events which are NOT essential to sequencing the given events.

It's very important to remember that you are looking for the best of the four possible choices, and that the best choice of all may not even be one of the answers you're given to choose from.

There is no one right way to solve these problems. Many people have found it helpful to first write out the order of the sentences, as they would have arranged them, on their scrap paper before looking at the possible answers. If their optimum answer is there, this can save them some time. If it isn't, this method can still give insight into solving the problem. Others find it most helpful to just go through each of the possible choices, contrasting each as they go along. You should use whatever method feels comfortable, and works, for you.

While most of these types of questions are not that difficult, we've added a higher percentage of the difficult type, just to give you more practice. Usually there are only one or two questions on this section that contain such subtle distinctions that you're unable to answer confidently, and you then may find yourself stuck deciding between two possible choices, neither of which you're sure about.

———

Preparing Written Material

EXAMINATION SECTION
TEST 1

DIRECTIONS: The following groups of sentences need to be arranged in an order that makes sense. Select the letter preceding the sequence that represents the best sentence order. *PRINT THE LETTER OF THE CORRECT ANSWER IN THE SPACE AT THE RIGHT.*

Question 1   1.____

1. The ostrich egg shell's legendary toughness makes it an excellent substitute for certain types of dishes or dinnerware, and in parts of Africa ostrich shells are cut and decorated for use as containers for water.
2. Since prehistoric times, people have used the enormous egg of the ostrich as a part of their diet, a practice which has required much patience and hard work-to hard-boil an ostrich egg takes about four hours.
3. Opening the egg's shell, which is rock hard and nearly an inch thick, requires heavy tools, such as a saw or chisel; from inside, a baby ostrich must use a hornlike projection on its beak as a miniature pick-axe to escape from the egg.
4. The offspring of all higher-order animals originate from single egg cells that are carried by mothers, and most of these eggs are relatively small, often microscopic.
5. The egg of the African ostrich, however, weighs a massive thirty pounds, making it the largest single cell on earth, and a common object of human curiosity and wonder.

The best order is

A. 5 4 1 2 3
B. 1 4 5 3 2
C. 4 2 3 5 1
D. 4 5 2 3 1

Question 2   2.____

1. Typically only a few feet high on the open sea, individual tsunami have been known to circle the entire globe two or three times if their progress is not interrupted, but are not usually dangerous until they approach the shallow water that surrounds land masses.
2. Some of the most terrifying and damaging hazards caused by earthquakes are tsunami, which were once called "tidal waves"— a poorly chosen name, since these waves have nothing to do with tides.
3. Then a wave, slowed by the sudden drag on the lower part of its moving water column, will pile upon itself, sometimes reaching a height of over 100 feet.
4. Tsunami (Japanese for "great harbor wave") are seismic waves that are caused by earthquakes near oceanic trenches, and once triggered, can travel up to 600 miles an hour on the open ocean.
5. A land-shoaling tsunami is capable of extraordinary destruction; some tsunami have deposited large boats miles inland, washed out two-foot-thick seawalls, and scattered locomotive trains over long distances.

The best order is

A. 4 1 3 2 5
B. 1 3 4 2 5
C. 5 1 3 2 4
D. 2 4 1 3 5

Question 3   3.__

1. Soon, by the 1940's, jazz was the most popular type of music among American intellectu-
   als and college students.
2. In the early days of jazz, it was considered "lowdown" music, or music that was played only
   in rough, disreputable bars and taverns.
3. However, jazz didn't take long to develop from early ragtime melodies into more complex,
   sophisticated forms, such as Charlie Parker's "bebop" style of jazz.
4. After charismatic band leaders such as Duke Ellington and Count Basic brought jazz to a
   larger audience, and jazz continued to evolve into more complicated forms, white audi-
   ences began to accept and even to enjoy the new American art form.
5. Many white Americans, who then dictated the tastes of society, were wary of music that
   was played almost exclusively in black clubs in the poorer sections of cities and towns.

The best order is

A. 5 4 3 2 1
B. 2 5 3 4 1
C. 4 5 3 1 2
D. 1 2 4 3 5

Question 4   4.__

1. Then, hanging in a windless place, the magnetized end of the needle would always point to
   the south.
2. The needle could then be balanced on the rim of a cup, or the edge of a fingernail, but this
   balancing act was hard to maintain, and the needle often fell off.
3. Other needles would point to the north, and it was important for any traveler finding his way
   with a compass to remember which kind of magnetized needle he was carrying.
4. To make some of the earliest compasses in recorded history, ancient Chinese "magicians"
   would rub a needle with a piece of magnetized iron called a lodestone.
5. A more effective method of keeping the needle free to swing with its magnetic pull was to
   attach a strand of silk to the center of the needle with a tiny piece of wax.

The best order is

A. 4 2 5 1 3
B. 4 3 5 2 1
C. 4 5 2 1 3
D. 4 1 3 5 2

Question 5

5.____

1. The now-famous first mate of the *HMS Bounty,* Fletcher Christian, founded one of the world's most peculiar civilizations in 1790.
2. The men knew they had just committed a crime for which they could be hanged, so they set sail for Pitcairn, a remote, abandoned island in the far eastern region of the Polynesian archipelago, accompanied by twelve Polynesian women and six men.
3. In a mutiny that has become legendary, Christian and the others forced Captain Bligh into a lifeboat and set him adrift off the coast of Tonga in April of 1789.
4. In early 1790, the *Bounty* landed at Pitcairn Island, where the men lived out the rest of their lives and founded an isolated community which to this day includes direct descendants of Christian and the other crewmen.
5. The *Bounty,* commanded by Captain William Bligh, was in the middle of a global voyage, and Christian and his shipmates had come to the conclusion that Bligh was a reckless madman who would lead them to their deaths unless they took the ship from him.

The best order is

A. 4 5 3 2 1
B. 1 3 5 2 4
C. 1 5 3 2 4
D. 3 1 5 4 2

Question 6

6.____

1. But once the vines had been led to make orchids, the flowers had to be carefully hand-pollinated, because unpollinated orchids usually lasted less than a day, wilting and dropping off the vine before it had even become dark.
2. The Totonac farmers discovered that looping a vine back around once it reached a five-foot height on its host tree would cause the vine to flower.
3. Though they knew how to process the fruit pods and extract vanilla's flavoring agent, the Totonacs also knew that a wild vanilla vine did not produce abundant flowers or fruit.
4. Wild vines climbed along the trunks and canopies of trees, and this constant upward growth diverted most of the vine's energy to making leaves instead of the orchid flowers that, once pollinated, would produce the flavorful pods.
5. Hundreds of years before vanilla became a prized food flavoring in Europe and the Western World, the Totonac Indians of the Mexican Gulf Coast were skilled cultivators of the vanilla vine, whose fruit they literally worshipped as a goddess.

The best order is

A. 2 3 4 1 5
B. 2 4 3 1 5
C. 5 3 4 2 1
D. 3 4 1 2 5

Question 7

1. Once airborne, the spider is at the mercy of the air currents—usually the spider takes a brief journey, traveling close to the ground, but some have been found in air samples collected as high as 10,000 feet, or been reported landing on ships far out at sea.
2. Once a young spider has hatched, it must leave the environment into which it was born as quickly as possible, in order to avoid competing with its hundreds of brothers and sisters for food.
3. The silk rises into warm air currents, and as soon as the pull feels adequate the spider lets go and drifts up into the air, suspended from the silk strand in the same way that a person might parasail.
4. To help young spiders do this, many species have adapted a practice known as "aerial dispersal," or, in common speech, "ballooning."
5. A spider that wants to leave its surroundings quickly will climb to the top of a grass stem or twig, face into the wind, and aim its back end into the air, releasing a long stream of silk from the glands near the tip of its abdomen.

The best order is

A. 5 4 2 3 1
B. 5 2 4 1 3
C. 2 5 4 3 1
D. 2 4 5 3 1

Question 8

1. For about a year, Tycho worked at a castle in Prague with a scientist named Johannes Kepler, but their association was cut short by another argument that drove Kepler out of the castle, to later develop, on his own, the theory of planetary orbits.
2. Tycho found life without a nose embarrassing, so he made a new nose for himself out of silver, which reportedly remained glued to his face for the rest of his life.
3. Tycho Brahe, the 17th-century Danish astronomer, is today more famous for his odd and arrogant personality than for any contribution he has made to our knowledge of the stars and planets.
4. Early in his career, as a student at Rostock University, Tycho got into an argument with the another student about who was the better mathematician, and the two became so angry that the argument turned into a sword fight, during which Tycho's nose was sliced off.
5. Later in his life, Tycho's arrogance may have kept him from playing a part in one of the greatest astronomical discoveries in history: the elliptical orbits of the solar system's planets.

The best order is

A. 1 4 2 3 5
B. 4 2 3 5 1
C. 4 2 1 3 5
D. 3 4 2 5 1

Question 9   9.____

1. The processionaries are so used to this routine that if a person picks up the end of a silk line and brings it back to the origin–creating a closed circle—the caterpillars may travel around and around for days, sometimes starving ar freezing, without changing course.
2. Rather than relying on sight or sound, the other caterpillars, who are lined up end-to-end behind the leader, travel to and from their nests by walking on this silk line, and each will reinforce it by laying down its own marking line as it passes over.
3. In order to insure the safety of individuals, the processionary caterpillar nests in a tree with dozens of other caterpillars, and at night, when it is safest, they all leave together in search of food.
4. The processionary caterpillar of the European continent is a perfect illustration of how much some insect species rely on instinct in their daily routines.
5. As they leave their nests, the processionaries form a single-file line behind a leader who spins and lays out a silk line to mark the chosen path.

The best order is

A. 4 3 5 2 1
B. 3 5 4 2 1
C. 3 5 2 1 4
D. 4 5 3 1 2

Question 10   10.____

1. Often, the child is also given a handcrafted walker or push cart, to provide support for its first upright explorations.
2. In traditional Indian families, a child's first steps are celebrated as a ceremonial event, rooted in ancient myth.
3. These carts are often intricately designed to resemble the chariot of Krishna, an important figure in Indian mythology.
4. The sound of these anklet bells is intended to mimic the footsteps of the legendary child Rama, who is celebrated in devotional songs throughout India.
5. When the child's parents see that the child is ready to begin walking, they will fit it with specially designed ankle bracelets, adorned with gently ringing bells.

The best order is

A. 2 3 4 1 5
B. 2 5 3 1 4
C. 5 4 1 3 2
D. 5 3 2 1 4

Question 11   11.__

1. The settlers planted Osage orange all across Middle America, and today long lines and rectangles of Osage orange trees can still be seen on the prairies, running along the former boundaries of farms that no longer exist.
2. After trying sod walls and water-filled ditches with no success, American farmers began to look for a plant that was adaptable to prairie weather, and that could be trimmed into a hedge that was "pig-tight, horse-high, and bull-strong."
3. The tree, so named because it bore a large (but inedible) fruit the size of an orange, was among the sturdiest and hardiest of American trees, and was prized among Native Americans for the strength and flexibility of bows which were made from its wood.
4. The first people to practice agriculture on the American flatlands were faced with an important problem: what would they use to fence their land in a place that was almost entirely without trees or rocks?
5. Finally, an Illinois farmer brought the settlers a tree that was native to the land between the Red and Arkansas rivers, a tree called the Osage orange.

The best order is

    A. 2 1 5 3 4
    B. 1 2 3 4 5
    C. 4 2 5 3 1
    D. 4 2 1 3 5

Question 12   12.__

1. After about ten minutes of such spirited and complicated activity, the head dancer is free to make up his or her own movements while maintaining the interest of the New Year's crowd.
2. The dancer will then perform a series of leg kicks, while at the same time operating the lion's mouth with his own hand and moving the ears and eyes by means of a string which is attached to the dancer's own mouth.
3. The most difficult role of this dance belongs to the one who controls the lion's head; this person must lead all the other "parts" of the lion through the choreographed segments of the dance.
4. The head dancer begins with a complex series of steps, alternately stepping forward with the head raised, and then retreating a few steps while lowering the head, a movement that is intended to create the impression that the lion is keeping a watchful eye for anything evil.
5. When performing a traditional Chinese New Year's lion dance, several performers must fit themselves inside a large lion costume and work together to enact different parts of the dance.

The best order is

    A. 5 3 4 2 1
    B. 3 4 2 5 1
    C. 3 1 5 4 2
    D. 4 2 3 5 1

Question 13

13.____

1. For many years the shell of the chambered nautilus was treasured in Europe for its beauty and intricacy, but collectors were unaware that they were in possession of the structure that marked a "missing link" in the evolution of marine mollusks.
2. The nautilus, however, evolved a series of enclosed chambers in its shell, and invented a new use for the structure: the shell began to serve as a buoyancy device.
3. Equipped with this new flotation device, the nautilus did not need the single, muscular foot of its predecessors, but instead developed flaps, tentacles, and a gentle form of jet propulsion that transformed it into the first mollusk able to take command of its own destiny and explore a three-dimensional world.
4. By pumping and adjusting air pressure into the chambers, the nautilus could spend the day resting on the bottom, and then rise toward the surface at night in search of food.
5. The nautilus shell looks like a large snail shell, similar to those of its ancestors, who used their shells as protective coverings while they were anchored to the sea floor.

The best order is

   A. 5 2 4 1 3
   B. 5 1 2 3 4
   C. 1 2 5 3 4
   D. 1 5 2 4 3

Question 14

14.____

1. While France and England battled for control of the region, the Acadiens prospered on the fertile farmland, which was finally secured by England in 1713.
2. Early in the 17th century, settlers from western France founded a colony called Acadie in what is now the Canadian province of Nova Scotia.
3. At this time, English officials feared the presence of spies among the Acadiens who might be loyal to their French homeland, and the Acadiens were deported to spots along the Atlantic and Caribbean shores of America.
4. The French settlers remained on this land, under English rule, for around forty years, until the beginning of the French and Indian War, another conflict between France and England.
5. As the Acadien refugees drifted toward a final home in southern Louisiana, neighbors shortened their name to "Cadien," and finally "Cajun," the name which the descendants of early Acadiens still call themselves.

The best order is

   A. 1 4 2 3 5
   B. 2 1 3 5 4
   C. 2 1 4 3 5
   D. 5 2 3 4 1

Question 15   15.____

   1. Traditional households in the Eastern and Western regions of Africa serve two meals a day-one at around noon, and the other in the evening.

   2. The starch is then used in the way that Americans might use a spoon, to scoop up a portion of the main dish on the person's plate.

   3. The reason for the starch's inclusion in every meal has to do with taste as well as nutrition; African food can be very spicy, and the starch is known to cool the burning effect of the main dish.

   4. When serving these meals, the main dish is usually served on individual plates, and the starch is served on a communal plate, from which diners break off a piece of bread or scoop rice or fufu in their fingers.

   5. The typical meals usually consist of a thick stew or soup as the main course, and an accompanying starch—either bread, rice, or *fufu, a* starchy grain paste similar in consistency to mashed potatoes.

The best order is

    A. 5 2 3 4 1
    B. 5 1 4 3 2
    C. 1 4 5 3 2
    D. 1 5 4 2 3

Question 16   16.____

   1. In the early days of the American Midwest, Indiana settlers sometimes came together to hold an event called an apple peeling, where neighboring settlers gathered at the homestead of a host family to help prepare the hosts' apple crop for cooking, canning, and making apple butter.

   2. At the beginning of the event, each peeler sat down in front of a ten- or twenty-gallon stone jar and was given a crock of apples and a paring knife.

   3. Once a peeler had finished with a crock, another was placed next to him; if the peeler was an unmarried man, he kept a strict count of the number of apples he had peeled, because the winner was allowed to kiss the girl of his choice.

   4. The peeling usually ended by 9:30 in the evening, when the neighbors gathered in the host family's parlor for a dance social.

   5. The apples were peeled, cored, and quartered, and then placed into the jar.

The best order is

    A. 1 5 3 4 2
    B. 2 5 3 4 1
    C. 1 2 5 3 4
    D. 2 1 5 4 3

Question 17   17._____

1. If your pet turtle is a land turtle and is native to temperate climates, it will stop eating some time in October, which should be your cue to prepare the turtle for hibernation.
2. The box should then be covered with a wire screen, which will protect the turtle from any rodents or predators that might want to take advantage of a motionless and helpless animal.
3. When your turtle hasn't eaten for a while and appears ready to hibernate, it should be moved to its winter quarters, most likely a cellar or garage, where the temperature should range between 40° and 45° F.
4. Instead of feeding the turtle, you should bathe it every day in warm water, to encourage the turtle to empty its intestines in preparation for its long winter sleep.
5. Here the turtle should be placed in a well-ventilated box whose bottom is covered with a moisture-absorbing layer of clay beads, and then filled three-fourths full with almost dry peat moss or wood chips, into which the turtle will burrow and sleep for several months.

The best order is

A. 1 4 3 5 2
B. 3 4 2 5 1
C. 3 2 4 1 5
D. 4 5 2 3 1

Question 18   18._____

1. Once he has reached the nest, the hunter uses two sturdy bamboo poles like huge chopsticks to pull the nest away from the mountainside, into a large basket that will be lowered to people waiting below.
2. The world's largest honeybees colonize the Nepalese mountainsides, building honeycombs as large as a person on sheer rock faces that are often hundreds of feet high.
3. In the remote mountain country of Nepal, a small band of "honey hunters" carry out a tradition so ancient that 10,000 year-old drawings of the practice have been found in the caves of Nepal.
4. To harvest the honey and beeswax from these combs, a honey hunter climbs above the nests, lowers a long bamboo-fiber ladder over the cliff, and then climbs down.
5. Throughout this dangerous practice, the hunter is stung repeatedly, and only the veterans, with skin that has been toughened over the years, are able to return from a hunt without the painful swelling caused by stings.

The best order is

A. 2 4 3 5 1
B. 2 4 1 5 3
C. 5 3 2 4 1
D. 3 2 4 1 5

Question 19   19.___

1. After the Romans left Britain, there were relentless attacks on the islands from the barbarian tribes of northern Germany–the Angles, Saxons, and Jutes.
2. As the empire weakened, Roman soldiers withdrew from Britain, leaving behind a country that continued to practice the Christian religion that had been introduced by the Romans.
3. Early Latin writings tell of a Christian warrior named Arturius (Arthur, in English) who led the British citizens to defeat these barbarian invaders, and brought an extended period of peace to the lands of Britain.
4. Long ago, the British Isles were part of the far-flung Roman Empire that extended across most of Europe and into Africa and Asia.
5. The romantic legend of King Arthur and his knights of the Round Table, one of the most popular and widespread stories of all time, appears to have some foundation in history.

The best order is

A. 5 4 3 2 1
B. 5 4 2 1 3
C. 4 5 2 3 1
D. 4 3 2 1 5

Question 20   20.___

1. The cylinder was allowed to cool until it sould stand on its own, and then it was cut from the tube and split down the side with a single straight cut.
2. Nineteenth-century glassmakers, who had not yet discovered the glazier's modern techniques for making panes of glass, had to create a method for converting their blown glass into flat sheets.
3. The bubble was then pierced at the end to make a hole that opened up while the glassmaker gently spun it, creating a cylinder of glass.
4. Turned on its side and laid on a conveyor belt, the cylinder was strengthened, or tempered, by being heated again and cooled very slowly, eventually flattening out into a single rectangular piece of glass.
5. To do this, the glassmaker dipped the end of a long tube into melted glass and blew into the other end of the tube, creating an expanding bubble of glass.

The best order is

A. 2 5 3 4 1
B. 2 4 5 3 1
C. 3 5 2 4 1
D. 3 1 4 5 2

Question 21   21.____

1. The splints are almost always hidden, but horses are occasionally born whose splinted toes project from the leg on either side, just above the hoof.
2. The second and fourth toes remained, but shrank to thin splints of bone that fused invisibly to the horse's leg bone.
3. Horses are unique among mammals, having evolved feet that each end in what is essentially a single toe, capped by a large, sturdy hoof.
4. Julius Caesar, an emperor of ancient Rome, was said to have owned one of these three-toed horses, and considered it so special that he would not permit anyone else to ride it.
5. Though the horse's earlier ancestors possessed the traditional mammalian set of five toes on each foot, the horse has retained only its third toe; its first and fifth toes disappeared completely as the horse evolved.

The best order is

A. 3 5 2 1 4
B. 5 3 2 4 1
C. 3 2 5 1 4
D. 5 2 3 1 4

Question 22   22.____

1. The new building materials—some of which are twenty feet long, and weigh nearly six tons—were transported to Pohnpei on rafts, and were brought into their present position by using hibiscus fiber ropes and leverage to move the stone columns upward along the inclined trunks of coconut palm trees.
2. The ancestors built great fires to heat the stone, and then poured cool seawater on the columns, which caused the stone to contract and split along natural fracture lines.
3. The now-abandoned enclave of Nan Madol, a group of 92 man-made islands off the shore of the Micronesian island of Pohnpei, is estimated to have been built around the year 500 A.D.
4. The islanders say their ancestors quarried stone columns from a nearby island, where large basalt columns were formed by the cooling of molten lava.
5. The structures of Nan Madol are remarkable for the sheer size of some of the stone "logs" or columns that were used to create the walls of the offshore community, and today anthropologists can only rely on the information of existing local people for clues about how Nan Madol was built.

The best order is

A. 5 4 3 2 1
B. 5 3 1 4 2
C. 3 5 4 2 1
D. 3 1 4 2 5

Question 23

23.___

1. One of the most easily manipulated substances on earth, glass can be made into ceramic tiles that are composed of over 90% air.
2. NASA's space shuttles are the first spacecraft ever designed to leave and re-enter the earth's atmosphere while remaining intact.
3. These ceramic tiles are such effective insulators that when a tile emerges from the oven in which it was fired, it can be held safely in a person's hand by the edges while its interior still glows at a temperature well over 2000° F.
4. Eventually, the engineers were led to a material that is as old as our most ancient civiliza- tionsglass.
5. Because the temperature during atmospheric re-entry is so incredibly hot, it took NASA's engineers some time to find a substance capable of protecting the shuttles.

The best order is

A. 5 2 1 3 4
B. 2 5 4 1 3
C. 2 3 1 2 5
D. 5 4 3 1 2

Question 24

24.___

1. The secret to teaching any parakeet to talk is patience, and the understanding that when a bird "talks," it is simply imitating what it hears, rather than putting ideas into words.
2. You should stay just out of sight of the bird and repeat the phrase you want it to learn, for at least fifteen minutes every morning and evening.
3. It is important to leave the bird without any words of encouragement or farewell; otherwise it might combine stray remarks or phrases, such as "Good night," with the phrase you are trying to teach it.
4. For this reason, to train your bird to imitate your words you should keep it free of any dis- tractions, especially other noises, while you are giving it "lessons."
5. After your repetition, you should quietly leave the bird alone for a while, to think over what it has just heard.

The best order is

A. 1 4 2 5 3
B. 1 2 4 3 5
C. 3 2 1 5 4
D. 3 1 5 4 2

Question 25   25.____

1. As a school approaches, fishermen from neighboring communities join their fishing boats together as a fleet, and string their gill nets together to make a huge fence that is held up by cork floats.
2. At a signal from the party leaders, or *nakura,* the family members pound the sides of the boats or beat the water with long poles, creating a sudden and deafening noise.
3. The fishermen work together to drag the trap into a half-circle that may reach 300 yards in diameter, and then the families move their boats to form the other half of the circle around the school of fish.
4. The school of fish flee from the commotion into the awaiting trap, where a final wall of net is thrown over the open end of the half-circle, securing the day's haul.
5. Indonesian people from the area around the Sulu islands live on the sea, in floating villages made of lashed-together or stilted homes, and make much of their living by fishing their home waters for migrating schools of snapper, scad, and other fish.

The best order is

A. 1 5 3 4 2
B. 1 2 4 3 5
C. 5 1 2 3 4
D. 5 1 3 2 4

––––––––––

KEY (CORRECT ANSWERS)

1.	D		11.	C
2.	D		12.	A
3.	B		13.	D
4.	A		14.	C
5.	C		15.	D
6.	C		16.	C
7.	D		17.	A
8.	D		18.	D
9.	A		19.	B
10.	B		20.	A

21. A
22. C
23. B
24. A
25. D

––––––––––

INTERPRETING STATISTICAL DATA
GRAPHS, CHARTS AND TABLES
TEST 1

DIRECTIONS: Each question or incomplete statement is followed by several suggested answers or completions. Select the one that BEST answers the question or completes the statement. *PRINT THE LETTER OF THE CORRECT ANSWER IN THE SPACE AT THE RIGHT.*

Questions 1-10.

DIRECTIONS: Questions 1 through 10 are to be answered SOLELY on the basis of the following table showing the amounts purchased by various purchasing units during 2018.

DOLLAR VOLUME PURCHASED BY EACH PURCHASING UNIT DURING EACH QUARTER OF 2018 (FIGURES SHOWN REPRESENT THOUSANDS OF DOLLARS)				
Purchasing Unit	First Quarter	Second Quarter	Third Quarter	Fourth Quarter
A	578	924	698	312
B	1,426	1,972	1,586	1,704
C	366	494	430	716
D	1,238	1,708	1,884	1,546
E	730	742	818	774
F	948	1,118	1,256	788

1. The total dollar volume purchased by all of the purchasing units during 2018 approximated MOST NEARLY

   A. $2,000,000   B. $4,000,000
   C. $20,000,000   D. $40,000,000

1._____

2. During which quarter was the GREATEST total dollar amount of purchases made? _____ quarter.

   A. First   B. Second   C. Third   D. Fourth

2._____

3. Assume that the dollar volume purchased by Unit F during 2018 exceeded the dollar volume purchased by Unit F during 2017 by 50%.
Then, the dollar volume purchased by Unit F during 2017 was

   A. $2,055,000   B. $2,550,000
   C. $2,740,000   D. $6,165,000

3._____

4. Which one of the following purchasing units showed the sharpest DECREASE in the amount purchased during the fourth quarter as compared with the third quarter?
Unit

   A. A   B. B   C. D   D. E

4._____

5. Comparing the dollar volume purchased in the second quarter with the dollar volume purchased in the third quarter, the decrease in the dollar volume during the third quarter was PRIMARILY due to the decrease in the dollar volume purchased by Units _____ and _____ .

    A. A; B   B. C;D   C. C; E   D. C;F

6. Of the following, the unit which had the LARGEST number of dollars of increased purchases from any one quarter to the next following qua.rter was Unit

    A. A   B. B   C. C   D. D

7. Of the following, the unit with the LARGEST dollar volume of purchases during the second half of 2018 was Unit

    A. A   B. B   C. D   D. F

8. Which one of the following MOST closely approximates the percentage which Unit B's total 2018 purchases represents of the total 2018 purchases of all units, including Unit B?

    A. 10%   B. 15%   C. 25%   D. 45%

9. Assume that research showed that each ten thousand dollars ($10,000) of purchases by Unit D during 2018 required an average of thirteen (13) man-hours of buyers' staff time. On that basis, which one of the following MOST closely approximates the number of man-hours of buyers' staff time required by Unit D during 2018? _____ man-hours.

    A. 1,800   B. 8,000   C. 68,000   D. 78,000

10. Assume that research showed that each ten thousand dollars ($10,000) of purchases by Unit C during 2018 required an average of ten (10) man-hours of buyers' staff time. This research also showed that during 2018 the average man-hours of buyers' staff time per ten thousand dollars of purchases required by Unit C exceeded by 25% the average man-hours of buyers' staff time per ten thousand dollars of purchases required by Unit E. On that basis, which one of the following MOST closely approximates the number of buyers' staff man-hours required by Unit E during 2018? _____ man-hours.

    A. 2,200   B. 2,400   C. 3,000   D. 3,700

_____

KEY (CORRECT ANSWERS)

1.	C		6.	B
2.	B		7.	C
3.	C		8.	C
4.	A		9.	B
5.	A		10.	B

_____

TEST 2

Questions 1-6.

DIRECTIONS: Questions 1 through 6 are to be answered SOLELY on the basis of the information contained in the five charts below.

NUMBER OF UNITS OF WORK PRODUCED IN THE BUREAU PER YEAR

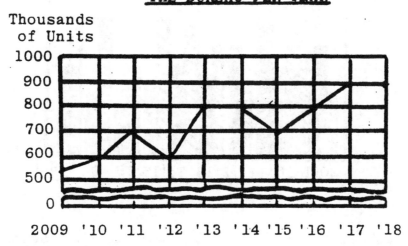

INCREASE IN THE NUMBER OF UNITS OF WORK PRODUCED IN 2018 OVER THE NUMBER PRODUCED IN 2009, BY BOROUGH

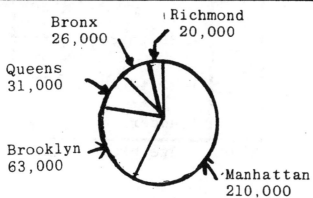

Bronx 26,000
Richmond 20,000
Queens 31,000
Brooklyn 63,000
Manhattan 210,000

NUMBER OF MALE AND FEMALE EMPLOYEES PRODUCING THE UNITS
OF WORK IN THE BUREAU PER YEAR

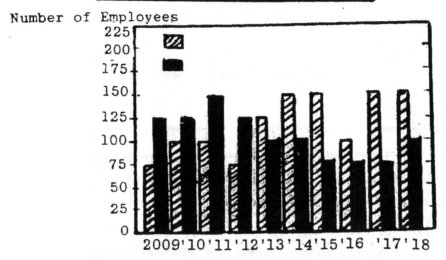

Number of Employees

DISTRIBUTION OF THE AGES BY PER CENT. OF EMPLOYEES
ASSIGNED TO PRODUCE THE UNITS OF WORK IN THE YEARS
2009 AND 2018

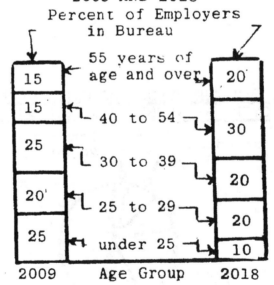

Percent of Employers
in Bureau

2009	Age Group	2018
15	55 years of age and over	20
15	40 to 54	30
25	30 to 39	20
20	25 to 29	20
25	under 25	10

TOTAL SALARIES PAID PER YEAR TO EMPLOYEES ASSIGNED
TO PRODUCE THE UNITS OF WORK IN THE BUREAU

Thousands of Dollars

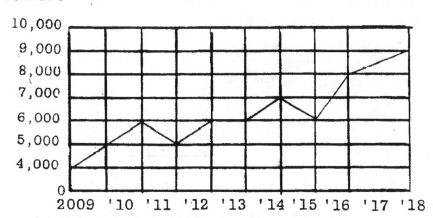

Thousands of Dollars

1. The information contained in the charts is sufficient to determine the   1.____

   A. amount of money paid in salaries to employees working in Richmond in 2018
   B. difference between the average annual salary of employees in the Bureau in 2018 and their average annual salary in 2017
   C. number of female employees in the Bureau between 30 and 39 years of age who were employed in 2009
   D. cost, in salary, for the average male employee in the Bureau to produce 100 units of work in 2014

2. The one of the following which was GREATER, in the Bureau, in 2014 than it was in 2012   2.____
   was the

   A. cost, in salaries, of producing a unit of work
   B. units of work produced annually per employee
   C. proportion of female employees to total number of employees
   D. average annual salary per employee

3. If, in 2018, one-half of the employees in the Bureau 55 years of age and over each   3.____
   earned an annual salary of $42,000, then the average annual salary of all the remaining
   employees in the Bureau was MOST NEARLY

   A. $31,750   B. $34,500   C. $35,300   D. $35,800

4. Assume that, in 2009, the offices in Richmond and the Bronx each produced the same   4.____
   number of units of work. Also assume that, in 2009, the offices in Brooklyn, Manhattan,
   and Queens each produced twice as many units of work as were produced in either of
   the other two boroughs.
   Then, the number of units of work produced in Brooklyn in 2008 was MOST NEARLY

   A. 69,000   B. 138,000   C. 201,000   D. 225,000

5. If, in 2006, the average annual salary of the female employees in the Bureau was four-fifths as large as the average annual salary of the male employees, then the average annual salary of the female employees in that year was

   A. $37,500   B. $31,000   C. $30,500   D. $30,000

5.____

6. Of the total number of employees in the Bureau who were 30 years of age and over in 2009, _____ must have been _____ .

   A. at least 35; females
   B. less than 75; males
   C. no more than 100; females
   D. more than 15; males

6.____

———

KEY (CORRECT ANSWERS)

1.	B		4.	C
2.	B		5.	D
3.	C		6.	A

———

TEST 3

Questions 1-10.

DIRECTIONS: Questions 1 through 10 are to be answered SOLELY on the basis of the REPORT OF TELEPHONE CALLS table given below.

	No. of Stations	No. of Employees	No. of Incoming Calls		No. of Long Distance Calls		No. of Divisions
Dept.			2017	2018	2017	2018	
I	11	40	3421	4292	72	54	5
II	36	330	10392	10191	75	78	18
III	53	250	85243	85084	103	98	8
IV	24	60	9675	10123	82	85	6
V	13	30	5208	5492	54	48	6
VI	25	35	7472	8109	86	90	5
VII	37	195	11412	11299	68	72	11
VIII	36	54	8467	8674	59	68	4
IX	163	306	294321	289968	289	321	13
X	40	83	9588	8266	93	89	5
XI	24	68	7867	7433	86	87	13
XII	50	248	10039	10208	101	95	30
XIII	10	230	7550	6941	28	21	10
XIV	25	103	14281	14392	48	40	5
XV	19	230	8475	9206	38	43	8
XVI	22	45	4684	5584	39	48	10
XVII	41	58	10102	9677	49	52	6
XVIII	82	106	106242	L05899	128	132	10
XIX	6	13	2649	2498	35	29	2
XX	16	30	1395	1468	78	90	2

(table title: TABLE - REPORT OF TELEPHONE CALLS)

1. The department which had more than 106,000 incoming calls in 2017 but fewer than 250,000 is

   A. II   B. IX   C. XVIII   D. III

   1.____

2. The department which has fewer than 8 divisions and more than 100 but fewer than 300 employees is

   A. VII   B. XIV   C. XV   D. XVIII

   2.____

3. The department which had an increase in 2018 over 2017 in the number of both incoming and long distance calls but had an increase in long distance calls of not more than 3 is

   A. IV   B. VI   C. XVII   D. XVIII

   3.____

4. The department which had a decrease in the number of incoming calls in 2018 as compared to 2017 and has not less than 6 nor more than 7 divisions is

   A. IV   B. V   C. XVII   D. III

   4.____

5. The department which has more than 7 divisions and more than 200 employees but fewer than 19 stations is

   A. XV   B. III   C. XX   D. XIII

   5.____

6. The department having more than 10 divisions and fewer than 36 stations, which had an increase in long distance calls in 2018 over 2017 is

    A. XI   B. VII   C. XVI   D. XVIII

6.____

7. The department which in 2018 had at least 7,250 incoming calls and a decrease in long distance calls from 2017, and has more than 50 stations is

    A. IX   B. XII   C. XVIII   D. III

7.____

8. The department which has fewer than 25 stations, fewer than 100 employees, 10 or more divisions, and showed an increase of at least 9 long distance calls in 2018 over 2017 is

    A. IX   B. XVI   C. XX   D. XIII

8.____

9. The department which has more than 50 but fewer than 125 employees and had more than 5,000 incoming calls in 2017 but not more than 10,000, and more than 60 long distance calls in 2018 but not more than 85, and has more than 24 stations is

    A. VIII   B. XIV   C. IV   D. XI

9.____

10. If the number of departments showing an increase in long distance calls in 2018 over 2017 exceeds the number showing a decrease in long distance calls in the same period, select the Roman numeral indicating the department having less than one station for each 10 employees, provided not more than 8 divisions are served by that department. If the number of departments showing an increase in long distance calls in 2018 over 2017 does not exceed the number showing a decrease in long distance calls in the same period, select the Roman numeral indicating the department having the SMALLEST number of incoming calls in 2018.

    A. III   B. XIII   C. XV   D. XX

10.____

KEY (CORRECT ANSWERS)

1.	C	6.	A
2.	B	7.	D
3.	A	8.	B
4.	C	9.	A
5.	D	10.	C

TEST 4

Questions 1-7.

DIRECTIONS: Questions 1 through 7 are to be answered SOLELY on the basis of the following chart.

EMPLOYABILITY CLASSIFICATION OF PERSONS RECEIVING HOME RELIEF
OR
VETERANS' ASSISTANCE AT WELFARE CENTER V, JANUARY 1, THIS YEAR

Employability Classification	Home Relief		Veterans' Assistance	
	Full	Supplementary	Full	Supplementary
Employable	369	207	15	42
Employed	330	83	2	35
Not Available For Employment	550	129	27	93
Awaiting employment conference	24	4	1	3
In rehabilitation	81	18	1	21
Attending school	26	16	3	13
In training	78	24	4	4
Temporary family care duties	32	19	6	7
Permanent family care duties	166	7	8	25
Unverified health condition	77	22	1	3
Temporary health condition	66	19	3	17
Permanently unemployable	47	8	1	37
TOTAL	1296	427	45	207

1. Of the persons on Home Relief who are either employed or employable, the percentage who are employable and are receiving full assistance is MOST NEARLY

    A. 30%   B. 35%   C. 50%   D. 65%

2. Assume that it is possible each month to reduce the number of Home Relief clients who are not available for employment and who are receiving full assistance by 10% from the previous month.
    By June 1, this year, the number of such Home Relief clients would be MOST NEARLY

    A. 225   B. 275   C. 325   D. 375

3. During the month of January, this year, of the full-assistance clients on Home Relief who were not available for employment because of temporary health conditions, 42% were removed from the relief rolls, and another 26% were reassigned to supplementary Home Relief assistance because of temporary health conditions.
    Taking figures to the nearest whole number, the number of all remaining Home Relief clients, including both full and supplementary assistance at Welfare Center V is MOST NEARLY

    A. 1250   B. 1265   C. 1675   D. 1695

4. The one of the following figures which is MOST likely to require checking for accuracy or investigating for significance is the figure for persons

1._____
2._____
3._____
4._____

A. not available for employment who are receiving supplementary Veterans' Assistance
B. receiving full Home Relief assistance who are employed
C. receiving supplementary Home Relief assistance who are not available for employment because they are in rehabilitation
D. receiving supplementary Veterans' Assistance who are permanently unemployable

5. With regard to clients receiving full Veterans' Assistance, the average monthly allotment per client in the various categories is as follows: Employable $168.06, Employed $194.92, Not Available for Employment $130.74, and Permanently Unemployable $112.56.
The average monthly allotment for all clients receiving full Veterans' Assistance at Welfare Center V is MOST NEARLY

    A. $140.06   B. $145.64   C. $151.58   D. $162.26

6. If all the Employable Home Relief clients on full assistance were to find employment so that 2/3 of them would no longer need any assistance and the rest would need only supplementary assistance, then the ratio of all Home Relief clients on full assistance to all Home Relief clients on supplementary assistance would be MOST NEARLY

    A. 2:1   B. 3:1   C. 3:2   D. 5:3

7. Assume that, for the category of Veterans' Assistance, the Federal government were to pay 2/3 of the first $60 of assistance given to each client, and 1/2 of the balance, on the basis of the average amount of assistance given to all veterans at a welfare center. Assume, further, that the average supplementary assistance given is $72, and the average full assistance is $140 at Welfare Center V. Under this plan, the amount of Veterans' Assistance given by Welfare Center V for which they would be reimbursed by the Federal government will be MOST NEARLY

    A. $8,000   B. $11,000   C. $13,000   D. $17,000

KEY (CORRECT ANSWERS)

1.	B		5.	B
2.	C		6.	D
3.	D		7.	C
4.	B			

TEST 5

Questions 1-10.

DIRECTIONS: Questions 1 through 10 are to be answered SOLELY on the basis of the Personnel Record of Division X shown below.

Employee	Bureau In Which Employed	Title	Annual Salary	On Vaca-tion	On Sick Leave	No. of Times Late
Abbott	Mail	Clerk	$31,200	18	0	1
Barnes	Mail	Clerk	25,200	25	3	7
Davis	Mail	Typist	24.000	21	9	2
Adams	Payroll	Accountant	42,500	10	0	2
Bell	Payroll	Bookkeeper	31,200	23	2	5
Duke	Payroll	Clerk	27,600	24	4	3
Gross	Payroll	Clerk	21,600	12	5	7
Lane	Payroll	Stenographer	26,400	19	16	20
Reed	Payroll	Typist	22.800	15	11	11
Arnold	Record	Clerk	32,400	6	15	9
Cane	Record	Clerk	24,500	14	3	4
Fay	Record	Clerk	21,100	20	0	4
Hale	Record	Typist	25.200	18	2	7
Baker	Supply	Clerk	30,000	20	3	2
Clark	Supply	Clerk	27,600	25	6	5
Ford	Supply	Typist	22,800	25	4	22

The table is titled:

DIVISION X
PERSONNEL RECORD – CURRENT YEAR

with a header group "No. of Days Absent" spanning the "On Vacation" and "On Sick Leave" columns.

1. The percentage of the total number of employees who are clerks is MOST NEARLY   1.____

    A. 25%   B. 33%   C. 38%   D. 56%

2. Of the following employees, the one who receives a monthly salary of $2,100 is   2.____

    A. Barnes   B. Gross   C. Reed   D. Clark

3. The difference between the annual salary of the highest paid clerk and that of the lowest   3.____
    paid clerk is

    A. $6,000   B. $8,400   C. $11,300   D. $20,900

4. The number of employees receiving more than $25,000 a year but less than $40,000 a   4.____
    year is

    A. 6   B. 9   C. 12   D. 15

5. The TOTAL annual salary of the employees of the Mail Bureau is _____ the total annual   5.____
    salary of the employees of the _____.

    A. one-half of; Payroll Bureau
    B. less than; Record Bureau by $21,600
    C. equal to; Supply Bureau
    D. less than; Payroll Bureau by $71,600

6. The average annual salary of the employees who are not clerks is MOST NEARLY   6.___

    A. $23,700   B. $25,450   C. $26,800   D. $27,850

7. If all the employees were given a 10% increase in pay, the annual salary of Lane would   7.___
then be

    A. *greater* than that of Barnes by $1,320
    B. *less* than that of Bell by $4,280
    C. *equal* to that of Clark
    D. *greater* than that of Ford by $3,600

8. Of the clerks who earned less than $30,000 a year, the one who was late the FEWEST   8.___
number of times was late _____ time(s).

    A. 1   B. 2   C. 3   D. 4

9. The bureau in which the employees were late the FEWEST number of times on an aver-   9.___
age is the _____ Bureau.

    A. Mail   B. Payroll   C. Record   D. Supply

10. The MOST accurate of the following statements is that   10.___

    A. Reed was late more often than any other typist
    B. Bell took more time off for vacation than any other employee earning $30,000 or
       more annually
    C. of the typists, Ford was the one who was absent the fewest number of times
       because of sickness
    D. three clerks took no time off because of sickness

KEY (CORRECT ANSWERS)

1.	D	6.	D
2.	A	7.	A
3.	C	8.	C
4.	B	9.	A
5.	C	10.	B

TEST 6

Questions 1-8.

DIRECTIONS: Questions 1 through 8 are to be answered SOLELY on the basis of the information contained in the chart and table shown below which relate to Bureau X in a certain public agency. The chart shows the percentage of the bureau's annual expenditures spent on equipment, supplies, and salaries for each of the years 2012-2016. The table shows the bureau's annual expenditures for each of the years 2012-2016.

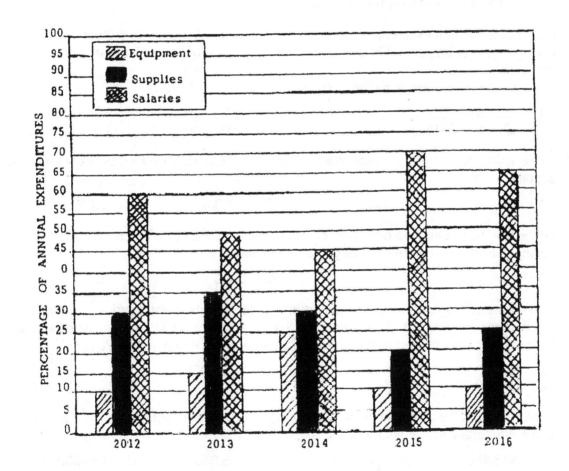

The bureau's annual expenditures for the years 2012-2016 are shown in the following table:

YEAR	EXPENDITURES
2012	$ 8,000,000
2013	$12,000,000
2014	$15,000,000
2015	$10,000,000
2016	$12,000,000

Equipment, supplies, and salaries were the only three categories for which the bureau spent money.

Candidates may find it useful to arrange their computations on their scratch paper in an orderly manner since the correct computations for one question may also be helpful in answering another question.

1. The information contained in the chart and table is sufficient to determine the   1._____

    A. average annual salary of an employee in the bureau in 2013
    B. decrease in the amount of money spent on supplies in the bureau in 2012 from the amount spent in the preceding year
    C. changes between 2014 and 2015 in the prices of supplies bought by the bureau
    D. increase in the amount of money spent on salaries in the bureau in 2016 over the amount spent in the preceding year

2. If the percentage of expenditures for salaries in one year is added to the percentage of expenditures for equipment in that year, a total of two percentages for that year is obtained.   2._____
The two years for which this total is the SAME are

    A. 2012 and 2014   B. 2013 and 2015
    C. 2012 and 2015   D. 2013 and 2016

3. Of the following, the year in which the bureau spent the GREATEST amount of money on supplies was   3._____

    A. 2016   B. 2014   C. 2013   D. 2012

4. Of the following years, the one in which there was the GREATEST increase over the preceding year in the amount of money spent on salaries is   4._____

    A. 2015   B. 2016   C. 2013   D. 2014

5. Of the bureau's expenditures for equipment in 2016, one-third was used for the purchase of mailroom equipment and the remainder was spent on miscellaneous office equipment. How much did the bureau spend on miscellaneous office equipment in 2016?   5._____

    A. $4,000,000   B. $400,000
    C. $8,000,000   D. $800,000

6. If there were 120 employees in the bureau in 2015, then the average annual salary paid to the employees in that year was MOST NEARLY   6._____

    A. $43,450   B. $49,600   C. $58,350   D. $80,800

7. In 2014, the bureau had 125 employees.   7._____
If 20 of the employees earned an average annual salary of $80,000, then the average salary of the other 105 employees was MOST NEARLY

    A. $49,000   B. $64,000   C. $41,000   D. $54,000

8. Assume that the bureau estimated that the amount of money it would spend on supplies   8.____
in 2017 would be the same as the amount it spent on that category in 2016. Similarly, the
bureau estimated that the amount of money it would spend on equipment in 2017 would
be the same as the amount it spent on that category in 2016. However, the bureau estimated that in 2017 the amount it would spend on salaries would be 10 percent higher
than the amount it spent on that category in 2016.
The percentage of its annual expenditures that the bureau estimated it would spend on
supplies in 2017 is MOST NEARLY

   A. 27.5%   B. 23.5%   C. 22.5%   D. 25%

―――――――

KEY (CORRECT ANSWERS)

1.	D	5.	D
2.	A	6.	C
3.	B	7.	A
4.	C	8.	B

―――――――

TEST 7

Questions 1-5.

DIRECTIONS: COLUMN I below lists five kinds of statistical data which are to be transformed into a chart or a graph for incorporation into the department annual report. COLUMN II lists nine different kinds of graphs or charts. For each type of information listed in COLUMN I, select the chart or graph from COLUMN II by means of which it should be demonstrated.

<u>COLUMN I</u>   <u>COLUMN II</u>

1. The relationship between employees' occupational classification and their salaries, for all employees by occupational classification, showing minimum, maximum, and average salary in each group.

A. 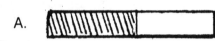   1.___

2. A comparison of the number of employees in the department, the departmental budget, the number of employees in the operating divisions and the operating division budget for each year over a ten-year period.

B.   2.___

3. The amount of money spent for each of the department's 10 most important functions during the past year.

C.   3.___

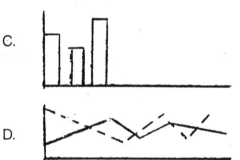

D.

4. The percentage of the department's budget spent for each of the department's activities for each year over a ten-year period.

E.    4.___

F.

210

5. The number of each kind of employee employed in the department over a period of twenty years and the total number of employees in the department for each of these periods.

G.

H.

5.____

KEY (CORRECT ANSWERS)

1. F
2. D
3. C
4. H
5. G